European Yearbook of International Economic Law

EYIEL Monographs - Studies in European and International Economic Law

Volume 30

Series Editors
Marc Bungenberg, Saarbrücken, Germany
Christoph Herrmann, Passau, Germany
Markus Krajewski, Erlangen, Germany
Jörg Philipp Terhechte, Lüneburg, Germany
Andreas R. Ziegler, Lausanne, Switzerland

EYIEL Monographs is a subseries of the European Yearbook of International Economic Law (EYIEL). It contains scholarly works in the fields of European and international economic law, in particular WTO law, international investment law, international monetary law, law of regional economic integration, external trade law of the EU and EU internal market law. The series does not include edited volumes. EYIEL Monographs are peer-reviewed by the series editors and external reviewers.

Deyan Draguiev

Interim Measures in Cross-Border Civil and Commercial Disputes

Interim Relief Proceedings in International Litigation and Arbitration

Deyan Draguiev
Sofia, Bulgaria

ISSN 2364-8392   ISSN 2364-8406 (electronic)
European Yearbook of International Economic Law
ISSN 2524-6658   ISSN 2524-6666 (electronic)
EYIEL Monographs - Studies in European and International Economic Law
ISBN 978-3-031-28703-9   ISBN 978-3-031-28704-6 (eBook)
https://doi.org/10.1007/978-3-031-28704-6

© The Editor(s) (if applicable) and The Author(s), under exclusive license to Springer Nature Switzerland AG 2023
This work is subject to copyright. All rights are solely and exclusively licensed by the Publisher, whether the whole or part of the material is concerned, specifically the rights of reprinting, reuse of illustrations, recitation, broadcasting, reproduction on microfilms or in any other physical way, and transmission or information storage and retrieval, electronic adaptation, computer software, or by similar or dissimilar methodology now known or hereafter developed.
The use of general descriptive names, registered names, trademarks, service marks, etc. in this publication does not imply, even in the absence of a specific statement, that such names are exempt from the relevant protective laws and regulations and therefore free for general use.
The publisher, the authors, and the editors are safe to assume that the advice and information in this book are believed to be true and accurate at the date of publication. Neither the publisher nor the authors or the editors give a warranty, expressed or implied, with respect to the material contained herein or for any errors or omissions that may have been made. The publisher remains neutral with regard to jurisdictional claims in published maps and institutional affiliations.

This Springer imprint is published by the registered company Springer Nature Switzerland AG
The registered company address is: Gewerbestrasse 11, 6330 Cham, Switzerland

Preface

The current book is predominantly based on a doctoral dissertation by the author pursued at and submitted to the University of Hamburg under the supervision of Prof. Peter Mankowski. To understand the underpinnings of the research and the conclusions that comprise the doctoral work and, hence, the present study, would mean to elaborate on the interim measures problem, which has sparked the interest of the author, how and where it has started and how it has developed.

The problem of interim measures in dispute resolution touches upon the very heart of procedural matters. Interim relief is a topic, which has been constantly alluring theoretical minds alongside practitioners seeking effective procedural moves and actions. This "double-sidedness" of the interim relief issues ensures that it is always within the focal point of scholars, analysts, legal counsel, etc. It is not difficult to find explanation of this phenomenon. Although it appears on its surface as an entirely procedural question, interim relief stands upon a cross-section of substantive and procedural law.

The substantive side is rooted in the actual or putative existence of substantive rights and obligations that, at least to some extent, have to be considered and reviewed when deciding an application for interim relief. Moreover, the ultimate implications of interim measures exert their effect, again, on the substantive rights and obligations of the parties.

In parallel to this, interim relief lives in a strict procedural framework. Within the entire matrix of a dispute resolution procedure, from establishing the jurisdiction of the seized body through conduct of procedure, issuing a determination (order/award/decision, etc.) and its enforcement in practice, the machinery of interim measures encompasses most, if not all, key procedural features, stages, and steps.

Hence, it is not difficult to imagine why the topic has enticed, entices, and will surely continue to entice many minds fascinated by theory and practice of legal proceedings alike. The mapping of interim relief, if we could reckon it laid down on an imaginary table as a map of a battlefield, could scope all their corners and entire territory. Undertaking the quest of analyzing interim relief, one can easily be drawn from valleys to mountains and down to deep oceans within this imaginary world of procedure, and to be always backed by issues of substantive law to make one's journey ever more challenging.

Bearing this unusual poetics in mind, it is also easy to understand why this author set his heart on the topic. However, it was far from the first topic the author considered to pursue (as a doctoral work). But it dawned at the author, at a particular point of his consideration about potential dissertation themes, that few other topics offer the same "marriage" of substantive and procedural law as interim relief. Furthermore, it is one of those topics that open up the entire spectrum from the very theoretical to the extremely practical. As the author has been a lawyer with both of these capacities and being seasoned through a multitude of interim measures proceedings, it quickly outshone any other potential dissertation topics and drove the author into following its thread for years.

The ultimate purpose of the study is to offer something that has been rarely pursued, or possibly never done at all. Continuing the metaphor of maps and knightly quests, the goal of the study, as it was devised by the author in its very beginning, is to draw an expansive map of interim measures proceedings on almost all existing levels.

First, on the level of national procedures. This is why the study focuses on a number of traits of such national procedures—the grounds and standards for granting interim relief in national courts, the types/categories of measures that are typically granted, etc. At such points, this study wades deep into the water of comparative law being led by the credo that a modern lawyer, no matter whether in academia or legal practice, inevitably needs to be aware of the variety of legal cultures, so there should be a merit into such a comparison.

Second, the next level relates to the question what happens if the interim relief proceedings feature an international/foreign element. As there is no uniform international instrument, the study puts focus on the EU regimes—the so-called Brussels system, as containing the single relatively uniform interim relief regime, and what forms its backbone. Here not only concepts of private international law but also key features of the EU law theory have to be brought in this part of the analysis.

The third relevant aspect is: what if the dispute is driven out of the system of state body adjudication, i.e. in the field of international arbitration. Hence, the study goes through the rules of major international arbitral institutions and arbitral case law, to the extent such is known and reported. In the author's view, it could not realistically deal solely with commercial arbitration, for which reason any arbitration problem has been also analysed from the perspective of ICSID as both an eminent arbitral institution and a pivot for investment arbitration, the latter being a sufficiently important branch of international arbitration where interim measures are a well-known phenomenon.

Finally, at the fourth level, the author decided to attempt to outline the main features, both common denominators and differentiating factors, of interim relief, measures, and procedures within the various realms analyzed. However, trying to reach out for such inferences was viewed by the author as not sufficiently well founded without making at least a (very) high level description of several interim relief proceedings which are outside the sphere of private law and private (civil and commercial) disputes. This is why and how institutions such as the International Court of Justice, ITLOS, and European Court of Human Rights became part of this study. In this author's view, making general conclusions about interim relief in proceedings with foreign or transnational element could not be justified without making at least some reference to such proceedings in adjudication bodies of public (international) law as well since both realms of private and of public international law disputes feature an international element, an "internationalization" of the dispute, and contact points, which purely national proceedings would not have.

The inferences, general remarks, and the dissection, which the author intended to put forward on basis of this extensive analysis, are contained at the end of the study. There the author also took the liberty to escape the field of law and make reference to theory of economics, etc. Indeed, this liberty is also taken at the very beginning of the study as well since the author shares the view that even a complex and very pragmatic matter of legal practice can find its backbone and rooting in the realms of philosophy, sociology, and psychology, and in legal theory, and so these sciences or fields of knowledge form helpful lenses through which we can see and scrutinize legal problems; hence we should utilize them.

What did bother the author, however, during the entire period of working on the study used to be whether to put some emphasis on details or seek broadness of the view. The author's view evolved towards the position that the modern world has adopted the approach of pigeonholing knowledge and has maybe lost the wider horizon of understanding. Therefore, an analysis that seeks to present the diversity of the problems, issues, and views in the particular field may have sufficient merit in the contemporary world which as if seeks to shed light on each and every niche but sometimes forgets about the wider breadth of the ocean (of knowledge and understanding).

Therefore, the structure of the study encapsulates these matters and its layers represent the cycle of interim relief, from its theoretical function and necessity down to its final realization.

Chapter 1 of the study creates the philosophical, sociological, conceptual, and terminological framework of the topic.

Chapter 2 is focused on the basis for issuance of interim relief—jurisdiction of competent bodies in cross-border litigation within EU as well as in international arbitration.

Chapter 3 covers the very essence of interim measures—what is the typology of measures, what categories of measures do exist, what are the standards applied by adjudicators in granting relief, and what are the procedural status and aspects of interim measures.

Chapter 4 deals with the procedure for enforcement of interim measures both in the EU law system and in international arbitration.

Chapter 5 compares grounds, procedures, and standards for interim relief in institutions founded on rules of public international law.

Chapter 6 draws inferences on basis of the review made in the previous parts, while Chapter 7 does outline concluding remarks.

As a result of all of this, the author hopes that the present study succeeds to comprise the said mapping of the problem of interim relief in proceedings of private/civil nature and having international implications, which has been conceived at its very beginning. The purpose is to be able to represent the groundwork of rules, proceedings, specific features, milestones, standards, concepts, and criteria, which a lawyer, no matter whether part of academia or legal practice, should bear in mind when confronted with such case, situation, issue, or question.

If the study fails to achieve this, it is entirely responsibility of its author. If the study succeeds to achieve this, the credit for this goes to a very significant extent to Prof. Peter Mankowski, without whom none of this could be possible.

Sofia, Bulgaria   Deyan Draguiev

Acknowledgments

This work is dedicated to the dear memory of Professor Peter Mankowski, long-standing professor of civil law, comparative law, private international law, and procedural law at the University of Hamburg. Professor Mankowski left us extremely early and suddenly, and the news of his passing was more than grievous and heart-wrenching. His infinite kindness is beyond the ability to describe. His stature on the field where he had developed his professional recognition is widely known and spawned repute and acclaim.

Prof. Mankowski has accepted the idea that I become his doctoral student under the most unusual circumstances. He did contact me about a scholarly article I had published in the "Journal of International Arbitration," which he wanted to cite in the profound commentary on the Brussels I Regulation that he edited. This is how our communication, afterwards cooperation started, where the professor accepted the student without previous relations and without studying under him beforehand. I will always remember Prof. Mankowski for the extremely courteous way of communicating his ideas, steering my interests forward, and suggesting the road to enhancement, as well as being always there to provide his wise advice. I believe this is how not only me, but also the entire wide family of his students and colleagues will remember him. His contribution to the present study, from accommodating my idea that he should become my supervisor, to his very refined remarks and ideas for embellishment, has done its positive impact and caused any draft of the study to become more complete and acceptable. My doctoral dissertation, the present study, and this book built upon it would not have existed, possibly, without Prof. Mankowski.

If I have to embark upon listing and enumeration of the various sources, which have influenced me and have contributed to this work and my ability to complete it, this would be a complex elaboration. It would have to entail various universities in different countries, incl. the University of Hamburg and its doctoral commission (comprising Prof. Eckart Brödermann, Prof. Tilman Repgen, and Prof. Julius Hinrich); many colleagues and friends at law firms; the clients, which have turned my mind to the practical implications of all written within this work; all my editors at various law journals and publishing houses, which have kindly helped me to hone my legal writing capacities; the publishing house "Springer", which welcomed the publication of this study as a book; and a myriad of sources within law, literature, history, philosophy, sociology, and psychology, which have, more or less, made me who I am.

But to shorten this, I would single out my parents, without whose love, care, and intellectual upbringing, nothing would have been possible down the long way.

Contents

1 Introduction on Interim Measures and Cross-Border Disputes 1
2 Basis and Jurisdiction to Grant Interim Measures 13
3 Nature, Operation, Types of Interim Measures 55
4 Enforcement of Interim Measures 107
5 Interim Measures in Other International Judicial and Quasi-Judicial Bodies 125
6 Assessment 141
7 Summary of Results. Conclusion 151

Abbreviations

AAA	American Arbitration Association
CIETAC	China International Economic and Trade Arbitration Commission
CJEU/ECJ	Court of Justice of the European Union
DIS	Deutsche Institution für Schiedsgerichtsbarkeit
EC	European Commission
ECHR	European Convention of Human Rights (Convention for the Protection of Human Rights and Fundamental Freedoms)
ECtHR	European Court of Human Rights
HKIAC	Hong Kong International Arbitration Centre
ICC	International Chamber of Commerce
ICDR	International Centre for Dispute Resolution
ICJ	International Court of Justice
ICSID	International Centre for Settlement of Investment Disputes
ITLOS	International Tribunal for the Law of the Sea
LCIA	London Court of International Arbitration
SCC	Stockholm Chamber of Commerce
SIAC	Singapore International Arbitration Centre
VIAC	Vienna International Arbitration Centre
UNCITRAL	United Nations Commission on International Trade Law
UNCLOS	United Nations Convention on the Law of the Sea

Chapter 1
Introduction on Interim Measures and Cross-Border Disputes

The role of this chapter of the present study is to lay down the wider framework for the operation of the analysis, which shall be put forth in the subsequent parts of this work. In order to understand the theoretical and further, the practical implications of the interim measure procedures, it is important to start from the conceptual underpinnings of interim relief. The latter is a fragment of the machinery of legal dispute resolution.

Moreover, dispute resolution serves a particular and very peculiar social role and can be perceived from the standpoint of philosophy, from the analytical viewpoint of psychology as studying the subjective understanding of relations arising from disputes, and the sociological prism to legal relationships and dispute resolution relations as particular types of phenomena pertaining to the field of social interaction and interplay among social agents.

Furthermore, this introductory part also serves the aim to delineate the key concepts that would be further analysed and to expound the arguments that the current study would seek to prove along the analysis it shall provide.

1.1 Developing Background of Relevant General Concepts

The current section seeks to provide a higher level of abstraction in dealing with the groundwork problem in the study. The section strives to outline several key concepts—what is a dispute, what is the nature and role of dispute resolution, and what are the legal aspects thereof, as these key concepts form the background to the particular and specific topic of interim relief.

The importance and operation of this explanation stems from the necessity to lay down understanding of such basic concepts that would be employed in delimiting peculiar features of interim measures. There is an interplay between the more philosophical understanding of these notions and some of the conclusions on interim relief, which shall be analysed in the course of this study. Prior to this, however, definitions forming the background should be clarified, and the first section of the study is the proper place for this.

1.1.1 General Understanding of Disputes: Philosophical, Psychological, Sociological Aspects

A dispute is, in philosophical terms, a contradiction between two or more parties regarding one and the same object.

Facts are the world.[1] These constitute states of affairs. A state of affairs is a combination of objects.[2] A proposition represents the existence and non-existence of states of affairs.[3] The sense of a proposition is its agreement and disagreement with possibilities of existence and non-existence of states of affairs.[4]

Hence, communication conveys the subjective representations of an understanding concerning the world, being an understanding of a particular state of affairs (i.e. ultimately objects). An accord means that certain existence/non-existence of a state of affairs is recognized by the parties participating in the respective flow of communication. A discord, however, means that to one party the state of affairs exists, while to another one—it does not (at all or in the same manner). The basis for discord is difference in perception. Perception is a cognition of an existential proposition; and it serves as a basis for inference, which uniformly exhibits the connection between propositions.[5]

The minimum requirements for a dispute to exist are: there are at least two parties in communication between each other; and these parties communicate regarding one and the same object. If there is no communication, there cannot be a dispute. Further, if the communication exists, but concerns different objects, i.e. the objects of the communication do not overlap, there is no actual dispute at all. Finally, the essence of the communication, if being a dispute, is controversy, contradiction, conflict. The communication is not collaboration but is expression of positions regarding one and the same object which do not coincide. Collaboration may ensue but is not an ingredient of dispute/communication.

Communication should be seen within the framework of social action, within existing social relationships. It is a form of social action, the latter being human action directed at the behaviour of other human beings.[6] Social action is action within social structure comprised of distinct human agents. Behaviour should be

---

[1] Wittgenstein (2001), para 1.1.
[2] Wittgenstein (2001), para 2.01.
[3] Wittgenstein (2001), para 4.1.
[4] Wittgenstein (2001), para 4.2.
[5] Moore (1899), pp. 176–193.
[6] Weber (1978), p. 22.

meaningful to be social. A social relationship is an orientation of meaningful inter-human behaviour. The content of a social relationship is its meaning.[7] The meaning is the one imputed by the social actors into the relationship. The imputed subjective meaning should not be one and the same for all actors; each may ascribe different meaning to the relationship.

Communication should be perceived in the terms of communicative action, action based upon deliberative process, where two or more individuals interact (through verbal or non-verbal means) and coordinate their action based upon agreed interpretations of the situation.[8] This is a form of social interaction, coordination of behaviour between the participants to the interaction. Social interaction might be perceived, indeed, as being comprised by communication flows between parties.

The primary interaction between the parties is a communication over certain object, which is a fact of human life and of social reality. The subject (i.e. subject matter) of this communication is the behaviour between the parties concerning the particular object (fact); their conduct is a set of rights and obligations, in general terms, which may be guided by various systems determining social interaction and inter-human behaviour (e.g. religion, morality, law, etc.).

An interaction is governed by a normative system. Any divergence in the understanding, interpretation of the object of the primary communication, as well as the subject of the primary communication, would lead to a secondary communication, i.e. communication purporting to resolve the divergence so as to realize (effect) the primary communication in the manner it ought to be conducted (effected). The essence of disagreement is difference in interpretation, including understanding (including subjective perception) of objects (facts) within the primary relationship, as well as understanding of what the norm governing the relationship prescribes. Thus difference may be termed as conflicting ontological interpretation (i.e. conflict over what a state of affairs is) and/or conflicting normative interpretation (i.e. conflict over what a state of affairs should be).

The essential purpose of communication is to reach understanding. To reach understanding would mean that parties to any disagreement return back to behaviour in conformity with the norm prescribing their behaviour, i.e. start acting as they ought to. This is either because their subjective perceptions concerning the object and the subject of the primary communication reach accord/coincide, or a third party binds them onto particular perception that the parties ought to conform to. This communication is secondary, based on the primary one, intertwined with the primary one, and governed by a set of rules prescribing particular rights and obligations. The object of the secondary communication is the primary one; and the subject of the secondary communication is the resolution of the contradiction so as to resolve and eliminate the secondary communication and revert back only to primary communication. The normative system that governs the primary communication is usually different from the normative system that governs the secondary one; the secondary

---

[7] Weber (1978), p. 28.
[8] Habermas (1984), p. 86.

one purports to govern how the conflict regarding the primary one should be resolved.

1.1.2 Defining Resolution of Disputes

The process of resolution may be described as solving a problem—to extinguish and do away with the problem. The non-existence of a problem denotes the existence of a solution ("the facts all contribute only to setting the problem, not to its solution"[9]). The solution of the problem is seen in the vanishing of the problem. ("Is not this the reason why those who have found after a long period of doubt that the sense of life became clear to them have then been unable to say what constituted that sense?").[10] Assuming the problem is the dispute, its solution will be that no dispute exists, i.e. that the difference is substituted by accord.

In the light of the understanding that dispute entails communication, and the resolution of a dispute is to have no discord, i.e. to reach accord, this would also mean that all parties to the communication see the facts, as objects of the communication, and the subject, as normatively prescribed behaviour, so that their perception coincides, i.e. accept subjectively one and the same as verified. If they cannot reach such subjective verification by themselves, they need a third party to verify it for them. Therefore, the process of dispute settlement by a third party, not participating in the dispute, is to reach a verification of the underlying state of affairs and communicate the verification. This, however, is not sufficient, as it should also be binding.

The third party holds authority over the disputants and this authority is the source of the binding force of the verification, i.e. that what is seen and communicated by the third party as verified should be accepted by the disputants as verified. Authority hinges on the ability of the third party to impose its verification, i.e. to have binding communication over the disputants. This is based on the participation of all parties—disputants and dispute resolver—into a single social structure (within the context of a social field where all parties participate), a composite flow of communication. This ensures enforcement of the verification, the understanding imposed by the third party. Any non-compliant disputant will be ousted out of this social structure, out of this matrix of communication. If a party wants to remain within the structure, it should comply. Non-compliance will be effected if the participation in the structure is no longer a subjective value for the disputant so the non-compliant party does not perceive the authority as binding as it does not fear being excluded from the structure. Otherwise, the mechanism of ensuring compliance with the authority of the third party is that normally parties value being part of this social structure and the communication flows within it. Being ousted from this social structure in practical

---

[9]Wittgenstein (2001), para 6.4321.
[10]Wittgenstein (2001), para 6.521.

1.1 Developing Background of Relevant General Concepts

terms would lead to disruption of a disputant's participation in a particular social field.[11]

If this line of thought is assumed, it would lead to the pivotal question how a dispute settlement is to be "enforced", what makes it binding, what is the source of authority, etc. These considerations have been widely discussed in the area of theory and philosophy of law.[12] However, at this theoretical level, the present study seeks to outline the social aspect of the dispute resolution process without delving into the water of law's authority and enforceability. At this stage, the study wants to suggest what is the social underpinning of this phenomenon. Borrowing, once more, from Pierre Bourdieu,[13] a disputant's compliance with a particular settlement of a dispute could have impact on the social capital of that party, this being "social obligations ("connections"), ... convertible, in certain conditions, into economic capital",[14] and "the aggregate of the actual or potential resources ... linked to possession of a durable network of more or less institutionalized relationships of mutual acquaintance and recognition—or in other words, to membership in a group—which provides each of its members with the backing of the collectively owned capital, a "credential" which entitles them to credit, in the various senses of the word. These relationships may exist only in the practical state, in material and/or symbolic exchanges which help to maintain them".[15] Since a party to a dispute may, theoretically, evade compliance with a resolution of a dispute, this also means that the party's social capital, which also determines the standing of that party on a particular social field, may be negatively affected, which would in effect negatively impact other social relations of that party, potential economic or societal opportunities of that party, etc.

By way of example, if the setting of the relations is a commercial one, and the parties to a dispute belong to a certain common social field of a particular type of trade, a disputant who fails to comply with contractual obligations, judgments or awards, etc., would be tarnished by bad reputation (as worsening its social, incl. symbolic, capital in the field). Even if a party may successfully evade obligations, this may affect negatively the party's standing on the social field of commerce. Globalization, mobility, electronic means of communication, interconnected supply chains, etc. in modern world economy boost the importance of a party's position and standing within the field of that party's business activities and add to the tools to ensure compliance. Hence, this model exemplifies that irrespective of legal means, there is a social context that drives parties to dispute resolution compliance.

---

[11] On social fields see generally Hilgers and Mangez (2014), pp. 1–37; also on social fields, Bourdieu (1999), pp. 5–27.

[12] The string of literature abounds of profound authors, among others see e.g. Weber (1954), pp. 33–41; Raz (1979), pp. 5–15; Oberdiek (1975), pp. 71–94.

[13] Bourdieu (1986), p. 241–58; also Bourdieu (1983), p. 183–98

[14] Bourdieu (1986), p. 242

[15] Bourdieu (1986), p. 247

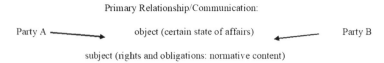

Fig. 1.1 Primary Relationship/Communication

Granted that compliance is effected, all parties involved have now a single and unified understanding of veracity regarding a certain state of affairs, so that there is nothing to dispute between themselves, i.e. accord is reached.

1.1.3 Legal Aspects of Disputes and Dispute Resolution

The legal backdrop of a dispute would mean certain elaboration of the elements stated hereabove. The content of the communication between the parties, and the respective object, is specific—legal rights and obligations; this means that there is a rule of law prescribing certain human conduct, in the form of rights and obligations, which form the subject of the primary communication, concerning the object of the primary communication, as provided by the rule of law governing this interaction. Hence, the situation is as follows:

(i) there is an existing relationship (based on communication) between the parties.
(ii) There is, additionally, a secondary communication with regard the pre-existing relationship (communication).
(iii) The pre-existing relationship is one of legal rights and obligations (see Fig. 1.1).
(iv) The secondary communication and set (complex) of relationships is the controversy concerning the pre-existing one. The communication which purports to deal with the pre-existing primary one may be conducted between only the original parties to the primary relationship but, most often, with the involvement of a third party; hence the secondary communication would involve not only one but usually a number of relationships, which is why it is possible to speak of a set or a complex of relationships (between the disputing parties; between each of the disputing parties and the third party). In other words, the object of the secondary communication, which comprises this complex or set of relationships, is the primary one of legal rights and obligations. The subject of this secondary scenario is, however, the resolution of the conflict regarding the primary one (see Fig. 1.2).
(v) A resolution of a dispute, i.e. of the secondary relationship, is the cessation of the dispute—that the secondary relationship be done away with. This is the "ought to" of the secondary relationship. The conduct of this relationship is, again, governed by rules of law.

1.1 Developing Background of Relevant General Concepts

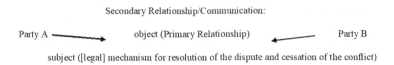

Fig. 1.2 Secondary Relationship/Communication

Against this theoretical concept, it is important to note that, since the purpose of the secondary scenario (communication) is to resolve a dispute within the primary one and bring the primary one back to peace, back to its state of conformity to what is normatively prescribed, this purpose should be ensured and there should be a mechanism in place to safeguard the possibility the primary relationship to exist. If there is a potential risk that the primary relationship be destroyed by the dispute, there would be no point in, and no value for, the realization of the secondary relationship.

Hence, the very essence of a secondary scenario and the set of relationships, which it entails, is that it needs a corollary in the form of a normative mechanism to ensure the existence of the elements of the primary relationship (communication) in the meantime before the secondary relationship is consummated and the dispute, or conflict, within the primary one is resolved.

Such mechanism is interim relief/interim measures, which is a requisite component of the mechanism how the secondary scenario operates. It is a tool that the secondary scenario needs in order to operate as to fulfil effectively its purpose.

1.1.4 Cross-Border Nature of a Dispute

The characterization of a cross-border dispute stems from the association of one of its defining elements with two or more jurisdictions (countries). The elements might be:

(i) Parties—that the parties are placed on the territory of different countries and/or are of different nationality;
(ii) Object—primary relationship; that the primary relationship is associated with two or more countries, which may mean that:

> The object (as fact) of the primary relationship is associated with more than one country;

> And/or the subject of the primary relationship, i.e. the associated rights and obligations, which are to be performed on the territory of more than one country.

The theoretical concept expounded hereabove should be exemplified by an illustration for better understanding. A, producer of goods, contracts with B, purchaser of goods. There is a primary relationship (communication) regarding the sale of the goods. The goods are the object of the relationship, and the subject is the set of rights and obligations concerning the transfer of ownership and physical delivery of the goods. In a non-ideal world, the goods might be found to be defective. There is ensuing communication between the parties as to (i) whether the goods are actually defective; and (ii) if found so, should be repaired or replaced, or the purchase price be refunded to the purchaser. This is the secondary relationship (communication) with object—the performance/non-performance of the primary one, and subject—resolution of the secondary one, so that any issue with the primary relationship is done away with.

Cross-border elements:

(i) A and/or B belong to different countries;
(ii) the goods and the place for their delivery are in different countries;
(iii) the goods and the place where they are established to have defects are in different countries (since this situation would place the proceedings and the objects in different countries and will trigger issues of cross-border implications).

1.2 The Concept of Interim Measures

1.2.1 Terminology

The phenomenon of interim measures is ubiquitous in national and transnational legal instruments and could be perceived under various names.

For example, EU Regulation 1215/2012 speaks under Article 35 of "provisional, including protective, measures", thus labelling the overarching phenomenon as "provisional measures". The same term is used in other EU cross-border regulations such as Regulation 2201/2003; Regulation 650/2012; Regulation 2016/1104, etc.

The various arbitral institutional rules use different accounts of this phenomenon. Article 26 of UNCITRAL Rules speak of interim measures. ICC Rules speak of interim and conservatory measures under the title of Article 29 thereof, which are called in the body of the provision interim or provisional, i.e. as separate and different phenomena. Article 28 of the LCIA Rules speaks of interim and conservatory measures. Article 37 of the SCC Rules calls this interim measures. Under Rule 30 of the SIAC Rules, interim measures may be granted. Article 23 of the HKIAC Rules regulate "interim measures of protection" while the body of the provision speaks of "interim or conservatory" measures. Article 23 of the CIETAC Rules is titled "conservatory and interim measures" while the body of the provision calls these "conservatory measures" under para 1 and "interim measures" under para 3. Article 24 of AAA Rules is labelled "interim measures" while the provision speaks of "interim or conservatory" measures. Article 20 of DIS Rules speaks of interim measures of protection. Rule 39 of ICSID Rules speaks of provisional measures for preservation.

Moreover, Article 41 of the Statute of the ICJ deals with provisional measures, as Article 290 does for UNCLOS. Under Rule 39 of the ECtHR rules of procedure, the

1.2 The Concept of Interim Measures

court may prescribe interim measures. Article 279 of TFEU grants the power to the CJEU to provide interim measures, too. Article 8 of Regulation 1/2003 gives powers of the EU Commission to provide interim measures.

The overview demonstrates that one and the same phenomenon is termed in a variety of ways although there is a relatively single and uniform concept that stands behind it. For the purpose of this study, the following analysis and clarification should be made regarding terminology:

Principle qualifications/labelling of measures:

(1) "protective", "conservatory", "preservation", "precaution/cautionary"—the emphasis is on the purpose of the measure to safeguard the status quo while the procedure is pending;
(2) "provisional"—the emphasis is on the time span of the measure, i.e. that it is effective only for a limited period of time (only "for the time being");
(3) "interim"—the emphasis is on the function of the measure as relief granted prior to the final resolution of the procedure, relief effective in between arising dispute and its settlement.

This study shall make use of the term "interim" to label this concept. Interim is deemed to be an all-embracing term for this procedural phenomenon because it:

(i) suggests that the time span of the measure is temporary, i.e. reflects the time aspect of the phenomenon—that it is only temporary pending final resolution;
(ii) suggests that this is relief granted to regulate the situation as regards the parties while the dispute is pending, which encapsulates the status quo precautionary function of such measures;
(iii) not all measures are by their function conservatory (e.g. some evidence-taking is not); and not all measures have emphasis on time factor (again, some evidence-taking or a ruling that restrains parallel proceedings) and serve a variety of functions; therefore, a label that puts emphasis only on time, such as "provisional", or preservation of status of affairs, such as "conservatory", overlooks other aspects of this phenomenon.

Hence, the term "interim" reflects better and to a greater extent the full array of functions of the concept of these measures.

1.2.2 Definition of Interim Measures

The terminology overview may serve as basis for delimitation of the features of the concept of interim measures. First, these are measures that are aimed to maintain the status quo between the parties to the dispute and avert further aggravation of the rights at stake. However, this is not absolute. Some measures purport not to maintain the status quo but to maintain (help, facilitate, make more efficient) the dispute resolution procedure. Other target the pure safeguarding of the potential of one of the parties to enforce its rights after the settlement of the dispute, including as to costs rendered in the course of the proceedings.

The variety of these aspects of interim measures dictates that a definition of interim measures cannot reduce interim measures to a mere procedural tool; interim measures would most likely have significant effect on the substantive rights of the parties as well. However, the basis for interim measures is undeniably procedural and their life span is functionally intertwined with the main proceedings dealing with the dispute between the parties.

Therefore, the proposed definition of interim measures is: (i) a procedural instrument (ii) issued by a dispute resolution body (iii) in order to temporarily manage the parties to the dispute as well as, in some circumstances, third parties, (iv) while the procedure is pending and before the rendering of final ruling on the merits of the dispute (v) for the purpose of safeguarding the substantive rights of the parties at stake in the dispute as well as the procedure for settlement of the dispute.

Considered against the understanding of dispute given under Sect. 1.1 above, the interim measures are a tool called upon to ensure that there is a flow of communication between the parties and that communication would not cease. First, in order that the possibility of communication within the primary relationship may be ensured because otherwise, there would be no point in having secondary communication (relationship). Second, in order that there is actual communication effected within the secondary flow of communication (relationship). Interim measures should prevent total breakdown of communication, at both levels, and should ensure that any communication, at both levels would be meaningful.

On a higher level of theoretical abstraction, the ultimate purpose of interim measures is to ensure proper dispute/conflict management. Hence, this makes them a conflict management instrument.

1.3 Arguments Which This Study Seeks to Analyse and Find Proof for

The method selected by the author for the present study is to a certain extent inspired by the deductive testing theory of Karl Popper[16] (also known as "critical rationalism"), which posits a hypothesis/problem/argument and then deduces logically its implications, observes, tests and compares them to other propositions, and thus draws conclusions whether these operations of the mind prove and corroborate the initial hypothesis put forward. In a similar vein, in the course of analyzing the problem, this study would seek to outline, compare, and find proof in laws and regulations, case law and legal theory for a number of arguments, which at this preliminary stage of the study should be considered as conjectures (hypotheses) that need further evidence:

---

[16] Popper (2002), p. 9

First, the purpose of interim relief is to influence a dispute and manage the dispute/conflict until its final settlement in order to avoid greater aggravation and safeguard the rights of parties after the dispute is resolved.

Second, interim relief procedures hinge upon several criteria of appreciation: (i) assessment of the probability of the alleged rights and positions of the parties to the dispute; (ii) the risk of imminent/unavoidable harm in the absence of granting interim relief; (iii) proportionality/adequacy between the dispute, the rights at stake, and the measures imposed. In various shapes and forms, such assessment criteria are employed in the wide array of national and international dispute settlement procedures.

Third, as interim relief depends on the underlying dispute and its nature, interim measures are connected with, and modified by, the various rights at stake between the disputing parties. The characteristics of a dispute, its subject matter, its time and geographical span and other features have direct implications on the interim relief granted for the purpose of the particular dispute. There is direct interrelationship between the interim measures and the underlying dispute.

Finally, although all disputes with international implications share similarities and common ground as to interim relief granted, there are some differentia specifica. With regard to differentiating features of private cross-border disputes, compared to public international law disputes, the specifics of the underlying substantive rights at stake (being rooted in private law) are reflected in the manner and purpose of interim relief granted. The latter is usually tailored to safeguard various rights stemming from the domain of private law such as monetary claims, assets of particular financial value, IP rights, etc.

Since the study seeks to build affirmation of these propositions, the structure of the study and its elements reflect these propositions. Hence, while Chap. 2 deals with the jurisdictional grounds for interim relief in cross-border litigation and arbitration proceedings, Chap. 3, builds upon the basic concepts and legal framework laid down in the first two chapters, and is focused on the nature and content of measures, as the operation and the interplay between subject matter of dispute and character of the measures should be revealed therein. Further, Chap. 5 is the structural point where the overview of interim measures in public disputes should demonstrate how these disputes predetermine different role of interim relief compared to private disputes and to what extent there are criteria applicable to public disputes measures which are similar to those in private disputes. Finally, Chap. 6 is the part of the study where it will look back at these arguments and make evaluation if the suggested conjectures are sufficiently clarified and proven, while Chap. 7 wraps up the entire work with concluding remarks.

References

Bourdieu P (1983) Okonomisches Kapital, kulturelles Kapital, soziales Kapital. In: Kreckel R (ed) Soziale Ungleichheiten. Otto Schartz & Co, Goettingen

Bourdieu P (1986) The forms of capital. In: Richardson J (ed) Handbook of theory and research for the sociology of education. Greenwood, Westport
Bourdieu P (1999) Le Fonctionnement Du Champ Intellectuel. Regards Sociologiques 17(18):5–27
Habermas J (1984) Theory of communicative action. Beacon Press, Boston
Hilgers M, Mangez E (2014) Bourdieu's theory of social fields: concepts and applications. Routledge, London
Moore GE (1899) The nature of judgment. Mind 8(30):176–193
Oberdiek H (1975) The role of sanctions and coercion in understanding law and legal systems. Am J Jurisprud 21(1):71–94
Popper K (2002) The logic of scientific discovery. Routledge, London
Raz J (1979) The authority of law. Oxford University Press, Oxford
Weber M (1954) Law in economy and society. Harvard University Press, Cambridge
Weber M (1978) Economy and society. University of California Press, Los Angelis
Wittgenstein L (2001) Tractatus Logico-Philosophicus. Routledge, London

Chapter 2
Basis and Jurisdiction to Grant Interim Measures

Chapter 1 elucidated the general backdrop and framework within which the problem at the heart of the study operates. Moreover, the previous chapter also laid down the main questions and arguments that the study seeks to find proof for (or against).

This chapter functions to achieve different ends. This chapter strives to lay down the jurisdictional grounds for granting interim relief. This is where the practicalities of interim relief start: from the assessment which rules (of law) set the conditions adjudicating bodies to issue interim measures.

The first section of the chapter deals with the so called Brussels regimes, i.e. the corpus of regulations which the European Union has established in the area of civil and commercial disputes in cross-border situations. The forerunner of the entire system is Regulation Brussels Ibis (1215/2012), previously Brussels I, and based on the Brussels Convention, where the main concept of interim relief under the EU Brussels regime started taking form and was sourced to a number of other regulations, with some amendments and alterations depending on their scope of application. Such other regulations of the Brussels regime are reviewed, as well.

The second part of this chapter provides overview of the jurisdictional bases for interim relief in the area of (international) arbitration. There are some intrinsic complexities of arbitration that this study cannot evade. Due to arbitration's consensual nature at its foundation, this part of the study needs to make a brief overview of the general grounds for jurisdiction of arbitral tribunals, and only afterwards to move on to specific rules establishing jurisdiction to grant interim relief. This includes also a review of major arbitral institutions as well as the issue of coordination, concurrence, even competition between state courts and arbitral tribunals in granting interim relief, with a proposed possible solution for this situation. Due to the specific nature of ICSID (being an arbitral institution similar to others; dealing with international economic issues; but deciding on matters with some public international law bearing), there is a distinct section devoted to ICSID. This approach is to be followed in subsequent chapters as well.

© The Author(s), under exclusive license to Springer Nature Switzerland AG 2023
D. Draguiev, *Interim Measures in Cross-Border Civil and Commercial Disputes*, EYIEL Monographs - Studies in European and International Economic Law 30, https://doi.org/10.1007/978-3-031-28704-6_2

2.1 International Civil and Commercial Litigation

2.1.1 Overview of the Jurisdictional System of the Regulations Within EU Law

The EU law regime on international jurisdiction is yet not a coherent set of rules. It provides a variety of regulations with direct effect and application within EU Member States that relate to each other but do not create a comprehensive system of regulation of civil and commercial cases with international elements within the EU.

The jurisdictional system has been gradually developed around the cornerstone of the 1968 Brussels Convention. It started with the civil and commercial disputes, which formed the scope of the Brussels I, later Brussels Ibis regulation, and the EU law regime was subsequently expanded with adding up the field of matrimonial/family and succession issues. In result, two notionally separate "streams" within this jurisdictional system could be discerned: Brussels I and Brussels II regimes, with a set of additional regulations.

Regulation Brussels Ibis can be considered, to a certain degree, the backbone of the Brussels I regime (and to a large extent the groundwork for the entire Brussels EU law regime),[1] as a number of other regulations (e.g. Regulation (EC) No 1896/2006 of the European Parliament and of the Council of 12 December 2006 creating a European order for payment procedure; Regulation (EC) No 861/2007 of the European Parliament and of the Council of 11 July 2007 establishing a European Small Claims Procedure;) refer to its framework, but in no case does it operate as basis for the rest of EU regulations. Instead, Brussels Ibis provides, in certain matters, groundwork for development of some concepts, which have been employed by other regulations, too; and in other matters such as matrimonial issues, insolvency, maintenance, the provisions of the respective regulations divulge from Brussels Ibis—e.g. Regulation 2201/2003, later 2019/1111; Regulation 2015/848 on Insolvency.

This analysis is relevant to the area of interim measures. The Brussels I regime regulates the jurisdiction of EU Member States' courts to grant interim measures; and the enforcement of such measures abroad. There is not yet a single system of rules and not all regulations follow one and the same pattern.

Jurisdictional rules are rules of law featuring the essential elements that rules of law have. Following Kelsen,[2] a legal rule is an "ought", a command, which permit human behaviour or authorize it. To map this theory against the specifics of procedure, procedural rules will fall within the scope of the second proposition, authorization of certain behaviour, and more particularly conferral of authority on a dispute resolution body to handle disputes and bind parties to disputes with rulings

---

[1] Mankowski and Magnus (2011), p. 11.
[2] Kelsen (2005), pp. 4–5.

that the parties ought to follow subsequently. The jurisdictional rule functions within the procedural set of rules, i.e. has procedural impact. The impact it has is effectuated only on the grounds for exercising jurisdiction. The jurisdictional rule incorporates the prerequisites for a decision-making body to conduct proceedings and issue binding ruling on the subject matter it is seized for.

In the context of interim measures, a jurisdictional rule shall mean a rule that provides the conditions for establishing court jurisdiction to impose interim measures.

Interim measures may be granted on two separate bases within the EU: first, on basis of the respective EU regulation; second, on basis of national procedural law. The EU regulations do not override national procedural law, they run in parallel (with some limited exceptions – e.g. some grounds of special jurisdiction under Article 7 of Regulation Brussels Ibis). Therefore, the policy legislative methods of the EU regulations are that they may:

(i) provide a coherent set of jurisdictional rules on interim measures;
(ii) regulate the matter to certain extent, and usually refer to another EU instrument, or employ the pattern and concepts as developed by another EU instrument; or
(iii) leave the matter to national law.

In reality, it is a mix between the three options.

First, some regulations feature autonomous and independent jurisdictional rules. A notable example is Regulation Brussels Ibis, which in its Article 35 regulates the grounds for exercising court jurisdiction to grant interim measures: "Application may be made to the courts of a Member State for such provisional, including protective, measures as may be available under the law of that Member State, even if the courts of another Member State have jurisdiction as to the substance of the matter." This rule operates as jurisdictional rule as it provides conditions for exercise of judicial competence. The rule effectively enshrines grounds for international jurisdiction, i.e. establishes the grounds to provide measures in cross-border situations, as a part of the wider jurisdictional framework of Regulation Brussels Ibis. In order that Article 35 is triggered as jurisdictional basis, the entire Brussels I regime should be applicable along its own specific concepts developed through theory and case law. The rule is relevant as to jurisdiction but do not regulate handling of proceedings nor guarantee the subsequent cross-border (international) enforcement of a decision. Regulation Brussels Ibis is, however, featuring a separate set of rules, which render enforcement of measures granted under this jurisdiction abroad subject to other conditions. The interpretation of Regulation Brussels Ibis (previously Brussels I) has given rise to the development of key concepts (e.g. the real connecting link doctrine) related to interim relief within EU law. Some of these concepts do not remain solely encapsulated within the framework of Regulation Brussels Ibis but may influence other regulations and have wider impact.

There are also regulations featuring rules that do not confer jurisdiction on their own strictu sensu, but refer to other jurisdictional grounds and thus have some procedural impact on court jurisdiction set up under national law. This is where a regulation provides some qualification on the jurisdiction that may be exercised under the relevant applicable national law.

For instance, under the Brussels II regime—Article 20 of Regulation 2201/2003, later Article 15 of Regulation 1111/2019—the matter of interim measures is referred to any court with principle jurisdiction under respective national procedural law with one qualification: only for urgent situations. The Regulation makes a reference to lex fori without providing jurisdiction on its own, and the matter is not regulated by the Regulation as long as it is "urgent". This is so because once jurisdiction on the substance is established in accordance with the Regulation, only the court with such jurisdiction will have competence to grant interim measures, as part of its general jurisdictional powers. The rationale behind is that any competent court may grant interim measures when time is of the essence; once the urgency is gone and the matter is brought to court on its substance, i.e. the court with jurisdiction under the Regulation Brussels II, the interim measures jurisdiction referred to as per Article 20 (Article 15) will be divested so that no clash of jurisdictions (and measures imposed) may occur. Therefore, the Regulation Brussels II does not provide specific own jurisdictional rules but a qualification on the jurisdictional rule, stemming from national law provisions, e.g. as to time span of interim measures jurisdiction. To be contrasted, Art. 35 of Regulation Brussels Ibis does not impose, on its own, explicit jurisdictional requirements that would qualify a national court's jurisdiction, as long as the national court's jurisdiction is generally congruent with the framework and applicability of Regulation Brussels Ibis; if Regulation Brussels Ibis employs urgency, it is as a standard for proper measures but not as a condition to establishing jurisdiction. Hence, the procedural rule is not actually jurisdictional as it does not lay down the prerequisites for establishing jurisdiction but outline additional requirements to a jurisdiction established under other jurisdictional (local, national) rules. Furthermore, it is a rule that presents rather an exception to the framework of the entire Regulation Brussels II and is not dependent on the overall application of that regulation. This is why it may not be deemed as a "pure" jurisdictional rule but as a procedural rule with impact on establishing jurisdiction (with jurisdictional impact). The measures provided under this jurisdiction are capable of cross-border enforcement but, again, subject to additional (even stricter than under Regulation Brussels Ibis) conditions and criteria.

Third, some regulations do not provide independent jurisdictional rules dealing with interim measures. Their provisions replicate the jurisdictional approach of another EU law regulation and the interpretation elaborated on its basis becomes applicable mutatis mutandi. This is relevant especially as to Regulation Brussels Ibis, which thus operates as backbone default source of jurisdictional concepts for a number of other regulations. However, these may follow the jurisdictional approach of Brussels Ibis, but do not follow the enforceability rules of Brussels Ibis.

An example is Article 14 of Regulation 4/2009. It does not contain an autonomous concept for interim relief and by employing identical language, effectively incorporates the approach of Regulation Brussels I (prior to Brussels Ibis). In such case the Regulation Brussels Ibis concepts and their interpretation remain relevant although Regulation 4/2009 makes no reference to Regulation Brussels I. The same

2.1 International Civil and Commercial Litigation   17

Table 2.1 Typology of jurisdictional rules and examples within EU Regulations regime

Type of rule	Source/Legal basis
A. Specific jurisdictional rule re interim measures enshrined by the respective regulation	E.g. Regulation Brussels Ibis
B. Qualified jurisdictional rule: no general grounds for establishing jurisdiction for interim measures enshrined by the respective regulation but explicit qualification for specifically indicated instances (qualification: "urgent cases")	E.g. Regulation 2201/2003, subsequently Regulation 2019/1111
C. Regulations without autonomous approach to jurisdictional rules	Features the language and terminology of another regulation (e.g. Regulation Brussels I), thus borrowing the interpretation that has been developed on its basis—e.g. Regulation 4/2009

approach is incorporated under Article 19 of Regulation 650/2012 on succession for instance. Unlike Regulation Brussels Ibis, however, these regulations do not feature grounds for cross-border enforcement of measures granted under their jurisdiction.

See Table 2.1 for the classification of procedural rules establishing jurisdiction regarding interim measures within EU Regulations framework—typology and examples:

2.1.2 Jurisdiction to Obtain Interim Measures Under Regulation Brussels Ibis

2.1.2.1 General Jurisdiction

The Regulation Brussels Ibis does not explicitly regulate a uniform jurisdiction, as it can be inferred on basis of interpreting Article 35 in conjunction with Article 42 of the Regulation. These are the two rules that can govern issues of interim measures within the framework of the Regulation.

There are two parallel regimes.[3]

First, this is the general jurisdiction under Regulation Brussels Ibis which may entail grounds for granting interim measures as part of the general dispute resolution jurisdiction of courts under the Regulation, as naturally there is a functional link between the general jurisdiction to resolve the dispute and the jurisdiction to protect its subject matter by interim measures.[4] Article 42 (2) provides for grounds for enforcement of a judgment ordering interim measures. According to Article 2 (a), 'judgment' includes provisional, including protective, measures ordered by a court or tribunal that by virtue of the Regulation has jurisdiction as to the substance of the

---

[3] Garcimartin (2014/2015), p. 57.
[4] Garcimartin (2014/2015), p. 59.

matter. Hence, Article 42 could regulate only judgments incorporating interim measures that are provided by courts with jurisdiction under Articles 4-26, i.e. as to the substance of the proceedings. This policy has been previously confirmed by the dicta in the case of Van Uden,[5] para 19, according to which "it is accepted that a court having jurisdiction as to the substance of a case in accordance with Articles 2 and 5 to 18 of the Convention also has jurisdiction to order any provisional or protective measures which may prove necessary".

Second, the special rule of Article 35 deals with, as outlined below in Sect. 2.1.3, a jurisdiction separate from the jurisdictional system of Articles 4-26 of the Regulation. This is a jurisdiction regarding the substance of the matter. Article 35 regulates only a jurisdiction of courts that are not competent under Articles 4-26. However, those courts with jurisdiction on the merits of the dispute are entitled to provide the full spectrum of relief, including interim relief.

Therefore, Regulation Brussels Ibis regulates two avenues for obtaining interim measures. First, the court that should have jurisdiction on basis of Articles 4-26 is entitled to entertain a request for interim measures besides dealing with the substance of the case. The requisite conditions for establishing the jurisdiction under this heading are the same as for dealing with the substance of the case. Moreover, the Regulation provides that courts not having jurisdiction under Articles 4-26 can also provide interim measures but only as long as the requirements of Article 35 are met. So this is the specific interim measures jurisdiction of the Regulation.

The general rules on jurisdiction under Articles 4-26 of Regulation Brussels Ibis are not discussed in details below as they do not deal with any specifics of provision of interim measures. The only specific interim relief-related rule within the general framework of Regulation Brussels Ibis is an enforcement rule (Article 42) which is discussed under Sect. 4.1 below.

Two points should be noted though. First, the interim measures proceedings may be brought before the court with jurisdiction on the merits even before the proceedings on the substance are effectively brought. Hence, the applicant may turn for interim relief to one court having (potential) jurisdiction on the substance before instituting the proceedings, and then bring the case on the substance to another court having jurisdiction on the merits.[6]

Second, the designation of competent court by prorogation, or selection, or arbitration, will have impact on the route for obtaining interim measures. In the former case the court having jurisdiction as a general rule will be the court selected for proceedings on the merits. In the latter case, no court may grant interim measures under the general rule, as the judicial jurisdiction on the merits of the dispute is excluded.[7]

---

[5] Judgment of the Court of 17 November 1998. - Van Uden Maritime BV, trading as Van Uden Africa Line v Kommanditgesellschaft in Firma Deco-Line and Another Case C-391/95.

[6] Garcimartin (2014/2015), p. 61.

[7] Garcimartin (2014/2015), p. 61.

2.1.3 Jurisdiction Under Article 35 of Regulation Brussels Ibis

2.1.3.1 General Remarks

Article 35 of Regulation Brussels Ibis is a distinct and specific jurisdictional basis although it is part of the jurisdictional matrix of Regulation Brussels Ibis. It is a jurisdictional rule with autonomous functioning within the jurisdictional system of Regulation Brussels Ibis and, indeed, within the entire framework of EU Regulations. Nevertheless, it interacts with the rest of the jurisdictional rules of Regulation Brussels Ibis. In some cases it may have wider or more limited application than the rest of the jurisdictional rules of the Regulation Brussels Ibis. This makes Article 35 jurisdiction more specific since it both follows a logic pertaining to the entire system, and also creates peculiar grounds for establishing jurisdiction.

It should be noted preliminarily that this is a jurisdictional rule and not an enforcement rule. It provides only for the basis of judicial competence to deal with an application for interim measures and does not provide for the enforcement of a judgment on such application. Although Article 35 creates a forum *sui generis*, i.e. court competence based on territoriality, it does not purport to create a rule of enforcement (execution).[8] This distinction is important as in some cases, as it will be analysed herein, there may be jurisdictional basis but yet there may be no option for enforcement of a judgment handed down by the court duly competent under the jurisdictional rule of Article 35. Hence, the interim measures under Article 35 cannot circulate[9] across borders on its own absent other conditions fulfilled.

As a jurisdictional rule, Article 35 of Regulation Brussels Ibis sets out the prerequisites (conditions) for a court bound by the Regulation Brussels Ibis to deal with an application for interim measures. It is framed as a completely separate basis which is not directly corresponding to the general provisions on jurisdiction (Articles 2-6 of Regulation Brussels Ibis), or the special grounds (Articles 7-24), or the prorogation of jurisdiction. Indeed, the wording of Article 35 indicates that the jurisdictional basis regulated therein is complementary one. This marks this interplay between the Art. 35 grounds and the rest of the jurisdictional bases: Art. 35 could not operate without the existence of the rest if the jurisdictional bases in the framework, but also enshrines a separate and additional jurisdictional option for the applicant. A contrario, the inherent and foremost interim measures jurisdiction that should be considered, then, is the jurisdiction of the court that has jurisdiction over the substance of the case. The Article 35 jurisdiction may be excluded by agreement between parties[10] which demonstrates its complementary and optional nature.

---

[8] Bureau and Muir Watt (2017), p. 103.
[9] E.g. see Lazić and Stuij (2017), p. 113.
[10] Garcimartin (2014/2015), p. 73.

This is a starting point for consideration of the parameters of the jurisdiction provided for in Article 35. It has the following aspects: ratione loci (territorii); ratione materiae; ratione temporis.

2.1.3.2 Territorial Scope

At first glance the jurisdiction under Article 35 should be considered as part of the system of the Regulation, and therefore should be governed by the basic principle of its applicability: the Regulation Brussels Ibis comes to play in case of an action brought against a respondent domiciled in a Member State of the EU (Article 4, paragraph 1), subject to the exceptions provided under Article 24 where not a subjective criterion (the domicile of the party) but an objective one (the subject matter of dispute) applies. The textual analysis, supported by a logical one, however, indicates that what Article 35 provides for is a jurisdiction which interacts within the framework of the Regulation Brussels Ibis, at one hand, and the national law of the Member States, at the other hand. Hence, this is an interim measures jurisdiction which aims to deal with requests to the courts of the Member States where the seized court is not the one having jurisdiction under the rest of the jurisdictional rules of Regulation Brussels Ibis.

But what if no Member State has jurisdiction under the particular dispute? For example, a US company, X, would like to bring action against a Chinese company, Y. Neither of them would qualify as EU Member State domiciles. Would it be possible that X may obtain interim measures from EU Member State courts? The independent nature of Article 35 might imply that any request to a Member State court should be entertained regardless of the Article 4 principle. However, this may push Article 35 too far from its original policy and stretch it to a length that has not been envisioned. Being a part of the Brussels Ibis system, it seems to be very unnatural to assume that it provides for an unrestrained application contrary to Article 4. After all, this is a jurisdictional system to encapsulate standard rules governing the EU Member States. Any rule or interpretation to the contrary would lead to exorbitance, which is not a policy of the Brussels Ibis system.

Furthermore, the real connecting link doctrine of the ECJ, which shall be analysed below, implies that an interpretation of Article 35 as a rule detached from the domicile principle of Article 4 of Regulation Brussels Ibis cannot be correct. Instead, a compromissory middle ground may be found. In practice, a party would not seek interim relief from EU Member State courts in case of absolutely no ties to the EU territory. Even where the respondent to the dispute is not domiciled in the EU, there would be a link to the EU; in practical terms, it may be contractual performance within the EU, a tort (delict) with effect within the EU, property in EU, etc. So, in order to separate frivolous applications from admissible ones, the territorial scope of Article 35 should be defined as sitting one step further from the Article 4 principle and within the bounds of the real connecting link doctrine: in order that Article 35 be triggered, the requisites of Article 4 ("persons domiciled in a Member State shall, whatever their nationality, be sued in the courts of that Member

State"—rei actor sequitur condition) or Article 24 (grounds for exclusive jurisdiction) should be met; however, even if these are not met, in practice the facts of the underlying dispute and/or the claimed rights at stake would fit into the general policy of the Brussels Ibis regime to seek connecting link with the EU territory. In the latter case, however, there would be a case-by-case analysis, which may not favour predictability but may enhance justice.

Hence, the jurisdictional basis of Art. 35 shall be (i) what the Regulation provides for; (ii) what applicable local procedural law provides for, but granted the limitation that in the absence of real connecting link with territorial implications, the jurisdiction will be exorbitant[11] and the measures may fail to be enforced in another EU Member State.

2.1.3.3 Time Span

The pertinent questions time-wise are: (i) when can interim measures be requested; and (ii) how long would they stay. The former one can be linked to the issue of jurisdiction as to the moment when the jurisdiction under Article 35 of Brussels Ibis Regulation is established; and the second will be reviewed accordingly below.

The textual analysis of Article 35 reveals that interim measures jurisdiction is detached from the main proceedings and so can be established regardless of the jurisdiction on the substance of the case. The policy of interim measures provisions is widely known to accept jurisdiction lead by the urgency and the need for measures to be imposed as soon as possible, so it would not be acceptable that jurisdiction be delayed until the main proceedings are instituted.

This policy can be interpreted against the background of timing so that an application for interim measures can be made prior to the proceedings on the substance of the dispute or while the proceedings on the substance of the dispute are pending. This argument is relatively widely accepted. The next question to it is, however, whether this would possibly lead to a clash if: the court second in time imposes measures conflicting with the measures imposed by the one first in time. This clash/collision will be dealt with further.

Some authors have argued that the time span of the Article 35 jurisdiction is limited only for the period until a court with jurisdiction on the merits of the case deals with it.[12] It has been suggested that when recast, Regulation Brussels Ibis should have featured a provision empowering the jurisdiction on the merits to modify or revoke the Article 35 court.[13]

In this author's view, the interpretation of Article 35 does not disclose any particular rule as to coordination of jurisdiction time-wise. Hence, there is no basis within the Brussels Ibis Regulation to consider that the Article 35 jurisdiction is

---

[11] See discussion on exorbitant jurisdiction (Garcimartin 2014/2015, p. 83).
[12] Lazić and Stuij (2017), p. 114.
[13] Burkhard Hess et al. (2005), Article 35.

existent until the court with jurisdiction on the substance handles the matter. This scenario does not cover the equally possible scenario of having an already established jurisdiction on the merits and a party willing to bypass enforcement issues by turning to the court at the place of potential enforcement on basis of Article 35. This is why Article 35 is in parallel to the general jurisdiction under Regulation Brussels Ibis. Moreover, a provision that the court with general jurisdiction can modify the measures provided by the Article 35 court would lead to a situation where the court of one EU Member State has say over rulings of another court of EU Member State which may lead to issues with mutual trust and regard between courts of Member States.

The discrepancies between Member States procedure-wise would make the task very difficult to be implemented in practice. The potential solution should be found by coordination under the law of the place where the measures would be implemented. E.g. if a party obtains measure in country X, and afterwards the court of country Y with general jurisdiction rules a different and conflicting measure, the measure which is second in time will have to be enforced, and the other party will be able to raise defences regarding the existing measure provided in country X. The issue would be decided under the lex fori of the seized court of country X. But what is important is that the matter will be solved by the courts of a single EU Member State, i.e. one jurisdictional system. This resolves the issue of coordination between the laws and courts of different countries.

2.1.3.4 Proper Forum

The textual analysis of Article 35 also demonstrates that an application for interim measures can be entertained by a number of courts.[14] First, this is the court with jurisdiction over the substance of the dispute. This is not stated explicitly but can be evinced a fortiori as Article 35 states that it regulates a jurisdictional basis parallel to the one of the court with jurisdiction over the substance of the matter. Second, the independent and complementary nature of Article 35 indicates that it is a "second option" while the main avenue for redress should be, normally, the court dealing with the dispute itself. After all, this is residual jurisdiction not deciding on the merits of the dispute. Hence, the claimant may seek relief from either the court which has jurisdiction under Regulation Brussels Ibis on the merits of the dispute, or to seek interim relief under Article 35 from another EU Member State court. The problem with clash/collision of jurisdiction surfaces again as one court may refuse to allow certain measures while the other may grant them, or each may allow conflicting measures. This issue shall be reviewed further below.

The reasoning here applies to prorogation of jurisdiction as well. Thus, under Article 25 of Regulation Brussels Ibis, the parties may agree on a specific court to handle their dispute. On its own, this does not derogate from Article 35, as this

---

[14] Bureau and Muir Watt (2017), p. 103.

situation does not substantially differ from the situation where the jurisdiction is based on the default rules of the Regulation Brussels Ibis. However, in this author's view, which is supported by doctrine and case law, the parties to a prorogation may agree on exclusion of the application of Article 35. There is a good reason behind this as parties would prefer to concentrate any issues of dispute and any powers of adjudication to a single forum. However, barring express derogation, Article 35 will allow that other courts apart from the prorogated forum, may handle the dispute between the parties.

The situation with arbitration agreements seems as analogous although in fact the arbitration agreement's effect is to derogate the entire application of the Brussels regime and so to exempt the parties from the powers of interim measures jurisdiction of national courts. Therefore, the mere presence of arbitration agreement would exclude the application of Article 35. This is analysed further below.

The same logic applies to the exclusive grounds of jurisdiction—Article 24. The exclusivity does not derogate from the application of Article 35. Hence, if there is a real estate or shareholding dispute, it shall be settled by the court envisioned in Article 24 while other EU Member State courts may grant interim measures as to such a dispute. However, the existence of such jurisdiction does not ensure the enforcement of the interim measure, as will be analysed further. Second, the real connecting link requirement may prevent this jurisdiction from being established. This is why theoretically the application of Article 35 is possible; however, in practice either the connection will not suffice or may be useless in the face of enforcement difficulties.

2.1.3.5 Substantive Scope

Article 35's application is within the scope of the Regulation Brussels Ibis. In fact, the Regulation operates on two levels in this respect. First, it sets base for the area of civil and commercial cases (matters). Second, its ambit has been gradually reduced and interfered with by the rest of the Brussels regime. This is why a number of matters falling within the penumbra of civil and commercial matters (such as maintenance, matrimonial and child abduction issues, insolvency, etc.) have been relocated to other regulations so that Brussels Ibis would not apply to them.

However, Article 35 operates on the first abovementioned level. It is the jurisdictional basis for the entire Brussels regime in case of civil and commercial disputes. Hence, whatever the dispute is, as long as it can be qualified as civil and commercial matter, the courts of the EU Member States would have jurisdiction to impose interim measures[15] (Provisional including protective measures filed as a

---

[15] e.g. Jacques de Cavel v. Louise de Cavel, (Case 143/78) (1979) ECR 1055; W. v. H., (Case 25/81) (1982) ECR 1189; Belgium: Trib. Nivelles Div. Act. 1995, 78; CA Bruxelles Div. Act. 1996, 57 (interim maintenance claim during divorce proceedings) In the Netherlands: Hoge Raad NIPR 1993, 390 (interim maintenance claim).

result of insolvency fall outside the scope of Art. 24 Brussels Convention (or Art. 31)[16]).

In order that Regulation Brussels Ibis is triggered, the scope and nature of the dispute should be of a civil and commercial nature. Regulation Brussels Ibis does not provide a definition of 'civil and commercial matters', hence such definition should be gleaned by way of interpretation. It is deemed that the relationship between the parties and their interests is denominator of what should be taken as civil and commercial, i.e. whether the interests concerned are private or not ("nature of the legal relationships between the parties to the action and the subject matter of the action or, alternatively, the basis of the action and the detailed rules applicable to it" according to CJEU[17]).

2.1.3.6 Interim Measures in the Scope of Article 35

Article 35 functions to refer the substance of measures available to an applicant to the domestic law, i.e. the lex fori, of the seized court.[18] However, this should not be taken as a mere referral as, if this is assumed, then any domestic measures would be available, which may not fit with the policy and principles of Regulation Brussels Ibis. The Brussels regime has an autonomous existence and requires autonomous interpretation.[19] Therefore, the concept of available interim measures that are within the jurisdiction under Article 35 should be analysed from the standpoint of the Regulation, not the lex fori.[20] The lex fori is the source, not the criterion for the measures—the ECJ case law has made characterization of interim measures ("measures which, in matters within the scope of the Convention, are intended to preserve a factual or legal situation so as to safeguard rights the recognition of which is sought elsewhere from the court having jurisdiction as to the substance of the matter."[21]) so the definition comes from the ECJ jurisprudence while the available measures are those provide by national law, which meet the definition given by the ECJ.

The preliminary issue is, however, whether the concept regulated in Article 35 applies to the entire Regulation Brussels Ibis. I.e. if the applicant seeks relief from a court competent on the merits of the dispute, would the same be applicable, would the court making assessment under, for instance, Article 4, be guided by the same concept as the one in Article 35. In this author's view, yes. This is so because there is no logic or policy in incorporating different concepts within the Regulation. Moreover, the only provision regarding interim measures under the Regulation, is in

---

[16] Trib.comm. Paris Gaz. Pal. 1985, 1, 185.
[17] CJEU Judgement under Case C-73/19, para 37.
[18] Garcimartin (2014/2015), p. 73.
[19] Krüger and Rauscher (MüKoZPO) (2020), Article 35, marginal number 2, 3.
[20] Vorwerk et al. (BeckOK) (2018), Article 35, Rn. 5-8.
[21] Judgment under Case C-261/90, Reichart II.

2.1 International Civil and Commercial Litigation

Article 35. Hence, the correct application of the Regulation is to apply the concept in any case of interim measures where the Regulation has applicability as well.

Interim measures are termed by the Regulation Brussels Ibis as provisional, including protective, measures. This is a wide-reaching concept that would encapsulate the traditional measures sought for obtaining interim relief. It would also include measures for collection of evidence. ECJ in the Reichert II case defined such measures as "measures which, in matters within the scope of the Convention, are intended to preserve a factual or legal situation so as to safeguard rights the recognition of which is sought elsewhere from the court having jurisdiction as to the substance of the matter." Some authors argue that the key characteristic of interim measures under Regulation Brussels Ibis is provisionality, i.e. time factor[22] as the measure should be procedurally limited in time. E.g. measures may coincide with measures to be ordered by the judgment on the merits—it would not preclude their preliminary nature, but these should be procedurally necessary for the safeguarding of substantive rights for the time period before final adjudication.[23] Moreover, it has been submitted that interim measures are characterized by a double-condition if the true function of the relief is to prevent future problems with the enforcement of the final decision (or to prevent the risk that relevant evidence becomes unavailable); and if the measure is to be enforced in a jurisdiction different from the one empowered to decide on the merits.[24] Some authors confirm that urgency is not a prerequisite for such measures.[25]

It should also be clarified what is the precise backbone of the standard which Article 35 incorporates. The literal meaning delineates provisional measures as a wide category, which should feature protective measures as its apparent subcategory. The French language version of the Regulation deals with these categories in a different manner: these are treated as equal, separate and alternative concepts ("provisoires ou conservatoires"). The same approaches is undertaken in the Spanish and Italian versions as well, for instance. There are grounds to conceive these as separate categories since such have been employed as separate notions rooted in Roman law: "fumus boni iuris" as protective measures and "periculum in mora" as provisional ones. Hence, it is assumed that both types of measures, protective and provisional ones, can exist as autonomous legal phenomena. The next step is to determine if these should be subordinated. The case law developed by the ECJ (e.g. Reichart II case) on the matter clearly demonstrates that the first and ubiquitous mark of the measures falling within the scope of Article 35 is their timeliness, which makes the element of provisionality leading when making assessment whether a particular measure could qualify under Article 35.[26] Therefore, the overarching principle to be inferred should be that these measures are employed only to have

---

[22] Lazić and Stuij (2017), p. 102.
[23] Jacques de Cavel v. Louise de Cavel, (Case 143/78) (1979) ECR 1055, para 6-10.
[24] Lazić and Stuij (2017), p. 111.
[25] Bureau and Muir Watt (2017), p. 188.
[26] Lazić and Stuij (2017), p. 102.

temporary effect on the substance of the dispute. However, what begs further clarification is: what could be defined as a "protective" measure? It has been argued that protective are those measures that ensure safeguarding the rights at stake in the dispute.[27] The interpretation of Article 35 in the Reichert II case seems to corroborate this ("intended to preserve a factual or legal situation so as to safeguard rights"). This understanding is supported by this author's view as well. Protective measures are those measures which target ensuring the procedure on the substance of the dispute, and the rights and obligations disputed thereof, will be implemented in an orderly manner. This may require as diverse measures as seizure of goods, freezing of money accounts, or preservation of evidence. Some more specific means for ensuring performance pertaining to some lex fori are, however, excluded. This is the so called référé within the systems of French, Belgian, Luxembourg law, where provisional contractual performance may be ordered by court as an interim relief. This is admissible under Regulation Brussels Ibis as long as the performance does not lead to an irreversible result. It reaffirms the interpretation that provisionality/temporary effect is the leading denominator of Article 35 measures. If a measure creates a new, irreversible or a difficult to reverse status quo between the parties, it should not fall within the scope of Article 35.

A certain manner of collection of evidence is known to be excluded as well: in St. Paul Dairy v. Unibel Exser case the ECJ decided that a measure ordering the hearing of a witness for the purpose of enabling the applicant to decide whether to bring a case, determine whether it would be well founded and assess the relevance of evidence which might be adduced in that regard is not covered by the notion of "provisional, including protective, measures". Recital 25 of Regulation Brussels Ibis added further qualification: "The notion of provisional, including protective, measures ... should not include measures which are not of a protective nature, such as measures ordering the hearing of a witness".

Are ex parte measures enforceable in the same manner as any other interim measures? Under ECJ case law, not, as it was stated in Denilauler./.Couchet Frères case[28]: "Judicial decisions authorizing provisional or protective measures, which are delivered without the party against which they are directed having been summoned to appear and which are intended to be enforced without prior service do not come within the system of recognition and enforcement [provided for by the Judgment Convention].[29] Some case law from national courts suggests that it is not, but under some circumstances this is possible: Cour d'Appel Bourges[30] recognised a foreign interim measure granted in unilateral proceedings but served upon the respondent—as the respondent was allowed to oppose it, this according to the court made it admissible.

---

[27] Mankowski and Magnus (2011), p. 531.
[28] Judgment of May, 21st 1980, 125/79, ECR 1980, 1553, 1555.
[29] See also: Hartley (2009), p. 434.
[30] Dated 02/22/2005, unpublished, referred to by the French reporter Sinopoli, French report, 3rd questionnaire, question 4.1.3 in: Hess (2005).

Does Article 35 incorporate some independent substantive standards on its own, regardless of the national law? It has not been expressly dealt with, but the case law[31] has considered that Article 35 could be triggered only in case of urgency. Without urgency, there is no underlying policy reason why a court different from the one having jurisdiction on the merits should grant interim measures on basis of Article 35. So, a standard of urgency is to be considered as necessarily incorporated within the concept of interim measures.

2.1.3.7 Real Connecting Link Doctrine

The ECJ exposed the view in the case of Van Uden Maritime BV v. Deco-Line[32] that there should be a real connecting link between the subject-matter of the measures sought and the territorial jurisdiction of the Member State of the court before which those measures are sought.

The ECJ dicta is rooted in a policy relating to the inter-State dimensions of the Regulation Brussels Ibis. As noted above, Article 35 is a jurisdictional rule. It does not deal with enforcement. Per se, a court may be competent under the set of jurisdictional rules but nevertheless the court's judgment may not be enforceable for one reason or another. However, in practical terms, it is useless to have judgments that cannot be implemented in reality. Therefore, a jurisdiction of a court should be able to lead to enforcement of that court's judgements. Otherwise the jurisdiction will be pointless, after all.

Second policy logic behind this reasoning is that the jurisdiction to grant interim measures is specific and should be distinguished from the general court competence to resolve disputes. To impose interim measures is to effectuate a significant interference in the parties to the dispute without the merits of the dispute being settled, i.e. before the adjudication of the legal and factual situation between the parties. This type of jurisdiction sits between the adjudicatory jurisdiction of courts and the execution jurisdiction. It combines elements of both.

Finally, the practical need for interim measures to be granted may lure a party to shop for a convenient jurisdiction. This can easily be escalated into frivolous applications aiming to take advantage of the differences between the legal systems of the EU Member States.

Taking into account all these considerations, it is not surprising that the ECJ elaborated the real connecting link rule. In its absence, a court of a Member State would have powers to order any interim measures that are entirely unrelated to the country where they would be effectuated. This is, a propos, the main argument against the anti-suit injunctions typical for the practice of UK courts. So, the rationale of the Brussels regime should prevent possible abuse. Furthermore, the

---

[31] Besix AG v. Kretzschmar, (Case C-256/00) (2002) ECR I-1699; Group Josi Reinsurance Company v. Universal General Reinsurance Company, (Case C-412/98) (2000) ECR I-5925.

[32] Case C-391/95) (1998) ECR I-3715.

enforcement of such a judgment would raise issues related to the sovereignty of Member States as a Member State would be able to impose execution measures on the territory of another Member State. Such a measure would be an unjustified intrusion into the sovereignty of the Member States.

The real connecting link doctrine answers all these concerns. Although the ECJ did not elucidate the precise ambits and content of this concept, and the recast Brussels Ibis did not provide explicit guidance, it is self-evident that the object towards which the measure is directed should bear some link with the Member State of the seized forum.[33] The link should have a territorial aspect.[34] This is why, in the most simplistic example, if a moveable good should be seized, the competent court is the court of the country where the moveable good is located; the same applies to real estate property. It is suggested that when the object is money in bank accounts, the location of the bank should be the decisive factor, or should be identified by reference to the IBAN code of the account (as expressly provided under Regulation 655/2014). Hence, the applicant should either seek relief on basis of Article 35 from the court in the country where the object of that relief is situated, or request relief from the court with jurisdiction on the merits, and then enforce the interim measure in the country where the object is located.[35]

It should be reiterated that the existence of a real connecting link is a jurisdictional requirement. Although it is intertwined with issues of enforcement, it is yet to be treated as a matter of jurisdiction. It regulates the court of which country should have competence under Article 35 of Regulation Brussels Ibis. The court at the place of the object of the interim measure has jurisdiction to impose the relevant interim measures. Or, in other words, if the court seized by an applicant does not have a territorial link with the object, therefore it shall lack jurisdiction regardless of other prerequisites under Article 35 being present or not. The rule does not state whether it regulates directly court jurisdiction or is a reference: in the former case it shall allocate competence to the court at the actual place of the object, and in the latter—to the courts in general of the country where the object is located. In this author's view, the second proposition should be supported. The Regulation sets up direct jurisdictional regulation in a few special rules (e.g. Article 6) and otherwise uses the technique of conflict rules: general reference to a country and not to a particular court having jurisdiction.

Only English case law prior to Brexit on the application of Article 35 of Regulation Brussels Ibis has diverted from the rationale of the territoriality of the notion of "real connecting link". The practice of granting freezing orders (under English Civil Procedure Rules, Rule 25), formerly Mareva injunctions, has spawned a number of cases where English court had to consider the application of Article 35. Under English law, some remedies, such as the freezing order, act in personam, i.e. the

---

[33] Vorwerk et al. (BeckOK) (2018), Article 35 Rn. 9.

[34] Hess et al. (2005), para 731; Gaudemet-Tallon (2010), p. 319. See: Cass. fr. 13 April 1999, Bull. I 133, p. 86.

[35] E.g. Heinze (2011), p. 612.

personal link between the respondent and the forum give rise to the jurisdiction of English courts.[36] A freezing order is deemed to be an instrument to prevent a respondent from swiftly stripping itself from its assets and should act only upon the respondent.

However, it has the practical side effect of affecting third parties that may be considered as assisting the respondent in dissipation of his assets, which is punishable by contempt of court. Moreover, the order affects assets outside the forum State. English dicta[37] accepts, though, that in personam link is sufficient to meet the territoriality requirement of Van Uden and Article 35. This may showcase some artificiality of the debate regarding freezing orders and real connecting link. Although the ECJ apparently framed the real connecting link in terms of territoriality, this can also capture the English notion of personal link, as English law adopts the understanding of in rem and in personam jurisdiction: the former dealing with placing of property, while the latter—with linking the forum with persons. Hence, the overarching principle yet is territoriality as the in rem and in personam jurisdictions are actually both dealing with jurisdiction based on territorial link between a person or property with the forum. The clash between Article 35 and English freezing orders would not lie with the personal link, which is actually a territorial link, but with the issue of enforcement of such orders while Article 35 is clearly not designated to deal with enforcement. Hence, the effect of such orders should be limited only as to the respondent as his behaviour is the actual object of the order, and cannot be enforced against the assets of the respondent in other States, or against third parties in other States.

2.1.4 Enforcement of Article 35 Based Interim Measures[38]

The enforcement framework under Regulation Brussels Ibis does not expressly refer to Article 35 measures.

Article 42 (2) (b) (i) requires that an interim measure which is subject to enforcement under Regulation Brussels Ibis should be capable of enforcement where declaration of jurisdiction on the substance could be obtained.

This rule, which underpins the enforcement framework under Article 42, is basis for inference what types of measures may avail of this enforcement mechanism under Regulation Brussels Ibis. The rule is in reality contrary to the logic of Article 35 jurisdiction as under Article 35 the competent court is (might be) one that does

---

[36] E.g. Banco Nacional de Comercio Exterior SNC v Empresa de Telecommunicaciones de Cuba SA [2007] EWCA Civ 662; Republic of Haiti v Duvalier [1990] 1 QB 202; Babanaft International Co SA v Bassatne [1990] Ch 13; Hartley (2009), pp. 411–448.

[37] Masri v Consolidated Contractors International Company SAL & Anor) [2008] EWCA Civ 303 (04 April 2008) para 106.

[38] Garcimartin (2014/2015), pp. 62–68; Lazić and Stuij (2017), pp. 112–115.

not necessarily have jurisdiction on the substance of the dispute. Therefore, Article 42 is not intended to be the tool for enforcement of interim measures granted under Article 35, as an Article 35 interim measure could not be incorporated in a judgment enforceable under Regulation Brussels Ibis.

In Recital 33 of the Recast Regulation, this has been stated explicitly:

> Where provisional, including protective, measures are ordered by a court having jurisdiction as to the substance of the matter, their free circulation should be ensured under this Regulation. However, provisional, including protective, measures which were ordered by such a court without the defendant being summoned to appear should not be recognised and enforced under this Regulation unless the judgment containing the measure is served on the defendant prior to enforcement. This should not preclude the recognition and enforcement of such measures under national law. Where provisional, including protective, measures are ordered by a court of a Member State not having jurisdiction as to the substance of the matter, the effect of such measures should be confined, under this Regulation, to the territory of that Member State.

It is to be noted that the case law of ECJ has also some bearing to this matter. As per the reasoning in the Bernard Denilauler—SNC Couchet Frère case, a measure, which is ex parte, would not be enforceable outside the country where it was granted. This interpretation is in line with the real connecting link doctrine which is firmly incorporated in ECJ case law and doctrine. The statement in Recital 33 follows these considerations already established in the course of the case law of ECJ.

Against this background, the proper understanding as to the status of enforcement under Article 35 should be as follows:

(i) Measures, which are granted by a court without jurisdiction on the substance of the matter, are not enforceable under Regulation Brussels Ibis. If national law at the place of enforcement would allow this, then they may nevertheless be enforced, but not on the grounds of the Regulation.
(ii) Measures, which are granted by a court not having jurisdiction on the substance of the matter, are in principle not enforceable, except where: (a) these are granted after inter partes procedure, or (b) the defendant is already notified of the measure prior to enforcement, so that there is no effect of surprise.

2.1.5 Brussels II Regime

The EU law features an additional "branch", additional "stream" of regulations, which mirror the concepts founded by, and elaborated by, Regulation Brussels Ibis, i.e. the Brussels I regime. This separate and parallel branch could be denominated as Brussels II regime. It encompasses a number of EU Regulations comprising jurisdictional rules, which cover the scope of civil disputes, as well, namely: a regulation on matrimonial matters and the matters of parental responsibility—first, the repealed Regulation (EC) No 1347/2000 (Regulation Brussels II); Council Regulation (EC) No 2201/2003 of 27 November 2003 concerning jurisdiction and the recognition and enforcement of judgments in matrimonial matters and the matters of parental responsibility, repealing Regulation (EC) No 1347/2000), known as Brussels IIbis, subsequently replaced by Council Regulation (EU) 2019/1111 of 25 June 2019 on jurisdiction, the recognition and enforcement of decisions in matrimonial matters and the matters of parental responsibility, and on international child abduction, known as Brussels IIter.

The Brussels II regime may form a separate and coherent system as these cover a particular distinct area of civil relations, and share specific logic and concepts, as well.

The Brussels II regime features provisions on interim relief on its own. Being part of the EU law regime, they interact with the underlying principles of Brussels I regime, e.g. Art. 35 of Brussels Ibis. However, there are major differences. This section of the study strives to outline these respective specifics, which differentiate Brussels II regime from the rest of the EU regulations.

2.1.5.1 Regulation 2201/2003 and Regulation 2019/1111[39]

The major regulation covering matrimonial matters was enacted as Regulation 2201/2003, also Brussels IIbis, which has been repealed in 2022 and recast as Regulation 2019/1111, also Brussels IIter. Both feature rules on interim relief and the evolution of the regime should be reviewed through the prism of both because the majority of case law accumulated on basis of Regulation Brussels IIbis has been subsequently reflected in the recasting of the regulation as Brussels IIter.

The substantive scope of Regulation 2201/2003 is set out within Art. 1, and includes inter alia divorce, legal separation or marriage annulment, attribution, exercise, delegation, restriction or termination of parental responsibility. This predetermines the scope of the interim relied available under Regulation 2201/2003. Interim measures granted under the Regulation should relate to the listed under Art. 1 matters, incl. rights of custody and rights of access, guardianship, curatorship and similar institutions.

Naturally, courts competent under Art. 3-15 of Regulation 2201/2003 have the powers and jurisdiction to grant interim relief. Similar to Art. 35 of Regulations Brussels Ibis, Regulation 2201/2003 encompasses a specific procedural rule (often qualified not as a real jurisdictional rule) under Art. 20 of the regulation, which targets interim relief: *"In urgent cases, the provisions of this Regulation shall not prevent the courts of a Member State from taking such provisional, including protective, measures in respect of persons or assets in that State as may be available under the law of that Member State, even if, under this Regulation, the court of another Member State has jurisdiction as to the substance of the matter."* (para. 1); and that *"The measures referred to in paragraph 1 shall cease to apply when the court of the Member State having jurisdiction under this Regulation as to the substance of the matter has taken the measures it considers appropriate."* (para. 2).

---

[39] See Pretelli (2018) Ancel and Muir Watt (2005); Honorati (2011), pp. 66–80; Feraci (2011).

The provision of Art. 20 plainly indicates that the grounds for establishing jurisdiction under that article adopt a more qualified approach compared to Art. 35 of Regulation Brussels Ibis. The ECJ has further elucidated the prerequisites for triggering Art. 35. As per the ECJ Purrucker case[40] (Case C-256/09), there should be three cumulative conditions (para. 77): (i) the measures must be urgent; (ii) should be taken in respect of persons or assets in the Member State where those courts are situated; and (iii) must be provisional. The ECJ declared this also under the Detiček case (C-403/09).[41]

First, unlike Art. 35 of Brussels Ibis, Regulation 2201/2003 severely restricts the scope of operation of Art. 20 by limiting it to only matters of urgency. While this has been indicated in case law (as analysed under Sect. 2.1.3.6), in Regulation 2201/2003 this has been poised on statutory footing. In the Detiček judgment, the concept of urgency relates both to the situation of the child and to the impossibility in practice of bringing the application concerning parental responsibility before the court with jurisdiction as to the substance (para.42 thereof). Thus a double test has been spawned: (i) the situation of the child should be of a nature that dictates immediate actions; and (ii) impossibility to seize the court having jurisdiction under Art. 3-15 of Regulation 2201/2003. These conditions could also be viewed from the standpoint of the Convention of 5 October 1961 concerning the powers of authorities and the law applicable in respect of the protection of infants, and the Convention of 19 October 1996 on Jurisdiction, Applicable Law, Recognition, Enforcement and Co-operation in Respect of Parental Responsibility and Measures for the Protection of Children, where urgency is indicated by the necessity to prevent irreparable harm. Apparently, the danger should be imminent, immediate. The ECJ also gave guidance in the judgment under case C-523/07[42] that it should be reasoned within the matrix of circumstances related to the physical, psychological and intellectual development of the child as well as likely development of the child and the effectiveness of the provisional or protective measures adopted (para. 59-60).

Second, without being expressly stated, and without the concept of "real connecting link" being employed under Regulation 2201/2003, a very similar interpretation of Art. 20 delimits the scope of the measures available under that provision. As declared by the ECJ in the Detiček judgment, provisional measures must be taken in respect of persons in the Member State in which the courts with jurisdiction to take such measures are located (para. 50). Hence, as the specific object of such measures are human beings (children, minors), these should be within the country of the court seized.

Third, the relief sought should be one of very temporary character. If it is not, then the urgency requirement would be undermined as well—bar any imminence of

---

[40] Judgment of the Court (Second Chamber) of 15 July 2010, Bianca Purrucker v Guillermo Vallés Pérez, C-256/09.
[41] Judgment of the Court (Third Chamber) of 23 December 2009, Jasna Detiček v Maurizio Sgueglia, C-403/09.
[42] Judgment of the Court (Third Chamber) of 2 April 2009.

harm, the application can wait to be filed with the court having jurisdiction on the substance of the matter. Therefore, the situation must require solely a very timely remedy to safeguard child's interests without harm. This is reaffirmed by para. 2 of Art. 20: as the measures endure until the court competent on the substance be seized, then timeliness is evidently enshrined as a factor under Art. 20.

The time span of the measures is expressly denoted. The explicit statement (under Art. 20 (2)), resolves the potential (positive) conflict between the court granting measures under Art. 20, and the one granting measures falling within the competence on the substance of the claim. The measures are having effect only as long as, and until, the court with jurisdiction under Art. 3-15 of Regulation 2201/2003 is seized.

Enforcement of measures under Art. 20 of Regulation 2201/2003. As noted under Sect. 2.1.4 hereabove, the Brussels I regime did not feature enforcement/circulation of interim relief under Art. 35 until recast. The recast regulation does feature the enhanced enforcement of measures. In a similar vein, currently Regulation 2201/2003 mirrors the situation under Regulation 44/2001, as both are products of a single stage in the historical development of the entire Brussels jurisdictional regime. On a strict literal and linguistic interpretation, a judgment under Art. 21 of Regulation 2201/2003 is defined as "divorce, legal separation or marriage annulment, as well as a judgment relating to parental responsibility, pronounced by a court of a Member State, whatever the judgment may be called, including a decree, order or decision" (Art. 2(4)). Similar expression was part of the matrix of Regulation 44/2001, and was further redefined under the current recast Regulation Brussels Ibis to include under Art. 2(2) provisional, including protective measures as well when given inter partes. Read together with the strict localization of the measure within the territory of jurisdiction of the granting court, this leads to the inference that the interim relief decisions under Regulation 2201/2003 is not subject to cross-border enforcement.

This was confirmed by the ECJ in the Purrucker case. Per para. 95, the right to be heard as an essential procedural feature defines whether measures should be allowed to circulate freely. Without the caveat which was included under Art. 2(2) of Brussels Ibis, interim relief granted under Art. 20 of Regulation 2201/2003 is yet not capable to qualify for enforcement. This ECJ expressly stated in that case (para. 100).

However, the Brussels II regime should follow suit after Brussels I regime recast the landscape of enforcement of interim measures. Council Regulation (EU) 2019/1111 of 25 June 2019 on jurisdiction, the recognition and enforcement of decisions in matrimonial matters and the matters of parental responsibility, and on international child abduction - Brussels IIter, has entered into force on 1 August 2022 replacing Brussels IIbis. It is being built upon the notions enshrined in Brussels IIbis and clarified and developed in the jurisprudence of the ECJ. It alters the position of interim measures and brings it in line with Regulation Brussels Ibis. Art. 20 of Regulation Brussels IIbis is reworked into Art. 15 of Regulation Brussels IIter, which elaborates, makes more specific and enhances the logic of the previous Art. 20. Urgency is retained as a leading and qualifying principle, which triggers interim relief jurisdiction. Furthermore, the requirement for territorial link/localization, is made explicit: courts have jurisdiction where (i) a child is present in that Member State; or (ii) property belonging to a child is located in that Member State. Thus Brussels IIbis posits the child as main linking factor, which to some extent departs and abrogates the earlier dicta in Deticek which interpreted the relevance of the localization of both child and parent.[43] The enhancement, which Regulation Brussels IIter encompasses, is, however, that Art. 2(1) lists provisional, including protective measures under the definition of "decision", which is subject of enforcement under that regulation, on the proviso that the decision on the measure should be served on the defendant to render it enforceable. Thus both Brussels I and II interim relief jurisdiction rules become aligned on the matter of cross-border circulation. However, the cross-border circulation of Article 15 measures is conditioned upon one more qualification—the measure granted under Article 15 should relate to return of a child and purport to protect the child from the grave risk. Hence, not each and every measure would be subject to extraterritorial enforcement, unlike Article 35 of Regulation Brussels Ibis measures which should only meet the first requirement, i.e. be a product of inter partes proceedings or at least served on the respondent prior to enforcement.

2.1.6 Other Regulations

Regulation 4/2009 (on maintenance obligations), Regulation 650/2012 (on succession matters), Regulation 2016/1103 (on matrimonial property regimes), and Regulation 2016/1104 (on registered property regimes) are tightly intertwined with the family law and inheritance issues, and each of them feature a uniform interim relief clause: "Application may be made to the courts of a Member State for such provisional, including protective, measures as may be available under the law of that State, even if under this Regulation, the courts of another Member State have jurisdiction as to the substance of the matter." (Art. 14 of Regulation 4/2009); Art. 19 of Regulation 2016/1104; Art. 19 of Regulation 2016/1103; Art. 19 of Regulation 650/2012). The provision is a reiteration of Art. 31 of Regulation 44/2001 prior to the recasting of Regulation Brussels Ibis, although the disputes within the scope of these regulations do not fall within the application of Regulation Brussels Ibis; some of them, such as Regulations 4/2009, 2016/1103 and 1104 have more touchpoints with the family law matters within Regulation Brussels II regime but do not fall within its scope, too. So these regulations occupy a territory outside both Brussels I and Brussels II regimes but as to their interim relief provisions, these (still) follow the pattern set by the earlier version of Brussels I.

Hence, it should be assumed that the specific characteristics of the interim relief rules as enshrined into Regulation 44/2001 are incorporated under the said regulations.

---

[43] De Sousa Goncalves AS (2022).

First, the substantive scope of the measures is predetermined by the respective scope of matters where the regulations are to be applied to.

Second, the catalogue of the available measures is set by the lex fori of the court seized.

Third, there should be a real connecting link between the object of the measures and the seized court, i.e. presence and localization of the object of the measure within the territory of the respective country of the court seized.

Fourth, and most importantly, these regulations mirror the lack of enforcement of interim measures which preceded Regulation Brussels Ibis. Within all these three regulations, "decision" is defined as "any decision [...] given by a court of a Member State, whatever the decision may be called, including a decision on the determination of costs or expenses by an officer of the court". None of these regulations includes the wider proviso that Regulation Brussels Ibis enshrined i.e. that a judgment incorporating measures is enforceable once notified to the defendant. It is to be inferred that the measures granted under Art. 14 of Regulation 4/2009, and Art. 19 of Regulations 650/2012; Regulation 2016/1103; and Regulation 2016/1104 cannot be circulated outside the territory of the country where provided.

2.2 International Arbitration

Arbitration rests on a number of cornerstones. A typical analysis of an arbitration problem inevitably needs to touch upon issues of (i) the source of arbitral jurisdiction, incl. valid consent to arbitrate; (ii) the jurisdiction of the arbitral tribunal/ arbitrator; (iii) the arbitral procedure; (iv) the arbitral award and its enforcement. The peculiarities of arbitration, incl. its consensual nature, require looking at most arbitration-related problems through the lenses of general concepts developed in relation to these cornerstones.

The analysis of interim relief within the framework of international arbitration shall go through these stages and be filtered through these concepts. However, as a preliminary matter, it should be first noted what temporary/working definition of interim measures and interim relief in arbitration would be employed.

There is no single overarching definition, and even the diverse national legislations as well as rules of arbitral institutions are reluctant to determine what interim measures are. It has been suggested that a possible theoretical definition is that such a measure provides "a remedy or a relief that is aimed at safeguarding the rights of parties to a dispute pending its final resolution".[44] In this author's view, too, this captures the essential characteristics of interim measures in arbitration, and this definition should be borne in mind at this stage of the current study. A more detailed

---

[44] Yesilirmak (2005), p. 5.

analysis, however, shall be provided thereof within the section dealing with the typology of measures and the rules of arbitral institutions.

2.2.1 Jurisdiction of Arbitral Tribunals to Grant Interim Measures

2.2.1.1 Source (Basis) of Arbitral Jurisdiction on Interim Measures

The main and general source of powers for arbitrators is consent, enshrined in the arbitration agreement.[45] In its absence, there would be no basis for their powers and hence the jurisdiction of the arbitral tribunal to decide on the particular dispute between the parties. Therefore, any powers of the arbitral tribunal, if existent, should stem from the arbitration agreement.[46]

Arbitration agreements, however, do rarely deal expressly with the issue of interim measures. If this is explicitly provided for in the arbitration agreement, it will do away with any potential gap or confusion. In the absence of explicit provision, would this preclude power to grant interim measures? It can be assumed that this power is implicit within the scope of the powers that the arbitrators should have in order to resolve the dispute.[47] The main power, right and obligation of the arbitral tribunal is to decide the case (dispute) at hand, i.e. to decide on the rights and duties between the parties to the arbitration agreement. To grant interim measures affecting and protecting these rights and duties is an ancillary matter to the general arbitral jurisdiction. Therefore, it is implied, if not expressly stated, that the arbitral tribunal may grant interim measures.

Furthermore, the arbitration agreement triggers the powers of the arbitral tribunal. However, these powers are within the bounds of the respective lex arbitri.[48] It provides what arbitrators governed by the procedural law of the seat of the arbitration have jurisdiction to do. If the lex arbitri provides for powers of the arbitral tribunal to grant interim measures, therefore there are grounds that are independent from the arbitration agreement for exercise of arbitral jurisdiction in this respect (but would not be triggered in the absence of an arbitration agreement at all).

The typical lex arbitri, being a national law based on the Model Law of UNCITRAL, expressly provides for the powers to grant interim measures. This model is the widely known and followed model of structuring the regulation on arbitral powers and arbitration procedure. Hence, given that an arbitration agreement is entered into as between the parties to the dispute, the arbitrators appointed by them

---

[45] Bermann (2017), pp. 24–34; 80–85.

[46] Blackaby et al. (2015), p. 305; Gaillard and Savage (1999), pp. 392–393; Yesilirmak (2005), pp. 53–55.

[47] Born, International Commercial Arbitration (2014), pp. 2427–2444; Yesilirmak (2005), p. 55.

[48] Born (2014), pp. 1533–1534; Blackaby et al. (2015), pp. 1–2.

will have powers to grant interim measures as the lex arbitri expressly provides and allows so.

Typically a lex arbitri allows interim measures while there are some countries where the lex arbitri expressly prohibits interim measures (Italy, China, Thailand, Argentina).

Under the Italian Code of Civil Procedure, Art. 818, "The arbitrators may not grant attachment or other interim measures of protection." (applicable only to proceedings brought prior to 28 Feruary 2023; subsequently, Art. 818 has been amended to allow conferrance of explicit powers to impose interim relief in the arbitration agreement).

According to Chinese Arbitration Law, Art. 68; and Thai Arbitration Act, §16, arbitrators lack authority to order interim relief.

Under Argentine National Code of Civil and Commercial Procedure, Art. 753:"Arbitrators cannot order compulsory measures or measures leading to enforcement. They must request them from the judge who will have to lend the support of his jurisdictional powers for the most swift and effective carrying out of the arbitral proceedings."

Is it possible that an arbitration agreement prohibits the arbitral interim measures jurisdiction? The voluntary nature of arbitration requires that the consent of parties be honoured as paramount. They would be able to opt-in and out of the arbitral regime as long as they do not contravene mandatory rules of the lex arbitri,[49] most likely overriding mandatory rules and public policy exception rules. Interim measures are, as noted above, an ancillary matter to dispute resolution but the relation between these is one way only: if the arbitral dispute resolution powers are present, the tribunal would be able to issue interim measures; however, absence of interim measures powers do not preclude general powers of arbitrators.

Hence, interim measures jurisdiction is a consensual component of the arbitral jurisdiction regime which can be abrogated given that the parties' consent is present. Should this be agreed, the arbitral tribunal would not be allowed to grant interim measures. This is applicable even if the lex arbitri expressly provides for interim measure jurisdiction. The restriction, being consensual, should override the statutory powers. This will not have effect, however, if the existence of interim measures jurisdiction is a matter of public policy. This is difficult to be assumed on basis of the typical and model provisions of lex arbitri.

This, however, would not affect the powers of state courts to grant interim measures. These are mandatory powers part of the lex arbitri governing the procedure. Waiver, even if consensual, can be assumed to be in breach of public policy and would not have effect. Nevertheless, a pro-arbitration theoretical outlook would favour such approach.[50]

---

[49] Bermann (2017), pp. 203–204.
[50] Born (2014), p. 2454.

Rules of arbitration institutions usually expressly provide for the powers of the tribunal to grant interim measures.[51] Therefore, selection of particular institutional rules can be deemed as sufficient to endow upon the arbitral tribunal powers to provide interim measures as envisioned under these rules. To the extent that institutional rules are optional for the parties—i.e. parties may modify them or elaborate their own set of rules for their dispute—parties are entitled to exclude the powers of tribunal to grant interim measures.

In spite of any express agreement on interim measures power of the tribunal, or providing for this in institutional rules, the lex arbitri may prohibit such powers. Some jurisdictions' arbitration laws do restrict interim measures powers only to courts[52] e.g., Italy, China, Thailand and Argentina. Therefore, in any event any consensus between the parties is subject to the applicable lex arbitri. It may prohibit interim measure powers of arbitrators at all or restrict them to some extent.

Interim Conclusion
The arbitral powers to grant interim measures are based on the arbitration agreement between the parties. If it is not expressly agreed, it is implicit from the general dispute resolution powers of the arbitrators. Apart from this, the law applicable to arbitral powers and procedure as well as relevant rules of arbitration, where the arbitration is under the auspices of a particular arbitral institution, usually expressly provide for interim measures jurisdiction of arbitral tribunals and can be basis for providing interim relief by arbitral tribunal. Express exclusion in the applicable can be effective but is very rare.

2.2.1.2 Scope of Arbitral Jurisdiction to Grant Interim Measures

As a general principle, the consensual nature of arbitration imposes significant limits onto arbitral jurisdiction. Since the powers of the tribunal are restricted to what the parties agreed to within the arbitration agreement, the limits of the jurisdiction are as follows.

Ratione Materiae The scope of the arbitral tribunal's jurisdiction should coincide with the dispute between the parties. Moreover, the dispute between the parties is predetermined by the scope of the arbitration agreement. Therefore, the arbitral tribunal should decide only within the matters in dispute between the parties and falling in the scope of the arbitration agreement. Moreover, the scope of the arbitration agreement should comprise substantive issues arising from the substantive provisions of the contractual relations between the parties.

---

[51] Article 26 UNCITRAL Model Rules on International Commercial Arbitration; Article 28 ICC Rules; Article 25 LCIA Rules; Article 26 Swiss Rules of Arbitration; Article 33 VIAC Rules; Section 20 DIS Rules; Article 23 HKIAC Rules; Article 23 CIETAC Rules; Rules 30 SIAC Rules; Article 32 SCC Rules; Rule 37 of AAA Rules, etc.
[52] Scherer and Richman (2015), p. 261.

2.2 International Arbitration

Most institutional rules do not have account of the substantive jurisdiction of the tribunal as it is implicitly deemed to stem from the general jurisdiction of the tribunal. However, the LCIA Rules for instance specify that the interim relief that the arbitrators are entitled to grant is the relief that they are empowered to grant by the final award.[53] But the situation is in fact different. The tribunal disposes of a different issue in its interim measures order/award than its final award. While the tribunal may decide on the existence or not of a particular debt, by its interim measures order/award the tribunal may enjoin a party from disposing of assets not entailed by the arbitration procedure. Therefore, the powers of the arbitral tribunal should be understood as even wider when granting interim measures as the tribunal does not decide on the substantive dispute although it is called to provide protective measures regarding that dispute. The key to understanding this is that the measure should be related to the subject-matter of the dispute, even if not directly part of the substantive relations between the parties.[54]

Ratione Personae The scope of personal jurisdiction is, again, predetermined by the scope of the arbitration agreement. The personal feature of the arbitration agreement relates to the parties having entered into the arbitration agreement. Their consent provides basis for the powers of the arbitral tribunal. Hence, the arbitral tribunal has powers only as to these parties, and only as to the subject matter within its jurisdiction ratione materiae.[55]

Therefore, the arbitral tribunal does not have jurisdiction to make binding interim measure orders on third parties, which are not bound by the arbitration agreement. This has been subject of discussions as to the potential options for consolidation/joinder of claims by or versus a number of parties within one and the same procedure. The issue is dependent on the approach to the mentioned notion of "party to arbitration agreement". Once this notion is widened, it may encapsulate a wider number of parties. If a restricted approach is adopted, the parties to the arbitration proceedings should strictly coincide with the parties to the arbitration agreement. Depending on this interpretation, the arbitral tribunal may impose measures as to parties that are not strictly parties to the arbitration agreement but nevertheless consent can be attributed to these parties. The essence of the matter is: who has given consent to the arbitration agreement, or whether it can be implied that that such consent is given, based on the circumstances.[56] For example, in ICC case no. 1434[57] the tribunal deduced the consent of the non-signatory defendants to be bound by the arbitration provision contained in the main agreement between contractor and employer from the close network of contractual relationships between the various companies of the contractor's corporate group and the absence

---

[53] Scherer and Richman (2015), p. 260.
[54] Scherer and Richman (2015), p. 272—Article 25.1(ii) LCIA Rules.
[55] Grierson and van Hooft (2012), p. 157; Scherer and Richman (2015), p. 262.
[56] Hanotiau (2006), p. 7.
[57] 03 J. Droit Int'l (Clunet) 978 (1976); 1 Collection of ICC Arbitral Awards 263.

of formalities in the determination of the parties to the various contracts. Claimant had contracted with a group of companies, and had no interest whatsoever in interfering in their internal organisation, as long as he received from the group the appropriate guarantees. Therefore no company of the group could object to the application of the arbitration clause in a dispute which concerned the whole group. No such consent could have been implied if various agreements of the contractual chain had contained incompatible arbitration or jurisdiction clauses. This is a simple example that the number of parties that can be assumed as bound by the arbitral tribunal's rulings, including those for interim measures, can be wider than the parties who formally signed the arbitration agreement. A tribunal may assume jurisdiction based on techniques such as incorporation of arbitration clause by reference, agency, piercing of corporate veil, estoppel, clause in favour of a third party, consent by conduct, etc.[58]

The foregoing analysis is based on the concept that the arbitration agreement is the source of the arbitral powers. As noted above (Sect. 2.2.1.1) there may be statutory grounds of arbitral jurisdiction. Such grounds are in a one-way connection to the arbitration agreement as source of jurisdiction. Without an arbitration agreement, the statutory powers would not come into play at all. Some lex arbitri such as UNCITRAL Model Law provides for the powers of arbitral tribunals to seek assistance from state courts for issuance of state court ordered interim measures on third parties.

Such provisions regulate a sua generis powers relating to the arbitral procedure. First, this is not a real arbitral jurisdiction power because it does not bestow powers on the arbitral tribunal to decide on a substantive matter. The only jurisdiction bestowed on the tribunal is a procedural power to request from a state court issuance of interim measures, respectively the rule provides for the state court duties to deal with such requests. The lex arbitri provides for a channel for tribunal-court communication. The actual jurisdiction to decide on the matter is provided to the state courts. This mechanism is necessary in order that third parties may be bound by interim measures. Being outside the rationae personae jurisdiction of the arbitral tribunal, third parties would not be bound unless this could be channelled via state courts. The extent of this power, as it is given to state courts, is regulated by the lex arbitri.

Is it possible that parties agree to widen the scope of personal jurisdiction, or restrict it? Parties may reach such agreement but it would be effective only within the bounds of the public policy/overriding mandatory rules of the lex arbitri. If it does not support alteration of personal jurisdiction on basis of consent, it would lead to partial invalidity or at least unenforceability of such a clause. Widening should also be premised upon consent by the respective "additional" parties.

Ratione Temporis The specifics of the time span of arbitral powers concern the moment when the jurisdiction of the arbitral tribunal is established. If the moment of

---

[58] For a detailed review Hanotiau (2006), pp. 7–48.

establishing the jurisdiction of tribunal as to the subject matter of the case, this would be the constitution/formation of the tribunal, which relates also to the appointment of arbitrators. However, if the interim measures jurisdiction of the tribunal is in question, it is possible that a preliminary jurisdiction is established in order to deal with interim measures as an emergency matter prior to the constitution of the arbitral tribunal. The rationale is that the emergency arbitration unit shall impose temporary interim measures before the matter moves on to the arbitrators who will deal with the substance of the dispute. They would rule on the interim measures as well. Hence, the purpose of the measures granted by the emergency arbitration unit would be to comprise the time period from the occurrence of the dispute and the respective need for interim measures, and the constitution of the tribunal.

2.2.1.3 Emergency Arbitrator Measures Under the Rules of Various Arbitral Institutions

Emergency arbitrator procedure was introduced first in the 2012 ICC Rules and was later adopted in other institutional rules, e.g. LCIA 2014 Rules, etc.

2.2.1.3.1 ICC

Under ICC Rules,[59] as amended in 2017, emergency arbitration applications are admissible prior to constitution of the arbitral tribunal (Article 29, para 1 ICC Rules). Hence, the interim period between filing a request for arbitration, and the constitution of the tribunal that is bound to take hold of the case file, is also covered by the jurisdiction of the emergency arbitrator (Article 29, para 1 ICC Rules in fine). Ratione temporis, the jurisdiction of emergency arbitrators stems only from arbitration agreements concluded prior to entry into force of the 2012 ICC Rules (1 January 2012). Further, the ratione materiae jurisdiction of the emergency arbitrator overlaps with the jurisdiction of the arbitration tribunal. Hence, it is governed by the arbitration agreement, the applicable arbitration rules and the mandatory rules of the lex arbitri. If the lex arbitri does not allow interim measures by arbitrators, an emergency arbitrator will not be competent to grant such as well. Parties are allowed to opt out of the emergency arbitration mechanism by consent; otherwise, it applies by default. Parties can replace the emergency arbitrator procedure by designation of another mechanism for pre-trial urgent relief.

After receipt of the application at the ICC Secretariat, the President of the ICC Court appoints an emergency arbitrator within as short a time as possible, normally within two days from the Secretariat's receipt of the Application (Article 2 of Appendix 5). Copy of the application is provided to the opposite party in the proceedings. The emergency arbitrator should comply with the same requirements

---

[59] Grierson and van Hooft (2012), pp. 63–72.

as an arbitrator. The Secretariat of ICC notifies the parties of the appointment and transmits the case file to the emergency arbitrator. The place of proceedings is determined by consensus between the parties or, in absence of such, can be determined by the President of the ICC Court. The emergency arbitrator decides on the manner of conduct of the proceedings by its own discretion and fixes timetable within the time frame of 2 days. The emergency arbitrator has the same powers for granting interim relief as the arbitrator, and hence applies the same standards and criteria. The emergency arbitrator decides on the application by way of order (Article 29, para 2 ICC Rules) within 15 days from the transmission of the file to the emergency arbitrator (Article 6, para 4 of Appendix V). Hence, even if the tribunal is constituted, it will not have powers to render interim relief if there is acting emergency arbitrator and the 15-day term has not elapsed yet. The order is not an award and is not subject to a mechanism of compulsory enforcement. Non—compliance with it may attract liability for damages. The emergency arbitrator may modify or terminator or annul its order made prior to the transmission of the matter to the arbitral tribunal. It will remain in force until, after the constitution of the tribunal, if it is not modified of terminated by the tribunal, until the final award is rendered. It will be terminated by the President of ICC Court if the requesting party does not file request for arbitration within 10 days from filing the emergency arbitration request.

The appointment of emergency arbitrator may be challenged (Article 3 of Appendix V). A challenge against the emergency arbitrator must be made within three days from receipt by the party making the challenge of the notification of the appointment or from the date when that party was informed of the facts and circumstances on which the challenge is based if such date is subsequent to the receipt of such notification. The challenge shall be decided by the Court after the Secretariat has afforded an opportunity for the emergency arbitrator and the other party or parties to provide comments in writing within a suitable period of time.

2.2.1.3.2 LCIA

Under LCIA Rules[60] (Article 9B, Rules 9.4-9.14), both the claimant and the respondent can seek appointment of an emergency arbitrator. The regulation of emergency arbitration procedure under LCIA Rules has a logic similar to ICC provisions with a few notable differences. The ratione temporis scope of the regime encompasses arbitration agreements concluded on or after 1 October 2014. Parties can opt out by explicit consensus; otherwise Article 9B applies by default. A party may seek appointment of emergency arbitrator prior to the constitution of the arbitral tribunal (Article 9.4) by application to the Registrar of the LCIA. The general prerequisite for emergency arbitrators under the LCIA Rules is the presence of emergency. Emergency is not defined. It can be understood as "necessity and

---

[60]Scherer and Richman (2015), pp. 133–166.

2.2 International Arbitration

time-pressure"[61] requiring urgent relief. The powers of the emergency arbitrator are broader under LCIA Rules compared to ICC Rules. In fact, these powers are not limited only to interim measures. In theory, the emergency arbitrator is entitled to any powers that the arbitral tribunal may have, and can grant any relief possible. However, given the expedited proceedings and the limitations on evidence in this regard, it is unlikely that the relief provided by an emergency arbitrator diverges substantially from what is usually deemed interim relief.

The Registrar appoints an emergency arbitrator within 3 days from receiving the application. The Emergency Arbitrator may conduct the emergency proceedings in any manner determined by the Emergency Arbitrator to be appropriate in the circumstances, taking account of the nature of such emergency proceedings, the need to afford to each party, if possible, an opportunity to be consulted on the claim for emergency relief (whether or not it avails itself of such opportunity), the claim and reasons for emergency relief and the parties' further submissions. The discretion of the emergency arbitrator is very wide and may not hold hearings at all; or may prefer to have the procedure ex parte. The emergency arbitrator decides the matter by rendering an award or order. The time frame of the procedure is 14 days from the appointment of the emergency arbitrator until rendering of the award/order. The award/order of the Emergency Arbitrator may be confirmed, varied, discharged or revoked, in whole or in part, by order or award made by the Arbitral Tribunal upon application by any party or upon its own initiative (Rule 9.11).

2.2.1.3.3 Swiss Rules

According to Article 43 of the Swiss rules of international arbitration, a party may apply to the court of the Arbitration Court of the Swiss Chambers' Arbitration Institution for appointment of an emergency arbitrator. Parties can opt out of this; otherwise the right exists by default. The powers of the emergency arbitrator encompass only granting urgent interim measure. The requesting party should outline the reasons for the urgency, i.e. why there is an urgent need for the measure applied for. The request for arbitration should be submitted within 10 days from submitting the application for emergency arbitrator. Emergency arbitrator may be appointed until the arbitral tribunal is constituted (Article 43 para 1). The Court appoints emergency arbitrator as soon as possible unless manifestly there is no arbitration agreement, or it is more appropriate to await the constitution of the tribunal. The emergency arbitrator may conduct the proceedings within broad discretion; nevertheless, Article 43, para 6 requires that the parties should have reasonable opportunity to be heard, hence there is no real room for ex parte measures. The emergency arbitrator issues a decision within 15 days from transmission of the file to him; the decision can be modified or terminated by the emergency

---

[61] Scherer and Richman (2015), p. 147.

arbitrator or, when the tribunal is constituted, by the arbitral tribunal. Otherwise the measure remains binding until the final award.

2.2.1.3.4 AAA

Under Article 6 para 1 of ICDR Rules, a party may seek emergency relief by emergency arbitrator on or prior to submission of notice of arbitration but in any case before the constitution of the arbitral tribunal. The ICDR Administrator appoints an emergency arbitrator within 1 day from receipt of the application. The emergency arbitrator fixes schedule of the procedure within 2 days from appointment. The emergency arbitrator has broad powers to conduct the proceedings but providing reasonable opportunity to all parties to be heard. The interim measure granted by the emergency arbitrator may be in the form of order or award. The emergency arbitrator or the tribunal may modify or vacate the award or order subsequently.

2.2.1.3.5 SCC

The 2017 SCC Rules regulate emergency arbitration procedure under Appendix II thereto.[62] A party may apply for emergency arbitrator appointment prior to the constitution of the arbitral tribunal. The powers of the emergency arbitrator coincide with the powers of the tribunal to grant interim measures (Article 1, para 2 of Appendix II referring to Article 37 SCC Rules). The SCC Board appoints emergency arbitrator within 24 hours from receipt of the application unless there is manifest lack of jurisdiction of SCC Board. The seat of the proceedings is as agreed by the parties; otherwise is determined by the SCC Board. The conduct of the proceedings is within the discretion of the emergency arbitrator but taking into account the urgency of the procedure. As generally SCC Rules (Article 23) require parties to have reasonable opportunity to be heard, the emergency arbitrator may have to balance between *audiatur et altera pars* and the urgency of the situation. Under Article 8 of Appendix II, the emergency arbitrator renders a "decision" within 5 days from appointment, which is binding on the parties. Cf, under Article 41 SCC Rules, where the Arbitral Tribunal consists of more than one arbitrator, any award or other decision shall be made by a majority of the arbitrators or, failing a majority, by the Chairperson. Hence, a "decision" under SCC Rules is a broader category than "award". The decision of the emergency arbitrator apparently falls under this category, so it should be taken not as an award but more like a procedural ruling/order. It can be amended by the emergency arbitrator or the tribunal; otherwise is effective until the award, within 90 days before the tribunal is not constituted or if within 30 days arbitration procedure is not commenced.

---

[62] Franke and Magnusson (2013), pp. 107–113.

2.2.1.3.6 SIAC

The 2016 SIAC Rules provide for emergency arbitration (Article 30 and Schedule 1). Under Article 1 to Schedule 1 to SIAC Rules, a party may apply for appointment of emergency arbitrator prior to constitution of the arbitral tribunal. The purpose should be emergency interim relief, i.e. a party may seek only an interim measure from the emergency arbitrator (cf LCIA Rules). The requesting party should specify nature and reasons for providing that relief. The SIAC President appoints an emergency arbitrator within 1 day from receipt of the application. The emergency arbitrator has broad discretion as to conduct of proceedings but should ensure reasonable opportunity for parties to present their cases (Article 7 to Schedule 1 to SIAC Rules). The emergency arbitrator sets schedule of the proceedings within 2 days from receipt of appointment. The place of arbitration is the one designated by the parties; otherwise, it is Singapore. The emergency arbitrator renders order or award within 14 days which is subject to scrutiny by the Registrar of SIAC. He has no powers after the formation of the arbitral tribunal. The tribunal may modify of vacate his order/award. If the tribunal is not constituted within 90 days, the order/award automatically ceases to be binding. Interestingly, according to Article 12 to Schedule 1 to SIAC Rules, the parties are bound to comply with the order/award without opposition.

2.2.1.3.7 CIETAC

Articles 23 and 77 of CIETAC Rules provide for emergency arbitrator procedure (Appendix III to CIETAC Rules). A party may request appointment of emergency arbitrator prior to the constitution of the arbitral tribunal (Article 2 of Appendix III). The party should outline the reasons for the emergency relief. The CIETAC Rules do not restrict emergency relief to interim measures only but it may be gleaned from the requirement to specify requested measures that the intended emergency relief is actually interim relief, i.e. the powers of the emergency arbitrator are limited to granting interim measures only. The President of CIETAC appoints the emergency arbitrator within 1 day. The emergency arbitrator should conduct the proceedings in the manner the emergency arbitrator considers to be appropriate, taking into account the nature and the urgency of the emergency relief, and shall ensure that each party has a reasonable opportunity to present its case (Article 5 of Appendix III), i.e. the emergency arbitrator has broad discretion. He should affix timetable for the proceedings within 2 days from receipt of the file. The emergency arbitrator issues order or award within 15 days from appointment. The tribunal may terminate the decision of the emergency arbitrator; the emergency arbitrator may terminate its own decision as well. Otherwise, the decision may stand until the final award (and even afterwards) or the tribunal is not constituted within 90 days from the date of the decision. The appointment of the emergency arbitrator can be challenged. A party which has justifiable doubts as to the impartiality or independence of the appointed emergency arbitrator may challenge that emergency arbitrator in writing and shall state the facts and reasons on which the challenge is based with supporting evidence (Article 3 of Appendix III).

2.2.1.3.8 HKIAC

Schedule 4 of the 2013 HKIAC Rules regulates emergency arbitration procedure. The application for emergency relief can be made on or after filing notice of arbitration, but in any event prior to the constitution of the tribunal (Article 1). The party should specify the reasons of urgency that require emergency relief. HKIAC appoints emergency arbitrator within 2 days from receipt of the application. Taking into account the urgency inherent in the emergency relief proceedings and ensuring that each party has a reasonable opportunity to be heard on the application, the emergency arbitrator may conduct such proceedings in such a manner as the emergency arbitrator considers appropriate (Article 11). The emergency arbitrator renders "decision, order or award" within 15 days from receipt of the file. It has the force of interim measure rendered by the tribunal and stands until amended by the emergency arbitrator, the tribunal or the final award unless the tribunal is not constituted within 90 days (Article 19).

2.2.1.3.9 Saudi Arabia Center for Commercial Arbitration

According to Article 6 of the Arbitration Rules (2018) of SCCA, a party may file request for interim relief before the constitution of the arbitral tribunal. The notice requesting such relief may be filed at the time of request for arbitration, or after its submission but not prior to that. The arbitral institution shall appoint a sole emergency arbitrator. The arbitrator has the full powers of a tribunal and the procedure is conducted hearing both parties. The arbitrator may grant any relief under the rules in the form of an arbitral award. After the constitution of the tribunal, the emergency arbitrator is divested from powers and the emergency relief may be modified or vacated by the tribunal. Seizing the judicial authorities does not preclude applying for emergency relief.

2.2.1.3.10 Dubai International Arbitration Center

Under the Dubai International Arbitration Center (DIAC) 2022 Rules, parties may apply for emergency relief. The Center shall appoint an emergency arbitrator in case that the Center finds prima facie grounds for this. The emergency arbitrator conducts procedure taking account of both parties and may issue a preliminary order. After the constitution of the tribunal, the emergency arbitrator loses powers and its order may be modified or cancelled by the tribunal in the course of the proceedings or by the final award in the end of it.

2.2.1.4 Interim Conclusions on Emergency Arbitrator Procedures

Emergency arbitrators' jurisdiction to provide relief encompasses the period prior to constitution of the arbitral tribunal. Some rules require that the application for emergency arbitrator is filed along with request for arbitration (HKIAC) while most require that request is filed within a very short time frame afterwards, usually 10 days. The applicant is usually required to specify reasons for urgency. The emergency arbitrator has broad powers. First, most rules specify that the emergency arbitrator is limited to granting interim measures. However, LCIA rules notably allow that any emergency relief is available from the emergency arbitrator, thus widening the scope of his jurisdiction. Second, the discretionary powers of the emergency arbitrator to conduct the procedure are broad. Most rules require that the parties should have reasonable opportunity to be heard, therefore the procedure should be inter partes. However, as the time frame is very tight and given the urgency of the situation, it is possible that the emergency arbitrator provides measures ex parte; these can be amended afterwards when the opposite party presents its case. The emergency arbitrator can be challenged. Most rules provide that the form of the emergency relief can be award or order, which is important for enforcement purposes. But given the urgency factor, enforcement of an award may be unrealistic so rendering an order should be sufficient. The measure can be modified or revoked by the tribunal afterwards or if tribunal is not constituted under a specified period of time (usually 90 days).

Under the ICC Rules, the earliest moment for providing interim measures is the transmission of the case file to the tribunal, which implies that by the moment of transmission the tribunal is already constituted.[63] The situation is similar under Article 25.3 LCIA Rules.[64]

In case that emergency relief is not available, the time moment when the tribunal's powers will come into force shall be the moment when the tribunal shall be constituted.

Interim relief is available to be provided by state courts and/or emergency unit where applicable rules designate one (e.g. ICC; LCIA rules) until the constitution of the arbitral tribunal. Once the tribunal is constituted and is in possession of the case (file), the tribunal may order interim measures until the case is decided on the merits by the final award. Under some rules (ICC, LCIA), a party would not be able to seek interim relief by courts once the tribunal is constituted unless exceptional circumstances are present; most rules, however, allow concurrent jurisdiction.

---

[63] Grierson and van Hooft (2012); Schwartz and Derains (2005), p. 299.
[64] Scherer and Richman (2015), p. 279.

2.2.2 Concurrent Arbitral and State Court Jurisdiction to Grant Interim Measures

As noted above, the first moment of time when the jurisdiction of the arbitral tribunal is established is the constitution of the arbitral tribunal (except when there is an emergency relief and imposed interim measures under such relief). Naturally, an aggrieved party would have to seek assistance from state courts to obtain interim measures if these are necessary prior to the date of constitution of the arbitral tribunal, i.e. are urgent.

(i) It is possible that the state courts impose interim measures, while subsequently the arbitral tribunal would impose some interim measures as well. As the state courts and the tribunal shall have concurrent jurisdiction, the measures imposed by each of these bodies may conflict with each other.

(ii) An alternative scenario for a potential conflict of jurisdictions is where both the arbitral tribunal and the state courts are empowered to grant interim measures. This is known to be so as under most leges arbitri state courts have powers to grant interim measures, consequently, there is room for potential conflicts.

Usually the powers of state courts to grant interim measures do not cease with the constitution of the arbitral tribunal and so parties can always seek assistance from the court. This allows the possibility for concurrence of jurisdiction.[65] This is the situation under most rules of arbitration with the notable exception of ICC and LCIA Rules that envision state-provided interim measures only in exceptional circumstances,[66] e.g. Article 28(2) ICC Rules. The situation is similar under Article 25.3 LCIA Rules.[67] Moreover, under established case law and doctrine, seeking measures from state courts would not preclude the jurisdiction of the arbitral tribunal and would not waive the rights of the parties to seek measures from the tribunal as well.[68]

The courts and the arbitral tribunals are separate and autonomous bodies. The tribunal, after being constituted, cannot revise the interim measures of the court, or revoke their effect or override them in any manner.[69]

Conflicts between concurrent jurisdictions would occur in practice at the moment when the various colliding interim measures have to be enforced, so that one and the same object will have to be affected by the conflicting measures.

Conflict between concurrent jurisdictions may be avoided by way of several regulatory approaches.

First, if the powers of courts to grant interim measures is restricted only as to the time limit before the arbitral tribunal is constituted, and, when it is constituted, only

---

[65] Yesilirmak (2005), pp. 66–107.
[66] Grierson and van Hooft (2012); Schwartz and Derains (2005), p. 299.
[67] Scherer and Richman (2015), p. 279.
[68] Born (2014), pp. 2548–2549.
[69] Ehle (2007); Binder (2005), p. 169.

as to matters and persons not covered by the arbitral jurisdiction, or in exceptional circumstances.[70] This approach is adopted by various institutional rules, e.g. ICC (Article 28(2)); LCIA (Rule 25.3), etc. Hence, if a party seeks interim measures regarding a third person, the state courts would have powers although the tribunal would be already constituted.

Second, could the same effect be achieved by contract, i.e. that the parties to the arbitration agreement restrict the powers of the state court to grant interim measures in concurrence with the arbitral tribunal? The validity of such an agreement may be of dubious nature. The state courts have statutory powers and jurisdiction based on statute. Although consent is paramount in arbitration-related matters, the exemption of court powers would be hard to be accepted by the lex arbitri (with some exceptions—e.g. UK law—under English Arbitration Act 1996, s. 42-44, parties' agreement is granted primacy over state authority to issue orders affecting the course of the arbitral proceedings; parties can agree to the contrary). However, the agreement may be drafted in a different manner so that the right of the parties to seek interim measures from courts on concurrent grounds may be restrained. Some lex arbitri may see the right to request interim measures as a procedural right which cannot be waived by way of contract, and as a contravention of public policy of the respective lex arbitri.

A third approach may suggest that although not expressly regulated in statutes or institutional rules, there is a certain coordination between the powers of state courts and tribunals. A court's powers are undeniably wider. However, this does not mean that it should override the powers of a tribunal.

In reality, the rule of 'first come, first served' would apply, i.e. the first measure to be enforced at the enforcement stage, would preclude and prevent the enforcement of the posterior measure. This could be grounded on several bases. First, if a res judicata approach is adopted, the issue decided by the interim measures ruling should be considered as settled by it and cannot be re-opened and decided. However, it is commonly held that interim measures rulings cannot have res judicata. The mirror image of this argument is an estoppel argument—once a certain measure is recognised, another conflicting one cannot be recognised as well. The same argument can be seen from the view point of lis pendens—deciding one and the same manner by different bodies in parallel should not be allowed. However, bodies in different countries can be coordinated with difficulty, as these are not parts of one and the same jurisdictional system and cannot be said that the lis pendens principle could be applied. Finally, and most importantly, there remains the public policy exception—it would be contrary to certainty of law, etc. to assume that conflicting interim measures would be recognised. Therefore, although it seems there may be a striking collision between interim measures granted by different bodies, in effect this, if it happens, would be naturally resolved in favour of the first to be imposed by way of enforcement interim measure.

---

[70] Yesilirmak (2005), pp. 92–93.

In this author's view, the proper approach is that of "concentration" of interim measure powers, i.e. that a single body should be entrusted with the powers of providing interim measures to the greatest extent possible. Parties' choice and will to arbitrate should be given primacy. A party should request interim measures from the arbitral tribunal in any event first unless the tribunal does not have any powers to provide such, or the requested relief is not within the scope of the powers of arbitrators. If the request is not granted or if the party does not have any other option, incl. that the tribunal does not have the relevant jurisdictional powers, the applicant should be entitled to request measures from the state court (see further Sect. 2.2.4 below).

2.2.3 Assessment of Jurisdiction/Law Applicable to Determination of Jurisdiction

The issues of jurisdiction are to be decided by the respective body (be it court or arbitral tribunal) by reference to the law governing the arbitration, the lex arbitri. It is the framework for deciding on matters relating to jurisdiction as well, including the jurisdiction to grant interim measures.

In most cases the lex arbitri would be the lex tribunalis siti. Hence, a tribunal will determine the limits of its powers to grant interim measures by reference to, and to the extent permissible, by the law of the seat of the tribunal.

Any issues regarding the grounds, or the scope, of the arbitral jurisdiction, will be subject to agreement between the parties to the extent this is permissible. Moreover the public policy and overriding mandatory rules of the lex arbitri will set the guidelines for the jurisdiction of the tribunal.

In reality, the most important rules on the jurisdiction to grant interim measures would be found within the set of rules of the relevant applicable rules of the arbitral institution governing the procedure. These would apply subject to consensual abrogation by agreement between the parties, inserted either in the arbitration agreement prior to the dispute, or specifically agreed upon after the dispute has arisen. Finally, these may not be in effect only if the lex arbitri is contravened.

2.2.4 Coordination Between Courts and Arbitral Tribunals. Role of Court as to Arbitral Power to Grant Interim Measures

It is noted above under Sect. 2.2.3 that state courts and arbitral tribunals have concurrent jurisdiction to grant interim measures. Most leges arbitri, especially those based on the UNCITRAL Model Law, endow the state courts with the powers to undertake interim measures independent from the powers of the arbitral tribunal.

The lex arbitri usually does not qualify such powers so that these can run in parallel to the powers of the tribunal or even counter to the powers of the tribunal. However, the actual role of the state court powers to grant interim measures is intertwined with the powers that an arbitral tribunal would not have. This is jurisdiction as to third parties. The tribunal would not be able to impose measures affecting third parties. However, the state courts have such power. This is why, strategically, the power to seize the state court, which both the parties to the dispute, and the tribunal itself, commonly have under the respective lex arbitri, should be used in these cases.

Same applies to interim measures regarding a subject matter which cannot be granted by the arbitral tribunal. Usually such are measures affecting real estate property, or measures that necessitate some registration or assistance from third parties. Although not third parties are affected, third parties are involved and for all practical purposes measures by the arbitral tribunal would not be enforceable if they concern such matters/objects.

Moreover, this power is also important since, as noted under Sect. 2.2.3, the time span of the interim measures jurisdiction of the arbitral tribunal very much depends on the moment of constitution of the arbitral tribunal. The availability of emergency relief unit may alleviate the problem but nevertheless, the necessity for a body empowered to grant interim measures in urgent situations and when the tribunal is not available to act, persists. This is why the ratione temporis jurisdiction of the courts is strategically important. The parties may have to seek interim measures from courts until the interim measures jurisdiction of the arbitral tribunal becomes available. This can cause further complications where the lex arbitri does not provide time limitations on the court imposed interim measures as these may collide with the measures the tribunal may grant. Ideally, the court measures should not lapse after the dispute is taken over by the arbitral tribunal. However, usually the lex arbitri does not contain such a rule for coordination of jurisdiction ratione personae.

2.3 Interim Measures in ICSID. Jurisdiction to Grant Interim Measures

Under Article 47 of the ICSID Convention, an ICSID tribunal has the power to recommend any provisional measures which should be taken to preserve the respective rights of either party.

Ratione materiae, the jurisdiction covers the investment disputes as defined in Article 25 of ICSID Convention ("any legal dispute arising directly out of an investment"), which is further defined in the ICSID case law as investment dispute.

Further, the ratione personae of the ICSID tribunal encapsulates a Contracting State and national of another Contracting State as defined in Article 25 (2) of the ICSID Convention. Therefore, the dispute within the jurisdiction of the ICSID tribunal should be between a party - individual, legal entity, Contracting State, and another Contracting State, hence, at least one of the parties should be a State.

Article 47 indicates that a tribunal may "recommend" measures. At the time of the drafting of the ICSID Convention, it was conceived of interim measures to be more recommendatory than obligatory,[71] which is why this language was used (also in line with the Statute of the ICJ). A number of tribunals have settled the law that Article 47, regardless how envisioned, should be now interpreted as giving jurisdiction for binding interim measures, e.g. Maffezzini v Spain;[72] Pey Casado v. Chile;[73] Tokios Tokel´es v. Ukraine;[74] Occidental v. Ecuador.[75]

Due to the issue of urgency which is most often implicated in interim measures proceedings, it is necessary to determine whether the tribunal should be satisfied that it has jurisdiction, or only a prima facie assessment of jurisdiction is sufficient. Some ICSID tribunals adopted the ICJ and ITLOS approach of examining whether there is a prima facie jurisdiction over the dispute—e.g. Occidental v. Ecuador;[76] Azurix v. Argentina.[77] In most cases, though, ICSID tribunals commented that jurisdictional objections and challenges do not preclude the power of the tribunal to grant interim measures (e.g. SGS v. Pakistan;[78] Holiday Inns v. Morocco;[79] Bayindir v. Pakistan[80]). The legal theory has also argued that Article 36 (3) of ICSID Convention supports the approach of tribunals since the Secretary-General ought to make examination as to jurisdiction because it should not register a case if it is manifestly outside the ICSID jurisdiction.[81] A contrario, a registered case should be, by a preliminary token, within the jurisdiction of ICSID to an arguable extent. Therefore, the ICSID case law does not state this as expressly as ICJ or ITLOS, but it can be inferred that: (1) at the moment of ruling on interim measures, the tribunal may not have examined its jurisdiction in full; (2) its jurisdiction may be challenged by one of the parties; (3) but as long as a prima facie existence of jurisdiction can be ascertained at that moment, the tribunal is entitled to entertain a request to grant interim measures under Article 47.

---

[71] Schreuer et al. (2009), p. 764.

[72] Maffezini v. Spain, Decision on Provisional Measures (Procedural Order No. 2), 28 October 1999, para. 9.

[73] Decision on Provisional Measures, 25 September 2001, paras. 17–26.

[74] Procedural Order No. 1, 1 July 2003, para. 4.

[75] Decision on Provisional Measures, 17 August 2007, para. 58.

[76] Decision on Provisional Measures, 17 August 2007, para. 55.

[77] Decision on Provisional Measures, 6 August 2003, para. 3.

[78] Procedural Order No. 2, 16 October 2002, 8 ICSID Reports 391.

[79] Decision on Jurisdiction, 12 May 1974, 1 ICSID Reports 658.

[80] Decision on Jurisdiction, 14 November 2005, para. 47.

[81] Schreuer et al. (2009), p. 772.

References

Ancel B, Muir Watt H (2005) L'intérêt supérieur de l'enfant dans le concert des juridictions: le Règlement Bruxelles II bis. Revue Critique de Droit International Privé (Rev. crit. dr. int. pr.) 4: 569–581

Bermann GA (2017) International arbitration and private international law. Brill Nijhoff, Leiden

Binder P (2005) International commercial arbitration and conciliation in UNCITRAL model law jurisdictions. Sweet & Maxwell Publishing, London

Blackaby N, Partasides C, Redfern A, Hunter JM (2015) Redfern and Hunter on international arbitration. Oxford University Press, Oxford

Born G (2014) International commercial arbitration. Kluwer Law international, The Hague

Bureau D, Muir Watt H (2017) Droit international prive, Tome I, Partie generale. Themis, Paris

De Sousa Goncalves AS (2022) The Recast of the Regulation on Jurisdiction, the Recognition and Enforcement of Decisions in Matrimonial Matters and the Matters of Parental Responsibility (Brussels IIb) In: Laimer S, Kronthaler C, Koch B (2022) Europäische und internationale Dimensionen des Privatrechts. Jan Sramek Verlag, Vienna

Ehle BD (2007) Concurrent jurisdiction: arbitral tribunals and courts granting interim relief. In: Alibekova A, Carrow R (eds) International arbitration and mediation - from the professional's perspective. Yorkhill Law Publishing

Feraci O (2011) Riconoscimento ed esecuzione all'estero dei provvedimenti provvisori in materia familiare: alcune riflessioni sulla sentenza Purrucker. Rivista di diritto internazionale privato e processuale (Rivdir. int. priv. proc.) 1:107–134

Franke U, Magnusson A (eds) (2013) International arbitration in Sweden: a practitioner's guide. Kluwer Law International, The Hague

Gaillard E, Savage J (eds) (1999) Fouchard Gaillard Goldman on international commercial arbitration. Kluwer Law International, The Hague

Garcimartin F (2014/2015) Provisional and protective measures in the Brussels I regulation recast. Yearb Priv Int Law (YbPIL) 16:57–84

Gaudemet-Tallon H (2010) Compétence et exécution des jugements en Europe. LGDJ, Paris

Grierson J, Van Hooft A (2012) Arbitrating under the 2012 ICC rules. Kluwer Law International, The Hague

Hanotiau B (2006) Complex arbitrations: multiparty, multicontract, multi-issue and class actions. Kluwer Law International, The Hague

Hartley T (2009) International commercial litigation. Cambridge University Press, Cambridge

Heinze C (2011) Choice of court agreements, coordination of proceedings and provisional measures in the reform of the Brussels I regulation. RabelsZ 75:581–618

Hess B, Pfeiffer T, Schlosser P (2005) Report on the Application of the Regulation Brussels I in the Member States. Study JLS/C4/2005/03

Honorati S (2011) Purrucker I e II ed il regime speciale dei provvedimenti provvisori e cautelari a tutela dei minori. Int'l Lis 2:66–80

Kelsen H (2005) Pure theory of law. The Lawbook Exchange Ltd, New Jersey

Krüger W, Rauscher T (eds) (2020) Münchener Kommentar zur Zivilprozessordnung. Beck, München

Lazić V, Stuij S (2017) Brussels ibis regulation: changes and challenges of the renewed procedural scheme. Springer, Berlin

Mankowski P, Magnus U (eds) (2011) Brussels I regulation – European commentaries on private international law. Sellier, Munich

Pretelli I (2018/2019) Provisional measures in family law and the Brussels II Ter regulation. Yearb Priv Int Law YbPIL 20:113–148

Scherer M, Richman L (eds) (2015) Arbitrating under the 2014 LCIA rules: a user's guide. Kluwer Law International, The Hague

Schreuer C, Malintoppi L, Reinisch A, Sinclair A (2009) The ICSID convention: a commentary. Cambridge University Press, Cambridge

Schwartz E, Derains Y (2005) Guide to the ICC rules of arbitration. Kluwer Law International, The Hague

Vorwerk V, Mayer H, Wolf C, Kessal-Wulf S, Bacher K, Dressler W, Hübsch G, Scheuch S, Toussaint G, Thode R (2018) Beckscher Online-Kommentar ZPO. Beck, München

Yesilirmak A (2005) Provisional measures in international commercial arbitration. Kluwer Law International, The Hague

Chapter 3
Nature, Operation, Types of Interim Measures

This chapter is intended to delve into another procedural aspect of interim relief. However, this aspect is the one which bears greatest relevance to matters of substantive law, as well. The purpose of this part of the study is to review several key matters:

First, what standards (i.e. criteria) national laws usually employ when deciding whether interim relief should be granted or not. The author strives to outline within this part several general benchmarks found in most national legislations and developed or reflected in the case law of various countries in order to glean if there are common reference points. The study has selected laws and practices of countries representing most continents, legal systems and traditions in order to reach well-grounded inferences. Since national adjudicating bodies may grant interim relief in cross-border disputes, incl. subject to arbitration, such review of national rules is relevant for the picture of interim relief in transnational disputes. Furthermore, this part also provides overview of various rules of arbitral institutions containing guidance on what measures may be granted under the respective rules.

Second, this chapter looks into the very procedural characteristics of interim measures before state courts and arbitral tribunals, i.e. interim relief proceedings in a very strict sense. This part deals with standards of proof, manner of conduct of procedure, issuance of final assessment/decision/order, its form and content, etc.

Third, in both national laws and arbitration law the content and scope of interim relief, i.e. what measures may be granted in practice, is rarely given as an exhaustive list. On the contrary, the powers of adjudicating bodies are rather wide and amorphous, so therefore legal scholarship and case law has further elucidated what particular measures may be implemented. This is being reviewed in that section of the chapter.

Finally, this chapter features a selection of particular types of disputes and what measures are typically granted to be implemented in such disputes. There is an additional rationale in including this part of the study since one of the main arguments/conjectures listed in the very beginning of the study seeks to prove that the nature of the disputed rights and obligations and the facts surrounding them are in correlation with the measures that should cater for the particular dispute.

3.1 Standards for Interim Measures

When deciding on an application for interim relief, adjudicators usually apply certain considerations and criteria to assess whether the relief requested should be granted. Various bodies of law contain very general standards to be applied when deciding on an interim measures application. The purpose of this section is to make review of the regulation on such standards in relevant national legislations and rules of arbitral institutions, and to discern those that seem to be the most common and important considerations applied.

3.1.1 Under National Law

The survey of the various systems of interim relief measures demonstrate that there are certain components of assessment for the purpose of granting interim relief that are, in one or another form, ubiquitously present in most systems of law.

The analysis below purports to outline the major elements that a decision-making body would seek when ruling on an interim measures application. In virtually all jurisdictions an interim measures application calls for a level of examination of the merits of the dispute and the measure would not be granted unless there is at least a level of probability of the claim of the applicant. It is not a full review of merits but merit should appear on basis of the evidence submitted. Further, most jurisdictions would also require that the interim measure is necessary as to avert negative consequences, with regard to the subject matter of the dispute; the liquidity of the debtor, etc. A time factor is usually present in most jurisdictions as well—in some, it is the urgency of the situation that must be present in order that an interim measure request is granted; in others, it is a factor that the dispute resolution body weighs when granting measures. Finally, all systems require some balancing between the interests of the parties, some proportionality between the measure and the aims it pursues.

Many of the comparative features of interim relief across various jurisdictions are reflected in soft law documents such as the ALI/UNIDROIT Principles of Transnational Civil Procedure[1] and ELI/UNIDROT Model European Rules of Civil Procedure.[2]

---

[1] Accessed at: https://www.unidroit.org/instruments/civil-procedure/ali-unidroit-principles/, last visited on 18 August 2022.

[2] Accessed at: https://www.unidroit.org/instruments/civil-procedure/eli-unidroit-rules/, last visited on 18 August 2022.

3.1.1.1 Proof of Significant Degree of Merit/Arguable Case

Most systems of law require that the court is satisfied to be established before it a certain degree of merit of the claim by the applicant. This can be termed in various ways but, generally speaking, in any event this is assessment that the claim is more likely to be successful than not, i.e. at least 50% of chance. Therefore, it can be inferred that the applicant should demonstrate (prove) before the court that its claim has as significant degree of likelihood of success on merits as at least 50%, i.e. more likely than not. The interim measures court will not be able, and should not be able, to review full merits of the claim but for the purpose of the interim relief review, the court should be able to discern a good arguable case, or, as common law often names it, a balance of the probabilities.

The national laws of reviewed countries differ on the issues whether 50% probability is sufficient, or more than 50% should be established. Albeit no system of law seeks 100% merit to be established, there are some systems that require very high level of probability—if not reaching 100%, in any event more than 50%.

For instance, under English law, it is necessary to establish that there is a serious issue to be tried, real prospects for success.[3] However, this does not always mean that the certainty to be established should be beyond 50%—for freezing orders, there should be a good arguable case as to the merits of the substantive claim—"one which is more than barely capable of serious argument, but not necessarily one which the judge considers would have a better than 50% chance of success".[4] As to search orders, for instance, the requirement is for extremely strong prima facie case[5] while for disclosure of documents—that there is prima facie existence of the claimed substantive rights for the proof of which the documents are produced.[6] Hence, as an overall standard, the proof of the substantive claim of the applicant should be prima facie, i.e. existence of substantive rights should be seriously proven to a significant probability, if not 50% or more.

Under s 389 (1) of Austrian Enforcement Act, the existence of a substantive claim should be established to an extent capable to persuade the court of its existence—a standard of less than 100% but more than 50% of probability of the claim.

Under Russian law, the applicant should not prove its right to the extent required in the substantive proceedings but it is necessary to submit sufficient evidence to support the existence of the respective claimed right.[7] Therefore, the claim should be evidenced on a credible level, if not to a 100% probability.

---

[3] E.g. Eng Mee Yong v Letchumann [1980] AC 331 at 337C-D; American Cynanamid Co. v Ethicon Ltd [1975] AC 396; Lumley v Wagner (1852) 1 De G M & G 604.

[4] Ninemia Maritime Corporation v Trave Schiffahrtsgesellschaft GmbH (The Niedersachsen) [1983] 2 Lloyd's Rep, 600 at 605.

[5] Anton Piller KG v Manufacturing Processes Ltd [1976] Ch 55, at 62.

[6] Mars UK Ltd v Waitrose [2004] EWHC 2264 (Ch); [2004] All ER (D) 136.

[7] Ruling of the Plenum of Supreme Arbitrazh Court No. 55 dated 12 October 2006.

Under the Swiss law, Debt Enforcement and Bankruptcy Law, Art. 272, the applicant should prove prima facie existence of claim.

In Italy, prima facie merits of the claim should be established (Article 669-8 of the Civil Procedure Code). Similarly, the Code of Civil Procedure of Sweden (Chapter 15, Sections 1–3) requires probability for the existence of the claimed substantive rights at hand.

In Japan, under Article 13 (2) of the Code of Civil Procedure, a prima facie case of the existence of the underlying rights should be made.

Under Article 590 of the Code of Civil Procedure of Columbia, at least appearance that the claimed substantive right exists should be established.

According to Queensland's Civil Proceedings Act, s 261A, in Australia, strong prima facie case should be made.

Some systems of law do not speak of prima facie merits of the underlying substantive claim but rather of a degree of risk to the rights of the applicant, which should be averted by way of the interim relief. The degree of threat varies—from the probability of its existence, to imminence of the threat. The magnitude of the threat varies as well—from possibility of threat to irreparable harm to rights of the applicant.

In Austrian law, it should be demonstrated that there are circumstances indicating actual threat to the rights of the applicant (Article 389 (1) of Enforcement Act).

In England, there should be strong evidence demonstrating real risk for dissipation of respondent's assets,[8] when freezing order is requested, and in case of search order, potential or actual very serious damage may ensue in the absence of the requested measure.[9] Similarly, according to Art 90(2) of the Arbitrazh Procedure Code of Russia, it should be established that material damage will occur.

Under Swiss Civil Procedure Code (Article 261), the interim measure should be granted only if the applicant's substantive rights will be prejudiced to extent that cannot be repaired, or at least cannot be easily repaired.

In France and French-influenced systems of law (France, Luxembourg, Belgium), interim measures are granted to avoid damage to the interests of the applicant.[10] Under Italian law, it should be evidenced that there is threat to the rights at stake that will be irreparably harmed pending outcome.[11]

According to Articles 362–363 of the Code of Civil Procedure of Portugal, interim relief is granted where there is threat of serious or irreparable harm to the substantive rights of the applicant.

The Civil Procedure Code of Sweden (Chapter 15, Sections 1–3) requires to be demonstrated risk to the underlying property rights at stake.

---

[8] Rossetti Marketing Ltd v Diamond Sofa Company Ltd and other [2012] EWHC 354 (QB).
[9] Anton Piller KG v Manufacturing Processes Ltd [1976] Ch 55, at 62.
[10] Miles (2017), pp. 26–27; generally Dumbauld (1932).
[11] Section 669 bis et seq. of Italian Civil Procedure Code.

3.1 Standards for Interim Measures

Under Art. 2 of the Federal Law concerning Civil Procedure of United Arab Emirates, a potential, if not fully proven, legal interest is sufficient to institute proceedings for the purpose to repel a forthcoming danger or to verify a right of which the evidence can be lost while the dispute is pending.

The risk of destruction of property is required under Order 39 of Code of Civil Procedure in India as well.

Under Queensland's Civil Proceedings Act 2011 (Australia), Section 9, interim measures should avert threatened or apprehended breach of the rights of the applicant.

Under Art. 8.2 of the ALI/UNIDROIT Principles of Transnational Civil Procedure,[12] a court is required to base interim relief grant on preponderance of considerations of fairness. The explanatory comment clarifies that "considerations of fairness include the strength of the merits of the applicant's claim" (comment P-8B), therefore it is expected that the court undertakes assessment of the underlying substantive rights at stake.

The overview demonstrates that most jurisdictions require not only that the existence of an underlying substantive right claimed to be established but also that the underlying substantive rights are put at risk by the respondent, and that the probability of the risk is proven by strong evidence. The risk should not be hypothetical or potential but actual and should pose realistic threat to the rights of the applicant. Few systems of law require that the harm that might be suffered is irreparable but the harm should be realistic, palpable, and indeed—significant.

3.1.1.2 Ensuring Enforcement of Judgment

Most jurisdictions adopt the standard that interim relief should purport to prevent potential actions of the respondent averting the effectiveness of the final decision on the merits of the dispute. Indeed, this is an essential component of interim relief without which the rationale of interim measures would be disrupted. The existence of an underlying claim does not suffice for the intrusion that interim measures present. The existence of a risk for the substantive rights claimed is not sufficient as well if the decision on the merits would be able to adequately put the parties to their initial position and repair any harm they might have suffered. There should be threat not only to the claimed substantive rights but also to the potential effect of the decision on the merits that resolves the dispute and establishes the parties' rights and obligations after the post resolution of the dispute. Therefore, although it may appear that the potential risk/threat is one and the same, it may overlap in some situations, but not in any and all. Hence, the proof of actual threat to the enforcement of the rights post-judgment is an autonomous standard. In some cases, the evidence may suffice to support both categories, but in some separate and different proof shall be necessary for meeting the distinct thresholds of both categories.

---

[12] UNIDROIT (2005).

Under English law, interim relief for the purpose of freezing injunction, should safeguard enforcement of the judgment on the merits and avert potential dissipation of assets by time the enforcement commences (per the English case of American Cyanamid Co (No 1) v Ethicon Ltd [1975] UKHL 1).

Under Articles 90–91 of Russian Arbitrazh Procedure Code, interim measures are provided where enforcement would be made more difficult or impossible.

Under Article 721 of the Spanish Civil Procedure Code, the interim relief requested should be able to ensure the effect of the outcome of the dispute on the merits.

Sections 916–917 of the German Procedural Rules[13] require that measures are provided where without them the enforcement of the decision on the merits is made more difficult or impossible. This could be the case if, considering the behavior of the debtor or based on other indications, there is a fear that the financial situation will deteriorate in the future. The seizure protects against stripping off substantial assets.[14] The existence of reasons for seizure is to be assessed from an objective point of view of an informed, conscientious observant person[15] The suspicion for sale of substantial assets, in particular the only physical asset, their relocation abroad, the concealment of their whereabouts, leaving a place of residence and an intended move abroad could also fall within the scope of that provision.[16] A sale of an asset constitutes a reason for seizure if the remaining assets of the debtor are not sufficient to satisfy the creditor and no substantial equivalent value flows into the assets of the debtor or enforcement of the proceeds is not possible; conversion of assets into money is a reason for arrest if there is a risk that the debtor will put the money aside.[17] Examples of such risks could also be existence of a realistic risk of deprivation of assets before access by creditors[18] or that the respondent may thwart enforcement by criminal means due to existing suspicions of criminal behaviour.[19] The risk may be associated with a third party and not only the debtor.[20] As to justify the fear of preventing or making enforcement more difficult, it must at least be credible that an unfavourable and not insignificant change in the debtor's financial circumstances is imminent.[21] § 917 ZPO does not focus on attitudes, but on the specific behavior of the debtor aimed at reducing, shifting or concealing assets that can be used for enforcement purposes. Under § 917 ZPO it is not a requirement that the debtor does nothing to improve his financial situation or that a large number of

---

[13] See generally Vorwerk V (BeckOK) (2022) ZPO § 916; 917; Krüger W et al (Munich Commentary on the ZPO) (2020), § 916–917.
[14] OLG Frankfurt am Main, decision of March 13, 2014—4 W 12/14.
[15] OLG Hamm, FamRZ 2012, 579.
[16] OLG Hamm, FamRZ 2012, 579; OLG Celle, FamRZ 2015, 160.
[17] KG, FamRZ 2014, 148.
[18] LG Traunstein, final judgment of March 17th, 2017—3 O 4524/16.
[19] LG Würzburg, decision v. 06.03.2017—11 O 386/17.
[20] Rostock Regional Court, decision of March 12, 2014—3 W 25/14.
[21] KG, FamRZ 2014, 148.

3.1 Standards for Interim Measures

creditors will have to satisfy themselves with relatively small assets or that the debtor's assets have already shrunk due to enforcement measures.[22] Intention to thwart enforcement can be indicated if a perpetrator has obtained an unlawful financial advantage through his acts and the acts were characterized by a fraudulent approach or an approach aimed at concealing the actual circumstances.[23]

Article 74 of the Civil Procedure Code of the Czech Republic requires that interim measures ensure enforcement of the judgment so it will not be compromised.

Under Chapter 15, Sections 1–3 of the Civil Procedure Code of Sweden, interim relief is granted where there is probability that the respondent will evade payment or will destroy the property at stake or, put more generally, the decision will not be implemented because of respondent's conduct.

In China, Article 92 of the Procedural Law requires interim relief to be granted if the decision on the merits will be impossible or more difficult to be enforced. Under Order 38 of Civil Procedure Code in India, the same requirement exists for granting attachment.

Under Article 20 (1) of the Civil Procedure Code of Japan, interim measures are provided to safeguard the subsequent enforcement of judgment on monetary claim.

According to Article 158 of the Civil Procedure Code of Kazakhstan, interim measures are granted if the enforcement of the decision will be made otherwise more difficult of impossible.

Under Order 30 of Federal High Court (Civil Procedure) Rules 2019 of Nigeria, where delay or obstruction of the enforcement of the decision on the merits may ensue, the court is entitled to grant interim relief.

Under Article 64 (a) of Federal Rules of Civil Procedure of the USA, interim measures are granted to secure satisfaction of the potential judgment.

In Argentinean Code of Civil and Commercial Procedure, Article 221, sequestration is granted to ensure effectiveness of rights at judgment enforcement. This standard is enacted in Brazil's Article 294 of the Civil Procedure Code and Chile's Article 290 of the Code of Civil Procedure.

Under Queensland's Civil Proceedings Act 2011, s 260A an order (a freezing order) for the purpose of preventing the frustration or inhibition of the court's process by seeking to meet a danger that a judgment or prospective judgment of the court will be wholly or partly.

The survey demonstrates that most jurisdictions do not speak only of a requirement that the underlying rights are threatened, but that the enforcement of the judgment on the merits is threatened, hence, this is rendered a separate standard to be met by interim relief applications. The wording of the requirement is very close from one jurisdiction to another, probably the most ubiquitous of all standards. In most cases it is clearly interpreted to mean evidence of transfer, dissipation and other actions of the respondent that hinder the possibilities for enforcement of the substantive rights awarded by the judgment. It may take the form of actions of the

---

[22] OLG Jena, 22.03.2006—6 U 442/05.
[23] Higher Regional Court Nuremberg, decision of April 16, 2013—2 Ws 10–11/13.

respondent directed at objects that are within the scope of the dispute on the merits itself, or actions of the respondent directed at its assets that will decrease the applicant's potential to be satisfied by a monetary judgment.

This requirement can also be termed as "necessity"—i.e. that there are such circumstances that necessitate provision of interim measures which will prevent greater harm to the interests of the applicant.

3.1.1.3 Urgency: Requirement for Granting Relief or Trigger for Faster Procedure

Urgency is a standard that is found in many systems of law but has different roles. In some jurisdictions urgency is an evidentiary standard which should be met in order that interim relief is obtained. In other jurisdictions, urgency is not a core standard and should not be proven at all costs. However, if established, it may have procedural implications as to the nature of the procedure for provision of the requested interim measures—whether ex parte (unilateral) or bilateral.

For instance, the systems of law rooted in French law[24] (France, Belgium, Luxembourg) require proof of urgency for interim relief to be granted.

Articles 362–363 Code of Civil Procedure of Portugal require urgency as well when the motion is brought prior to the claim on the merits of the dispute. Similarly, under Article 254 of the Dutch Civil Procedure Code, interim measures are provided in urgent situations.

Article 233 of the Law of Procedure before Sharia Courts of Saudi Arabia allows interim measures when urgency requires safeguard of rights that time delay may prejudice.

Under Art. 2 of the Federal Law concerning Civil Procedure of United Arab Emirates, interim relief is provided where there is a risk of forthcoming danger to the interests of the applicant.

In Article 219 of Code of Civil, Commercial, Administrative and Financial Procedure of Congo urgency is required as well.

Under Article 148 of the Code of Civil Procedure of Morocco interim measures are provided in emergency situations.

Article 233 of Code of Civil and Commercial Procedure of Argentina requires urgency for interim measures to be granted, same with Article 294 of Brazil's Code of Civil Procedure.

However, some systems of law include urgency only as a component that has procedural effect so that a party, having proven urgency, can obtain interim measures ex parte without notice to, and opposition by, the respondent.

For instance, in case of emergency, under the Spanish Code of Civil Procedure the interim measures can be provided ex parte (Article 730). Same applies under Sections 916–917 ZPO.

---

[24] Art. 484–492 of French Civil Procedure Code.

3.1 Standards for Interim Measures

The Swiss law requires the proof of urgency in order to provide measures that avert harm to the interests of the applicant.[25]

According to Chapter 15, section of Civil Procedure Code of Sweden, procedure is ex parte if delay places the applicant's motion at risk.

Under Article 93 of the Procedural Law of China, emergent cases of interim measures are ex parte. Same applies for India (Order XXXIX, Art. 3, Code of Civil Procedure, 1908 (Act No. 5 of 1908)). In Singapore, under Order 29 (2) cases of urgent interim measures are ex parte. Same is under Order 29 in Malaysia.

According to Art 65 (b) of Federal Rules of Civil Procedure in USA, in cases of immediate and irreparable injury, loss, or damage, applications for temporary restraining orders are treated ex parte.

Under Art. 8.2 of the ALI/UNIDROIT Principles of Transnational Litigation,[26] a court may issue an ex parte award of interim measures only where there is an urgent necessity. The restrictive language is further clarified by explanatory comment P-8C: the court should analyse "whether the applicant has made a reasonable and specific demonstration that such an order is required to prevent an irreparable deterioration in the situation to be addressed in the litigation, and that it would be imprudent to postpone the order until the opposing party has opportunity to be heard". Hence, it should not be considered as a general precondition but only as prerequisite for ex parte proceedings.

Similarly, Rule 186 of the ELI/UNIDROIT Model European Rules of Civil Procedure requires that ex parte proceedings be conducted only where inter partes procedure would frustrate the prospect of the applicant receiving effective protection of their interests.[27]

As a result, urgency can be treated in three different manners.

First, it can be a requisite element of proving the grounds to obtain interim measures.

Second, it may not be such element, but if proven, it will support an ex parte treatment of the application for interim measures.

However, there is a third role for emergency circumstances. These may not relate to the grounds but to be factor for considerations instead and to be taken into account along with other circumstances of the case. They can have persuasive effect to support arguments for existence of necessity to be provided interim measures, including arguments related to actual risk/threat to substantive rights/underlying claim, or relating to risks to potential enforcement of the decision on the merits. Then urgency simply adds up weight to the application.

---

[25] Art. 265 of Swiss Civil Procedure Code.

[26] ALI/UNIDROIT Principles of Transnational Civil Procedure, UNIDROIT (2005).

[27] ELI – UNIDROIT Model European Rules of Civil Procedure (2021).

3.1.1.4 Proportionality/Balance Between the Parties

Most systems of law provide for an additional requirement, which is the proportionality of the interim measure applied for. Interim measures intrude on the interests of the parties to the dispute. The intrusion may be allowed in order to prevent greater harm, but should not be present to extent that is irreversible or is disproportionate. This standard has been termed in various ways.

Under English law, the court should strike a balance of convenience between the parties (per the House of Lords in the case of American Cyanamid Co (No 1) v Ethicon Ltd [1975] UKHL 1), i.e. though the applicant's rights should be safeguarded by the interim measure, the respondent's rights should not be prejudiced without justification, disproportionately and without adequate remedy. Austrian law requires proportionality as well. Under Russian Arbitrazh Procedural Code, courts should grant measures that are proportionate and should not make respondent's position overly difficult.[28] Swiss law adopts the principle of proportionality, too.[29] Art 590 of Code of Civil Procedure of Columbia requires proportionality as well.

Under Art. 8.1 of the ALI/UNIDROIT Principle of Transnational Civil Litigation, it is expressly stated that provisional measures should be governed by the principle of proportionality.[30] As per Rule 185 of the ELI/UNIDROIT Model Rules of European Civil Procedure, interim relief should impose the least burden on the respondent. It has to be ensured that the measure's effects are not disproportionate to the interests it is requested in order to protect.[31]

3.1.1.5 Additional Categories

Provisionality/Timeliness
Various systems of law use some additional standards. Some use the broad language of interim measures to be just (and convenient) in order to be provided—Article 63 of Civil Procedure Act of Kenya (In order to prevent the ends of justice from being defeated); Article 64 of Civil Procedure Act of Uganda.

Some jurisdictions explicitly require that any admissible measure granted should have timely effect, i.e. be provisional, and should not render the position of the parties in a situation which cannot be altered—Article 730 of Spanish Code of Civil Procedure; Article 233 of Argentinean Code of Civil Procedure; Article 301 of Chilean Code of Civil Procedure; Article 384 of Federal Code of Civil Procedure of Mexico.

---

[28] Business impossible or very difficult; i.e. Ruling of the Plenum of Supreme Arbitrazh Court No. 11 dated 9 July 2003.

[29] Swiss Federal Supreme Court, 2 May 2005, BGE 131 III 473; 14 November 2008, case no 4A_367/2008 (unpublished); 3 January 2012, case no 4A_611/2011.

[30] ALI/UNIDROIT Principles of Transnational Civil Procedure, UNIDROIT (2005).

[31] ELI – UNIDROIT Model European Rules of Civil Procedure (2021).

3.1 Standards for Interim Measures

It is submitted that these additional standards overlap with some of the 'core' standards. Proportionality, timeliness and capability to alter interim measures indicate one and the same—interim measures should relate only to a status quo which is preserved during the pendency of the dispute and should not pre-judge the merits of the case, or render the judgment on the merits not enforceable.

3.1.1.6 Liability for Damages as a Means to Achieve Balance Between the Parties

A very common aspect of interim relief procedures across various jurisdictions is the requirement that the applicant is held liable for damages in the event that the end result of the dispute resolution procedure does not find merit in the claim of the applicant. Indeed, this does not feature as, to put it precisely, specific precondition to providing the requested interim measures, therefore, strictly speaking, it cannot be termed as part of the grounds or standards for granting interim relief. It is rather a legally entrenched, statutory based aspect of interim relief and consequence of providing such relief.

This is very logical as this is a liability, stemming from the operation of the law, which is based on the rationale of interim relief procedures. Interim relief has a restrictive impact on the sphere of the respondent and, in practical terms, it is improbable to assume a respondent would not suffer any damages or costs in relation to measures restricting the respondent. Hence, it would be an affront of basic principles of private law to conceive imposing measures for the benefit of the applicant without the necessary corollary being liability of the very same applicant towards the respondent. Hence, to put it in other words, the very existence of this liability is a prerequisite to having interim relief procedures in general. Otherwise, interim relief may become a tool for vexatious and unfounded applications, and the damnum iniuria (compensation of unlawful harm) principle of law would be compromised.

Most legislations across various systems of law contain express rules regulating liability for unjustified interim relief. Where not stated explicitly, other national laws ground this liability on different general principles and policy or have developed the notion of such liability incrementally via case law. Moreover, often the law can cast this as a procedural matter rather than expression of a fundamental substantive law notion—national laws combine such liability with a procedural requirement or prerequisite, for example posting a bond/security guarantee, making declaration or undertaking to pay damages sustained, etc. In such case, the general principle is the underpinning for the existence of the procedural rule and the requirement for submission of a bond, guarantee, etc.

Under English law, Civil Procedure Rules (CPR) Practice Direction 25A, para. 5.1(1) as well as case law[32] expressly requires a party undertaking to pay damages to the interim measures respondent.

---

[32] Sinclair v Cushnie [2004] EWHC 218 (Ch).

In French law this has been developed as a matter of case law and has been explicitly stated by the French Court of Cassation in a judgment of 24 February 2006.[33] According to it, the enforcement of an interim relief measure is at the risk of the party that seeks it and is subject to the obligation for that party to compensate the ensuing damages if the measure is cancelled.

German ZPO[34] similarly regulates under Section 945 that if a measure is found to be unjustified or cancelled, the party that has obtained the order is under obligation to compensate the opponent for the damages that suffered as a result of the measure; liability is no fault, risk-based.

Under Article 374(4) of Swiss Civil Procedure Code the applicant is liable for the harm caused by unjustified interim measures. If he or she proves, however, that the application for the measures was made in good faith, the arbitral tribunal or the state court may reduce the damages or relieve the applicant entirely from liability.

Per Section 394 of the Austrian Enforcement Act, in the case of unjustified interim measures the respondent has the right to seek damages, also confirmed by case law.[35]

Belgian civil procedure law expressly regulates civil liability for interim relief (Judicial Code, Art 1369 bis/3 § 2 and Article 1369 ter § 3).

In Italy, Art. 96 of the Civil Procedure Code requires compensatory damages in the event of an unjustified interim measure; the applicant could be found liable in the event he is found to have acted without ordinary care.

Art. 728.3 of Spanish Civil Procedure Law seeks sufficient guarantee from the applicant to cover potential damages liability of the applicant.

Under Polish Civil Procedure Law, Art. 98 § 1, general responsibility for damages stemming from the outcome of the judicial proceedings is provided for.

The Turkish Civil Procedure Code under Art. 399 regulates compensation damages claims for unjustified interim relief.

Under Article 98 of the Russian Arbitrazh Procedural Code there are grounds for the right of the respondent to obtain damages compensation for losses caused by interim measures.

Non-European jurisdictions follow the same policy to a similar extent. For instance, the national laws of the Latin American states feature such requirements. Under Art. 300 of the Civil Procedure Code of Brazil, the applicant is required to compensate damages that the respondent may incur. The Bolivian Civil Procedure Law (Art. 332) contains such provisions, too.

Art. 236 of the Law of Procedure before Sharia Courts in Saudi Arabia requires such liability as well.

Art. 165 of the Civil Procedure Code of the Republic of Kazakhstan provides that the court admitting security of a claim application may require from the applicant to post a security of possible damages to the respondent. The respondent may

---

[33] Appeal No. 05-12.679, Alain X v Epoux Y.
[34] Krüger W et al (MüKoZPO) (2020), ZPO § 945 Rn. 1-3.
[35] Austrian Supreme Court, 11 December 2007, 17 Ob 28/07b.

3.1 Standards for Interim Measures

subsequently bring a claim for compensation of damages caused by measures for security of a claim.

Under Article 105 of the Chinese Procedural Law the applicant must compensate the respondent for any losses incurred due to the granting of an interim measure, which is later found to be unjustified or erroneously granted.

According to Rule 65 (c) of the Federal Rules of Civil Procedure of USA, the court may issue a preliminary injunction or a temporary restraining order only if the applicant gives security in an amount that the court considers proper to pay the costs and damages sustained by any party found to have been wrongfully enjoined or restrained.

Both the ALI/UNIDROIT Principles of Transnational Civil Procedure (Art. 8.3) and the ELI/UNIDROIT Model European Rules of Civil Procedure (Rule 187) regulate provision of security to allow potential compensation for damages sustained by the respondent. Under both soft law instruments, it is a matter of court discretion whether to require posting a bond and is dependent on the particular circumstances of the case.

The overview also demonstrates that the liability for damages is of rather strict nature, i.e. the harmful event and result is sufficient to ground liability and fault of the applicant is not required. However, some legislations, for instance Swiss law, incorporate a good faith exception, i.e. that an applicant may avail itself from liability if acting on basis of good faith.

3.1.2 Characteristic Features of the Procedures to Obtain Interim Relief

Procedures for obtaining interim measures under various national systems of law usually differ from the typical/general claim procedure. As the purpose of the interim measures procedure is to safeguard the interests of the applicant from potential harm, interim measure procedures tend to divert from the fairness and equality principles and often national systems of law adopt a model for such procedures which encompasses fewer hearing opportunities or is ex parte from the onset. The rationale for this is the speediness of the procedure which will be compromised if interim measures are granted too late.

There are three approaches, which can be found in the various systems of law.

First, some do not adopt any specific rules enhancing speed and efficiency of the procedure.

Second, some jurisdictions provide that in specific circumstances applications for interim measures can be dealt with in greater haste and without notice to the respondent as to prevent the respondent from taking bad faith actions that will undermine the efficiency of the interim measures. It is to note that the factor of emergency can function in two directions: as a standard in favour of granting interim relief (as under Sect. 3.1.1.3 above) and as triggering a fast track procedure.

For instance, in case of emergency, under the Spanish Code of Civil Procedure the interim measures can be provided ex parte (Article 730). Same applies under §§ 916–917 ZPO.

According to Chapter 15 of Civil Procedure Code of Sweden, procedure is ex parte if delay places the applicant's motion at risk.

Under Article 93 of the Procedural Law of China, emergency cases of interim measures are ex parte. Same applies for India (Order XXXIX, Art. 3, Code of Civil Procedure, 1908 (Act No. 5 of 1908)). In Singapore, under Order 29 (2) cases of urgent interim measures are ex parte. Same is under Order 29 in Malaysia. According to Art 65 (b) of Federal Rules of Civil Procedure in USA, in cases of immediate and irreparable injury, loss, or damage, applications for temporary restraining orders are treated ex parte.

Similarly, some jurisdictions consider that specific categories of interim measure applications should be considered ex parte. For instance, under English law search order applications are ex parte. Under Swiss law, applications for attachment of pecuniary receivables are dealt with ex parte (Articles 274 and 276 of Debt Enforcement and Bankruptcy Act). In Morocco, payment order applications are ex parte.

Finally, many jurisdictions treat all interim measure applications always as ex parte, e.g. § 75c (3) of the Czech Civil Procedure Code; Article 23 of the Civil Procedure Code of Japan; Article 160 of the Civil Procedure Code of Kazakhstan; Article 219 of the Civil, Commercial, Administrative and Financial Procedural Code of Congo; Article 198 of Code of Civil and Commercial Procedure of Argentina; Article 384 of the Federal Code of Civil Procedure of Mexico.

3.2 In International Arbitration

As the basis of the powers to provide interim measures is contractual, the parties would be bound by any criteria for interim measures that may be included in their arbitration agreement. In default of this, the parties should be guided by the standards that are set by the relevant applicable institutional rules, whatever they may be. In addition, the arbitral case law has suggested a number of criteria that are usually invoked when assessing interim measure requests.

3.2.1 General Criteria Under Institutional Rules

Under Article 26, para. 3 of the UNCITRAL Arbitration Rules, the party requesting an interim measure should satisfy the arbitral tribunal that: (a) harm not adequately reparable by an award of damages is likely to result if the measure is not ordered, and such harm substantially outweighs the harm that is likely to result to the party against whom the measure is directed if the measure is granted; and (b) there is a reasonable possibility that the requesting party will succeed on the merits of the claim.

3.2 In International Arbitration

According to ICC Rules, Article 28.1, interim measures are granted as the tribunal considers appropriate.

Under Article 25.1 of the LCIA Rules, interim measures are granted where they are "appropriate in the circumstances".

Under Article 37 (1) of the SCC Rules, the tribunal grants any interim measures it deems appropriate.

According to Article 24 of AAA's International Center for Dispute Resolution Rules, a tribunal may grant interim measures it deems necessary.

Under Article 23.3 of the CIETAC Rules, the tribunal may provide any interim measure it deems necessary or proper in accordance with the applicable law or the agreement of the parties.

According to Article 23.2 of HKIAC Rules, at the request of either party, the arbitral tribunal may order any interim measures it deems necessary or appropriate.

Under Article 30.1 of SIAC Rules, the Tribunal may, at the request of a party, issue an order or an award granting an injunction or any other interim relief it deems appropriate.

Under Article 33 (1) of the VIAC Rules, the arbitral tribunal may, at the request of a party, grant interim or conservatory measures against another party; the rules does not include the discretionary language that most institutional rules employ, though. Nevertheless, this should be presumed.

Under Article 29 (1) of the Swiss Rules, the arbitral tribunal may grant any interim measures it deems necessary or appropriate.

Under Article 25 of the DIS Rules, the arbitral tribunal may, at the request of a party, order interim or conservatory measures.

Under Article 23 (1) of the Saudi Center for Commercial Arbitration Rules, any party may request interim, precautionary or preliminary measure it deems necessary. The rule is similar under Article 27.1 of the Rules of Conciliation and Arbitration of the Qatar International Center for Conciliation and Arbitration, and Article 28 of the Arbitration Regulations of the Abu Dhabi Global Market Arbitration Centre, and Appendix II, Article 1 of the Dubai International Arbitration Centre Arbitration Rules (a tribunal may, upon an application by a party, order interim measures on terms that it considers appropriate in the circumstances, and issue a preliminary order in support of such measures). These to a significant extent incorporate the approach of UNICITRAL Rules.

3.2.2 Particular Standards (Criteria and Factors)

The overview indicates that apart from the UNCITRAL Rules, most other institutional rules use the typical language of appropriate (and/or necessary) interim relief (or do not include such a criterion at all as with VIAC and DIS). Hence, the institutional rules do not give much clarity on the matter. The interpretation of the criteria for granting interim measures is rooted in theory and arbitral case law.

For instance, with regard to ICC Rules, it is noted that the relevant factors are:

- The party will suffer irreparable harm (i.e., damage that cannot subsequently be remedied by a damages award) or difficult to be repaired harm (damage that cannot be adequately repaired either by reference to amount, or by reference to period of time until the remedy is delivered) if the interim relief is not granted.
- Such harm will outweigh any harm that might be caused to the other party if the interim relief is granted. This is sometimes known as the 'balance of convenience' test.
- The requesting party has a reasonable chance of succeeding on the merits of the claim (i.e., in the final award). This is the most controversial part of the test: some commentators believe that it is dangerous for the arbitral tribunal to make any kind of prejudgment of the merits at this stage (i.e., generally, before the written submissions have been exchanged or any oral evidence heard); others consider that it is essential to weigh the strength of the parties' respective cases into the overall balance.[36]

As to LCIA Rules, it is considered that:

- There is no guidance in the LCIA Rules as to the relevant test arbitral tribunals must follow when deciding whether or not to order interim measures. This leaves the Arbitral Tribunal with wide discretion in this respect. Most arbitral tribunals will look into, and rely on, (1) the relevant law governing the arbitration (usually the law of the seat of arbitration); (2) the law of the possible place(s) of enforcement of the interim measure (if granted); and (3) more generally, case law from other arbitral tribunals to determine the requirements for granting interim measures.
- The common denominator of this requirement is that the circumstances of the case (i.e., the risk of harm) are such that the measure cannot await the final resolution of the dispute. For instance, this could be the case where not granting the interim measure and instead waiting for the final award might result in a loss which, if it occurs, will not be able to be addressed by damages (e.g., destruction of evidence) or will be addressed inadequately (e.g., sullied business reputation).
- National arbitration statutes and arbitral case law commonly also require a demonstration of proportionality, or 'balance of convenience'. For instance, under Article 17(A) of the UNCITRAL Model Law, the requesting party must show that the harm that it would suffer if the requested measure is not granted 'substantially outweighs' the harm that is likely to result to the other party if the interim measure is granted[37]

With regard to Swiss rules of arbitration:[38]

---

[36] Grierson and van Hooft (2012), p. 160.
[37] Scherer and Richman (2015), pp. 264–265.
[38] Zuberbühler and Muller (2005), pp. 230–231.

3.2 In International Arbitration

1. the tribunal should have prima facie jurisdiction;
2. there should be prima facie evidence of a risk of irreparable harm or injury to the requesting party;
3. such harm or injury should be imminent (urgency requirement);
4. there should be a reasonable chance of success on the merits; and
5. the requesting party needs to provide appropriate security.

The arbitral institutions from North Africa and the Gulf region, for instance, follow to a significant extent one and the same pattern set out by the UNCITRAL Rules:

The party requesting an interim measure is expected to satisfy the arbitral tribunal that:

(a) Harm not adequately reparable by an award of damages is likely to result if the measure is not ordered, and such harm substantially outweighs the harm that is likely to result to the party against whom the measure is directed if the measure is granted; and
(b) There is a reasonable possibility that the requesting party will succeed on the merits of the claim. The determination on this possibility shall not affect the discretion of the arbitral tribunal in making any subsequent determination

(for instance the rules of the Saudi Centre for Commercial Arbitration, the Qatar International Center for Conciliation and Arbitration, the Abu Dhabi Global Market Arbitration Centre, the DIAC Arbitration Rules, the Cairo Regional Centre for International Commercial Arbitration).

3.2.2.1 Prima Facie Merits of the Case

The arbitral case law has established that the tribunal should make assessment of the potential merits of the claim. The purpose of the assessment is to distinguish a vexatious, manifestly unfounded claim from a claim that has real possibility of success.[39] This is a preliminary appreciation of the case and it should not be as detailed and justified as the final award on the merits. Furthermore, the evidentiary basis and the legal submissions of the parties would never be as specific and developed as the ones that would form the basis for the tribunal's decision on the merits.

Hence, this is a preliminary stage of the procedure where on basis of what is made available by the parties, the tribunal should decide whether the case submitted before the tribunal has no merit at all; and if the tribunal finds that the case is not absolutely unfounded and vexatious, that the claimant's legal arguments and evidence supporting them indicate that it is more likely that the claim will be eventually granted. Of course, strong submissions and proof by the respondent may tip the scales and either demonstrate that the likelihood of success is not significant, or

---

[39] Born (2014), pp. 2477–2480; Yesilirmak (2005), pp. 176–178.

indicate that the arguments of the parties are at par and cannot be decided which party may prevail.

3.2.2.2 Risk for Irreparable or Significant Harm or Loss

This standard has been termed in various ways but regardless of the particular wording, it is focused on the harm/loss that the claimant (applicant) will suffer in the absence of the requested interim measures.[40] The tribunals should order provisional measures, if only the requesting party has substantiated the threat of a not easily reparable prejudice as otherwise the interim measures will not be necessary.[41] The particular threshold is a matter, which is not cast in stone as only the UNCITRAL Rules feature some criteria on it ("harm not adequately reparable by an award of damages"). In the world of commercial disputes where pecuniary rights form the subject matter of cases in almost any situation, it is difficult to have a situation of "irreparable" harm. In the view of this author, the precise standard should be serious, or significant harm, or harm that could not be easily repaired by the award, including awarding of damages.[42] Moreover, the precise standard may vary from case to case depending on the subject matter (i.e. the particular rights to be protected) of the dispute. Therefore, the proof of significant risk should be provided by the claimant and should substantiate real possibility for harm and not merely hypothetically existing risk. The risk may encompass the threat to enforcement of the award on the merits, i.e. that without the requested measures, when the award comes to enforcement stage, the claimant will not be able to utilize it on purpose. This can be, for instance, related to actions or transactions directed at depleting the potential assets of the respondent.

3.2.2.3 Urgency

Urgency is another standard that is very much intertwined with the risk of significant harm.[43] Both of them can form a composite standard of "necessity", i.e. requirement that without the requested measures the applicant's rights will be prejudiced. Necessity is not expressly stated in the UNCITRAL Rules but the arbitral case law unanimously adopts it. The degree of urgency is fact-specific. However, it can be gauged by two criteria. First, that the relief sought should be granted to preserve rights of the applicant before the rendering of the award, i.e. that the relief may be

---

[40] Born (2014), pp. 2468–2473; Yesilirmak (2005), pp. 179–181.

[41] Interim Award in ICC Case No. 8786, 11(1) ICC Ct. Bull. 81, 83–84 (2000) See also Interim Award in ICC Case No. 8894, 11(1) ICC Ct. Bull. 94, 97 (2000).

[42] Supported by arbitral case law, i.e. Interim Award in ICC Case No. 8786, 11(1) ICC Ct. Bull. 81, 83–84 (2000). See also Interim Award in ICC Case No. 8894, 11(1) ICC Ct. Bull. 94, 97 (2000).

[43] Born (2014), pp. 2473–2475; Yesilirmak (2005), pp. 178–179.

useless if it should be awaited by the time of the award.[44] Second, there should be real likelihood (not hypothetical) for the occurrence of prejudicial events that may impair the rights of the applicant.[45] Although some require the existence of imminence of the threat, it is generally not required that there should be a particular time frame in which the risk will materialize.

3.2.2.4 Proportionality/Balance Between the Interests of the Parties

The interim measure should cater for the interests of the claimant but at the same time should not impair the interests of the respondent disproportionately and inadequately. The tribunal should balance between the parties and the injury that the respondent may potentially suffer should be taken into account as well.[46]

Moreover, it is often stated that the interim measures should not prejudge the matters of the case.[47] This standard has been much discussed and it is submitted that its meaning should lie with the requirement that the interim relief should not preclude any award on the merits and should not put the parties into a state that cannot be subsequently reversed (including by award of damages). In the view of this author, this is tightly related to proportionality, as a proportionate interim measure would leave sufficient room for the parties and the tribunal to make submissions on the merits and decide on the merits and will not pre-judge the case.

3.2.2.5 Liability for Damages as a Means to Achieve Balance Between the Parties[48]

The arbitration law on interim relief does not diverge, as a matter of underlying rationale and as a matter of practice and most often, applicable rules, from the regime governing liability for damages caused by state court provided interim relief.

Under the UNCITRAL Model Law, Article 17G, the party requesting an interim measure or applying for a preliminary order shall be liable for any costs and damages caused by the measure or the order to any party if the arbitral tribunal later determines that, in the circumstances, the measure or the order should not have been granted. The arbitral tribunal may award such costs and damages at any point during the proceedings.

---

[44] Baker and David (1992), p. 139; Procedural Order No. 3 in ICSID Case No. ARB/02/18 of 18 January 2005, ¶8; Chevron Corp. v. Repub. of Ecuador, Second Interim Award on Interim Measures in PCA Case No. 2009-23 of 16 February 2012, ¶2.

[45] Tokios Tokelés v. Ukraine, Procedural Order No. 3 in ICSID Case No. ARB/02/18 of 18 January 2005.

[46] Yesilirmak (2005), p. 181.

[47] Born (2014), pp. 2476–2477.

[48] See generally Herinckx (2014); Bantekas et al. (2020), Article 17G.

The posting of a bond or security in general is a prerequisite for the award of interim measures, which is necessary to ensure the reimbursement of compensation from the respondent. Separately, an applicant's undertaking to provide security could be a factor in the test whether relief request to be granted.[49]

To the extent that the national law could be applicable as lex arbitri, the overview of various legislative approaches under Sect. 3.1.1.6 would apply mutatis mutandi as these provide substantive law grounds for liability within the purview of the respective jurisdictions for damages claims arising within these jurisdictions—such example is the approach of French case law.[50]

The position is similar under English law where the Arbitration Act 1996 does not regulate the matter expressly and the Civil Procedure Rules (CPR) Rules are followed by the case law.[51]

The law of the USA has expressly rendered the Federal Rules of Civil Procedure applicable to arbitration as well (Rule 81 (a)(6)).

The approach of other systems is to enshrine the same rule governing state courts but as part of the corpus of the arbitration law—such is Section 1041(4) ZPO that contains the same provision as Section 945 ZPO.

Article 374(4) of the Swiss Code of Civil Procedure features a third approach—it refers to both judicial and arbitral powers within one and the same provision bringing them into one composite rule.

Oddly, the Mexican law[52] provides that the arbitral tribunal may also be liable for damages caused by the provided interim relief.

However, what is a common feature is that liability for unjustified interim measures granted by an arbitral tribunal has footing in the applicable national law. Many legislations follow verbatim the model provision of the UNCITRAL Model Law (e.g. Belgium, Australia, etc.).

The various institutional rules deal with this as a procedural matter rather than as specific grounds for liability. For instance, Article 28 of the ICC Rules expressly states that the arbitral tribunal may make the granting of any such measure subject to appropriate security being furnished by the requesting party.

Similarly, under Article 25 of the LCIA Rules, the applicant may be required to post a cross-indemnity for any costs or losses incurred by the respondent party in complying with the interim measure.

As per Article 26 (6) of the UNCITRAL Arbitration Rules, the arbitral tribunal may require the party requesting an interim measure to provide appropriate security in connection with the measure.

---

[49] Bantekas et al. (2020), Article 17G.

[50] Cass., I" civ. ch., 23 April 2013, appeal No. 12-12.'101, Kura Shipping v Delta Lloyd Schadeverzekering, Rev. arb., 2013.

[51] SmithKline Beecham Plc, GlaxosmithKline UK Ltd and others v Apotex Europe Ltd and others [2006] EWCA Civ 658 (23 May 2006).

[52] Art. 1480 Commercial Law.

3.2 In International Arbitration

As per Article 37 of the SCC Rules, the arbitral tribunal may order the party requesting an interim measure to provide appropriate security in connection with the measure.

Under Article 30.1 of the SIAC Rules, the arbitral tribunal may order the party requesting interim relief to provide appropriate security in connection with the relief sought.

According to Article 23 of the CIETAC Rules, the arbitral tribunal may require the requesting party to provide appropriate security in connection with the measure.

Considering the criteria to gauge the amount of the security, it is expected to be able to cover the actual costs and the potential damages to the adverse party while taking into account the financial capability of the applicant[53]

While various arbitration rules refer only to presentation of security, guarantee or bond as a precondition to granting interim relief, UNCITRAL Arbitration Rules is perhaps the only set of rules that explicitly speaks of a party's damages liability (Art. 26 (8)). More importantly, the arbitral tribunal is provided with powers to order such damages compensation within the course of the arbitral proceedings even without the aggrieved party bringing a separate damages claim outside these proceedings.

The relevant arbitral case law on provision of security/guarantee/bond is scant. For instance, under ICC case 7544,[54] a party was ordered to make (preliminary) payment against delivery of a corresponding bank guarantee as to cover the risk that the final decision might not be consistent with the decision reached in the interim measures award.

Under another arbitration claim,[55] an arbitrator ordered the immediate payment of royalties in a dispute against provision of a bank guarantee by the claimant, under the conditions that the payment was to be made first and the bank guarantee was to be provided subsequently.

As per an order under unpublished AAA case from 1999 in a dispute under joint operations agreement, the respondent was required to comply with an injunction pending the final award and injunction's effect was based on posting of either cash or other kind of security.[56]

While in the case of damages stemming from state court ordered interim relief the question of jurisdiction would be decided by reference to the choice of court rules within the respective jurisdiction, it is a pertinent question which body should decide a dispute arising from arbitral interim relief damages. Both the UNCITRAL Model Law and the UNICTRAL Arbitration Rules expressly regulate that the arbitral tribunal granting the relief should be the proper forum and, even more, the same arbitral proceedings should be the proper avenue to seek compensation.

---

[53] Yesilirmak (2005), p. 188.

[54] ICC Second Interim Award 7544 of 1996, extracts published in 11(1) ICC Int'l Ct Arb Bull 56–60 (2000).

[55] NAI Case No. 3310, 15 October 2002, Yearbook Comm. Arb., 2008, vol. XXXIII, p. 160.

[56] Yesilirmak (2005), p. 188.

This logic has been followed by some arbitral case law as well. For instance, as per ICC case 12363[57] where the subject matter of the dispute was alleged violation of a license agreement, the "tortuous conduct of Claimant is deeply rooted in the agreement since Claimant obtained an interim injunction on the sole basis of an alleged violation by Respondent of (...) the agreement. (...) the Arbitral Tribunal is the sole competent jurisdiction to decide on the validity of the said clause; but the resolution of this issue constitutes for the Arbitral Tribunal the preliminary and necessary step prior to entering into the merits of Respondent's counterclaim because the question of an extra-contractual liability of Claimant would arise if and only if the aforesaid contractual provision is declared null and void by the Arbitral Tribunal; in the negative, Respondent's counterclaim would lack any legal basis. (....) this condition is obviously met in the present case. On the other hand, a denial by the Arbitral Tribunal of its competence with respect to Respondent's counterclaim would cause Respondent to address the said claim to the ordinary jurisdiction designated by the rules of international conflict of jurisdiction with the consequence that two judicial authorities, i.e. the Arbitral Tribunal and a State Court would be called to decide on a same issue, i.e. that of the validity of Article 74.3 of the licence agreement; such a consequence may involve the risk of contradictory decisions which can only be avoided if the Arbitral Tribunal's exclusive jurisdiction on Respondent's counterclaim". The approach of the case was affirmative, and so was under another ICC case,[58] case 14046, where costs to obtain interim measures before local state courts were awarded by the arbitral tribunal. Other reported arbitral case law expounded similar logic.[59]

The nature and scope of the liability is an important matter as well.

The case law review seems to point out that costs, incl. financial costs and legal fees, are recoverable; other damages may be sought, but as far as security is posted, the respondent would be able to avail of this guarantee to cover potential losses.

It is not cast in clear terms whether the liability stemming from unjustified interim measures is strict or fault-based. A certain view is that the UNCITRAL Model Law did intentionally evade any language implying strict liability. Instead, the Model Law rather sought to make liability dependent on improper, abusive acts by the applicant—the phrase "in the circumstances" denoting a more holistic subsequent evaluation by a dispute resolution body that, being better informed, would assess that a measure should not have been granted. This may have relevance only to the extent that the applicant made its application on grounds, which at that point appeared justified but later on might be established as unfounded, and there is either abuse by the applicant at the time of the application or at least lack of care to seek relief without being aware of all circumstances.[60] Another view is that the UNCITRAL

---

[57] Partial Award, ICC Case No. 12363, 23 December 2003, ASA Bull., 2006.

[58] Final Award, ICC Case No. 14046, Yearbook Comm. Arb., 201 a, vol. xxxv.

[59] Final Award, ICC Case No. 10509, 2000; Final Award, ICC Case No. 15248, Yearbook Comm. Arb., 20'13, vol. XXXVIII.

[60] To this end see Herinckx (2014), pp. 247–248.

Model Law is silent on this, the matter appears to be outside the scope of the Model Law, and it can be suggested that the nature of the liability would be determined by reference to the law applicable to a damages claim.[61]

In this author's view, the matter may be analysed from a different perspective. If an interim measure were found to be unjustified, this would imply that the preliminary assessment conducted by the arbitral tribunal reached a conclusion, which divulges from the end result of the arbitral procedure. Given the key factors for determining if a measures request should be allowed—prima facie merit, necessity to avert harm, potential urgency, etc.—the most likely difference would amount to a finding that the substantive rights which have first been honoured, are afterwards finally to be rejected at the end of the procedure. It is a truism that within a preliminary measures phase of a process the dispute resolution body would not be able to make a full and comprehensive evaluation, hence it is entirely possible that the substantive claim turns out to be unjustified in the end. Therefore, it is suggested that a risk-based approach should be adopted. The applicant benefits from an interim relief award, which is why it is the applicant's risk to embark upon interim relief procedure. If the claimed rights turn to be without merit at the end of the procedure, it is a risk to be assumed and borne by the applicant. However, strict liability is an exception from the general principles of tort law and, usually, is explicitly enshrined by statute. To the extent that such strict liability is not expressly regulated, it is suggested that it should be assumed the applicant may be allowed to exculpate itself by proving good faith upon requesting interim relief. The applicant should have based its request on good faith understanding of the relevant circumstances underpinning the claimed rights, all such facts should have been expounded to the best knowledge of the applicant, and the duty of care to lay down all circumstances that could have been reasonably presented to the tribunal should have been discharged. Such a defence, it is suggested, might negate the potential liability of an applicant.

3.2.3 Interim Measures in ICSID. Standards to Grant Interim Measures

The first requirement, which is absolute and cannot be compromised, for granting interim measures, is urgency. Urgency has been the most often argued standard for provision of interim relief (in 73% of all relief applications urgency has been relied upon[62]). As noted in Biwater Gauff v. Tanzania,[63] provisional measures are to be provided where the issue cannot await the outcome of the award on the merits. The legislative history of ICSID Convention confirms that it was intended that interim

---

[61] Bantekas et al. (2020), Article 17G.
[62] Goldberg (2019), pp. 16–17.
[63] Procedural Order No. 1, 31 March 2006, para. 68.

measures are adequate only for situations of absolute necessity.[64] The burden to prove urgency is on the party making the request. There should be an imminent threat on prejudice on the rights of the requesting party.[65] Degree of urgency will vary in accordance with the particular set of circumstances.[66] The threshold is by no means a low one; about half of all applications arguing urgency have been granted.[67] Situations where urgency has been found are, for instance, in order to avert a court decision that may lead to investor losing business,[68] and to stay on enforcement of debts that could aggravate the dispute.[69]

The measures should be urgent and necessary to preserve the status quo or to avoid irreparable damage.[70] Hence, necessity is the second absolute requirement. The measure should be necessary for the preservation of the rights at stake. The measure is necessary when it should avert irreparable harm to the rights invoked.[71] Possibility for a harm does not meet the threshold[72]—the threat should be imminent. Nearly in 70% of all cases where requests for interim relief were made, parties have relied on necessity as criterion.[73] Similar to urgency, parties have been successful on this in about half of all applications made. Examples can be risk of insolvency[74] or tax measures introduction that can ruin the business.[75]

Third, the level of harm should be at least substantial. Initially, ICSID tribunals[76] were closer to ICJ case law adopting the standard of irreparable harm, i.e. harm that cannot be compensated by damages, and since most claims are for damages, then this high threshold would rarely be met. Subsequent case law has started to move away from this dicta to indicate that a claim for damages may still necessitate interim measures if there will have to avert potential destruction of the investment as a going

---

[64] ICSID (1968), p. 523.

[65] Azurix v. Argentina, Decision on Provisional Measures, 6 August 2003, para. 33.

[66] Biwater Gauff v. Tanzania, Procedural Order No. 1, 31 March 2006, para. 76.

[67] Goldberg (2019), pp. 16–17.

[68] Merck Sharpe & Dohme (I.A.) Corporation v. The Republic of Ecuador (PCA Case No. 2012-10), Decision on Interim Measures dated 12 June 2012, para. 71.

[69] City Oriente Limited v. Republic of Ecuador and Empresa Estatal Petróleos del Ecuador (Petroecuador) ICSID Case No. ARB/06/21, Decision on Provisional Measures dated 19 November 2007, para. 69.

[70] Plama v. Bulgaria, Order on Provisional Measures, 6 September 2005, para. 38.

[71] Occidental v. Ecuador, Decision on Provisional Measures, 17 August 2007, paras. 59, 61.

[72] Occidental v. Ecuador, Decision on Provisional Measures, 17 August 2007, para. 89.

[73] Goldberg (2019), pp. 18–19.

[74] Sergei Paushok, CJSC Golden East Company and CJSC Vostokneftegaz Company v. The Government of Mongolia, UNCITRAL, Order dated 2 September 2008, para. 77.

[75] Lao Holdings N.V. v. Lao People's Democratic Republic (ICSID Case No. ARB(AF)/12/6), Decision on Claimant's Amended Application for Provisional Measures dated 17 September 2013, para. 21.

[76] Plama v Bulgaria, para. 46; Helnan International Hotels AIS v Arab Republic of Egypt, ICSID Case No ARB/05/19, Decision on Claimant's Request for Provisional Measures (17 May 2006), para. 34.

concern[77] as this could qualify as an irreparable harm. Hence, the issue is not that only rights not being capable of monetary compensation should be preserved by interim measures but interim measures should be granted only to prevent complete prejudice to the investment, i.e. its destruction. Harm should not be irreparable but should be very substantial.

It can be additionally noted that a number of tribunals have also cited proportionality of the measure (35%) and prima facie merit of the claim (6%)[78] as criteria to be taken into account.

3.2.4 Procedural Aspects of Interim Measures Granted in Arbitration

3.2.4.1 Procedure to Obtain Interim Measures

Procedures for interim measures can be (1) inter partes as a rule; (2) ex parte as a rule; or (3) inter partes but could be ex parte if some conditions are met. Usually interim measure procedures in arbitration are inter partes.[79] Most institutional rules do not regulate the matter but it is commonly understood that for instance ICC and LCIA rules do not approve of ex parte measures.[80] There should be a hearing/submission of the positions of the parties, in one form or another, in order that the tribunal rules on the interim measures application. In the VIAC Rules (Article 33(1)) and the DIS Rules (Article 25.1), it is explicitly stated an interim measure should be granted only after hearing both parties. This is dictated by a number of rationales. First, this is based on guaranteeing fairness and equal opportunity of the parties to present their cases.[81] Furthermore, it should be borne in mind that interim measures are not a mere procedural matter and are a very intrusive instrument. Hence, it is justified to be provided only after both parties present their submissions.

Second, ex parte measures are usually (as in domestic court litigation) intertwined with the issue of urgency. Urgency justifies ex parte procedure because the latter guarantees swift and prompt outcome that may avert negative consequences that a longer procedure would have. However, interim measures would avert such negative result as long as their enforceability is effective. Enforcement of arbitral interim measures is complex and in most cases these are not ready and easily enforced, sometimes not directly enforceable at all. Therefore, even if the procedure is

---

[77] Ioan Micula and Others v Romania, ICSID Case No ARB/05/20, Decision on Provisional Measures (2 March 2011), para. 41; Cemex Caracas Investment BV and Cemex Caracas II Investment BV v Bolivarian Republic of Venezuela, ICSID Case No ARB/08/15, Decision on the Claimant's Request for Provisional Measures (3 March 2010), para. 55.
[78] Goldberg (2019), pp. 18–19.
[79] Born (2014), pp. 2507–2510.
[80] Schwartz and Derains (2005), p. 298; Scherer and Richman (2015), p. 280.
[81] Yesilirmak (2005), pp. 221–222.

designated as ex parte—in order to safeguard fast enforcement—this targeted prompt enforcement will rarely come into effect. Hence, the ex parte procedure would have dubious importance.

Therefore, usually interim measures are provided by tribunals after inter partes procedure.

Under most institutional rules, measures should be granted by request of parties, which is logical given the paramount party autonomy in arbitration. However, some rules expressly provide for ex officio powers.[82]

3.2.4.2 Form of Interim Measures

Interim measures can take two forms: of an order or of an award.[83] An arbitration order usually connotes ruling of the arbitral tribunal on a procedural matter. An award, however, is typically the form to decide on a matter from the substance of the dispute pending before the tribunal. While orders are normally targeting organizational issues, awards settle disputed rights and obligations. Institutional rules usually give both options to the tribunal (Art 29 ICC Rules; LCIA; Art 37 SCC; Art 23 HKIAC Rules; Art 23 CIETAC Rules; Rule 30 SIAC Rules; Art 24 AAA Rules). Some rules require that all interim measures are provided as procedural orders—e.g. ICSID, Rule 19; VIAC Rules, Art. 33. As per the Swiss Rules, relief is granted by way of interim awards (Article 29(2)).

The order is an instrument for conduct of the arbitration procedure and is a flexible tool that does not have specific regulation on its use and utility (and related formalities). The award is, however, a very formal instrument. It is a final and binding ruling of the tribunal. But as noted, it does not necessarily mean that it should be the final and binding ruling on the merits of the case—it can be a final and binding ruling on a specific issue, for instance on a particular interim measures request.[84]

In favour of this position is a significant number of legal theory[85] and case law.[86] The views against include both doctrine[87] and case law,[88] and white papers,[89] too.

---

[82] Yesilirmak (2005), pp. 166–167.

[83] Born (2014), pp. 2505–2507; Yesilirmak (2005), pp. 190–196.

[84] Bermann (2017), pp. 437–438.

[85] Born (2014), p. 2512.

[86] S. Seas Navigation Ltd v. Petroleos Mexicanos of Mexico City, 606 F.Supp. 692 (S.D.N.Y. 1985). See also Metallgesellschaft AG v. M/V Capitan Constante, 790 F.2d 280, 282-83 (2d Cir. 1986).

[87] Boog (2011), para. 379; (interim measures do not fall within scope of Article I of New York Convention); Gaitis (2005), pp. 31–33; Lachmann (2008), para. 2060; Poudret et al. (2007), para. 633.

[88] Judgment of 13 April 2010, DFT 136 III 200, §2.3.3 (Swiss Federal Tribunal).

[89] UNCITRAL (1999), para. 121.

3.2 In International Arbitration   81

An order may be more swift and effective time and formality-wise but a ruling bound as an award has a higher degree of enforceability.

There is no set rule on how a tribunal should act. However, the due diligence of tribunal's work, it is submitted by scholars and also supported by this author, requires that regardless of what orders are issued, any interim measures ruling to be cast as an (interim) award as well which is in the best interest of the parties.[90]

In practice, surveys show that most parties comply with orders or awards even without enforcement actions as to avoid conflict with arbitrators, possible increase in cost allocation, and claim for breach of arbitration agreement due to non-compliance.[91]

3.2.4.3 Procedural Status

The life span of interim measures should endure the arbitral proceedings.[92] Interim measures are subject to revocation/reconsideration[93] by the same body that did render them. Even if the measures are in the form of arbitral awards—the final award can order that the status set by the interim award be amended.[94]

Interim awards possess res judicata effect.[95] The question may be answered only if the concept of res judicata is sufficiently clear. First, if it is understood as a more general notion, it would mean that a ruling on particular issue, raised by request, is binding on the parties to the issue and the same request cannot be ruled upon again as between the same parties.[96] Such a broad notion encapsulates issues of law and fact as well as procedural issues raised in the course of proceedings. Second, it is understood in the light of the underlying substantive rights and obligations, it would mean that the ruling establishing certain rights and obligations cannot be disputed between the parties and the parties are bound by what is established by the ruling—their substantive relationship is what the ruling indicates.[97] Since there is no unitary notion of res judicata, it is difficult to define whether res judicata applies to

---

[90] Redfern and Hunter (2015), paras. 5.48–5.66.

[91] Scherer and Richman (2015), pp. 277–278.

[92] Yesilirmak (2005), pp. 198–199.

[93] Yesilirmak (2005), pp. 199–201.

[94] Yesilirmak (2005), pp. 201–203.

[95] See e.g. Mayer (2004).

[96] Judicial decision between the same parties some issue which was in controversy between the parties and was incidental to the main decision has been decided, then that may create an estoppel per rem judicata (Carl-Zeiss-Stiftung v. Rayner & Keeler, Ltd [1966] 2 All E.R. 536); Bermann (2017), p. 457, footnote 1271.

[97] E.g. Article 1351 of the French Civil Code, according to which: "The authority of res judicata applies only to what was the object of a judgment. It is necessary that the thing claimed be the same; that the claim be based on the same cause; that the claim be between the same parties and brought by them and against them acting in the same qualities." Also France, New Code of Civil Procedure Article 480; in Belgium, Code of Civil Procedure Articles 23–27; in The Netherlands, Code of Civil

interim measures rulings. Some legislations explicitly rule it out: Article 1059(1) of the Netherland Code of Civil Procedure.

Therefore, taking into account the components of res judicata:

The interim measure ruling does not dispose of the substantive rights in dispute with any finality. Therefore, the interim measure rulings cannot create any effect as to substantive rights and obligations as between the parties. If an interim measures ruling is granted, there would not be, normally, a subsequent request with the same content. A party may request reconsideration instead. But if the request is not granted, i.e. is rejected? Does this preclude a subsequent application? The ruling rejecting interim measures request does not preclude subsequent request, which is not based on the same facts. If there is a change in the factual matrix, this will allow a new motion to be considered. Hence, there is a partial res judicata. A ruling rejecting application based on a particular set of facts is binding and precludes subsequent application on the same facts, therefore has an effect very similar to res judicata. But on the other hand, does not preclude application within the same proceedings but on different/changed facts.

3.2.4.4 Interim Measures in ICSID. Procedure to Obtain Interim Measures

The party requesting the interim measure should specify the particular right sought to be preserved (Rule 39 (1) of the Arbitration Rules). It may be not only a substantive right but also a procedural right (e.g. collection of evidence, the exclusive nature of ICSID arbitration, confidentiality of proceedings[98]).

On basis of the wording of Rule 39 (4) of the Arbitration Rules ("after giving each party an opportunity of presenting its observations") it can be inferred that the procedure for granting interim measures is bilateral and these could not be granted ex parte.[99] The practice of ICSID tribunals is to give opportunity to both parties to present statements in writing as well as hold hearings.[100]

Procedure Article 236; in Germany, Code of Civil Procedure Articles 322–327; in Italy, Code of Civil Procedure Article 324; in Sweden, Code of Judicial Procedure Articles 17:11 and 30:1.

[98] Schreuer et al. (2009), p. 779; Biwater Gauff v. Tanzania, Procedural Order No. 1, 31 March 2006, para. 71.

[99] see also ICSID Reports (1968), Note E to Arbitration Rule 39.

[100] Holiday Inns v. Morocco, Decision on Jurisdiction, 12 May 1974, 1 ICSID Reports 653–659; AGIP v. Congo, Award, 30 November 1979, para. 9; Amco v. Indonesia, Decision on Provisional Measures, 9 December 1983, para. 2; MINE v. Guinea, Award, 6 January 1988, 4 ICSID Reports 68/9; Atlantic Triton v. Guinea, see: Delaume, G. R., ICSID Tribunals and Provisional Measures— A Review of the Cases, 1 ICSID Review—FILJ 392 at 393 (1986); Vacuum Salt v. Ghana, Decision on Provisional Measures, 14 June 1993, 4 ICSID Reports 324; CSOB v. Slovakia, Decision on Jurisdiction, 24 May 1999, para. 14; Maffezini v. Spain, Decision on Provisional Measures, 28 October 1999, para. 26; Tanzania Electric v. IPTL, Decision on Provisional Measures, 20 December 1999, para. 4; Pey Casado v. Chile, Decision on Provisional Measures, 25 September 001, para. 34; SGS v. Pakistan, Procedural Order No. 2, 16 October 2002, 8 ICSID Reports 388;

It is possible to request interim measures even prior to the constitution of the arbitral tribunal. Under Rule 39 (5) of the Arbitration Rules, Secretary-General on the application of either party, fixes time limits for the parties to present observations on the request, so that the request and observations may be considered by the tribunal promptly upon its constitution. This would most often find application in cases of extreme urgency. On average, it takes about 6 months (sometimes less, sometimes considerably more) for a tribunal to render its order on request for interim measures.[101]

The interim measures granted by the tribunal are subject to modification and revocation. There is no res judicata[102] and this can be requested by the parties at any time granted there is change in the circumstances (material change, i.e. change that requires amendment).[103] Further, under Rule 39 (3) of the Arbitration Rules, the tribunal can act proprio motu to cancel or modify measures. If not altered or revoked, measures would stay until the rendering of the final award.

The review of case law demonstrates that about 60% of all granted measures are cast in the form of a decision, while 35% as orders and 5% have other form.[104]

3.3 Types of Interim Measures

Various sources of rules on interim relief tend to leave the precise scope of interim measures as rather an open-ended matter. Seldom do bodies of law enumerate precise lists of interim measures to be granted by an adjudicating body. Instead, what is more common is to leave the adjudicator to provide the measures which appear to be most adequate and appropriate for the particular dispute at hand.

However, this does not mean that there does not exist a range of measures, or put in other words, a classification of the categories of measures which adjudicating bodies may impose. Furthermore, national laws usually include some concrete measures although relief tend to be described with a very high level of generality. In arbitration, precise classes or measures are seldom used.

Zhinvali v. Georgia, Award, 24 January 2003, paras. 39–41; Azurix v. Argentina, Decision on Provisional Measures, 6 August 2003, para. 1; Tokios Tokel'es v. Ukraine, Decision on Jurisdiction, 29 April 2004, para. 11; Duke Energy v. Peru, Decision on Jurisdiction, 1 February 2006, para. 17; Biwater Gauff v. Tanzania, Procedural Order No. 1, 31 March 2006, paras. 21, 31–64; Saipem v. Bangladesh, Decision on Jurisdiction, 21 March 2007, paras. 163–169; Occidental v. Ecuador, Decision on Provisional Measures, 17 August 2007, para. 5.

[101] See case law review in Schreuer et al. (2009), pp. 770–771.

[102] Pey Casado v. Chile, Decision on Provisional Measures, 25 September 2001, para. 14.

[103] SGS v. Pakistan, Procedural Order No. 2, 16 October 2002, 8 ICSID Reports 396; Vacuum Salt v. Ghana, Decision on Provisional Measures, 14 June 1993, 4 ICSID Reports 328.

[104] Goldberg (2019), p. 28.

This section of the study purports to look into various national bodies of law and rules of arbitral institutions as to compare and contrast what categories of measures are explicitly included, and what typology of such measures can be drawn on this basis. Lastly, this section also sheds light on some measures that are typically granted in a number of cross-border disputes that are often conducted.

3.3.1 Under National Law

Interim measures may be classified by various types and according to various criteria. By no means exhaustive, the survey aims to outline the main types of interim measures. This analysis indicates the following basic parameters of interim measures: Timing/Time span; Addressee(s); Purpose; Subject Matter. These parameters serve as foundation and starting point for analysing the approaches of various jurisdictions to categorizing interim measures.

Under Section 381 of the Austrian Enforcement Act, there are three general categories of interim measures—preventive measures (to safeguard enforcement of decision on merits); regulatory measures (regulating the state of affairs between the parties while the case is pending); performance measures (for preliminary performance).

In English law, according to the Civil Procedure Rules 2011, s. 25.1 (1), these include: interim injunctions (ordering actions to be taken or to be avoided); interim declarations; orders regarding detention, custody, preservation, inspection, sampling, sale of or payment regarding a property; orders authorising the entry into any land or building; orders to give up goods; freezing orders and orders directing that a party provide information about the location of any property or assets which are the subject of such freezing order; search orders; orders for disclosure of documents or inspection of property prior to a claim being made against either an actual or potential opposing party and/or against an entity which is not party to the proceedings; orders for interim payment on account of any damages, debt or other sum the court may hold the defendant liable to pay; orders regarding the payment of monies in to the court pending the outcome of proceedings; orders directing a party to file an account or directing an account/inquiry be made by the court; and orders regarding the enforcement of intellectual property proceedings.

Possible categories of interim measures under Articles 90–91 of Russian Arbitrazh Procedural Code include: freezing bank accounts, seizure of money in cash, seizing property and other assets (including bank accounts) of the respondent; placing a restriction order on the respondent and third parties prohibiting certain conduct or acts related to the subject matter of the claim; obliging the respondent to perform certain acts in order to prevent spoilage and impairment of the property in dispute; ordering the placing of property in dispute into the custody of the applicant or a third party; suspending the enforcement of a writ of execution or any other enforcement document; suspending the sale of property if a claim on the release of property from seizure is filed.

3.3 Types of Interim Measures

Interim measures under Article 292 of the Swiss Civil Procedure Code include: prohibition, e.g. (1) on altering or disposing of the matter in dispute, (2) on performing a competing activity, (3) on selling a product, (4) on publishing an article or book, (5) on executing a board resolution and/or filing it with the corporate registry, (6) on paying out a bank guarantee, (7) on making certain statements; an order to remedy an unlawful situation, e.g. (1) seizure of the subject matter of the dispute or (2) confiscation of counterfeit goods; an order to an authority, e.g. (1) to the commercial registry to implement a register ban (provisional interdiction of certain register entries), (2) to the land registry to inscribe a restraint of disposal, (3) to the land registry to inscribe a certain right in rem, such as the statutory mortgage of contractors; an order to a third party, e.g. (1) to block a bank account, (2) to hand over shares, (3) to prohibit the debtor from paying before the court has decided on who is entitled to the claim; performance in kind, e.g. (1) the restitution of items taken away or kept back, (2) to continue or resume the delivery of goods.

Measures under Article 727 of Spanish Civil Procedure Code are measures necessary to secure the rights at hand or the enforcement of the judgment, inter alia: blocking of property to ensure enforcement of judgment; deposition of goods; inventory of goods; inscription in public registers; judicial order for cessation of activity or abstention or prohibition on cessation; deposition of IP objects.

Interim measures under Articles 362–363 of Civil Procedural Code of Portugal include provisional restitution of property; suspension of corporate resolutions; provisional payments; attachment; inventory of goods; blocking ships.

According to §§ 916–917 ZPO, interim measures may be: seizure—attachment of receivables/moveable property/ship; lien on real estate; injunction—to safeguard status quo preventing change that may frustrate or make impossible enforcement of right at stake.

Under Czech Civil Procedure Code, § 76, a preliminary measure may command that the participant in particular (a) pay maintenance in a necessary extent; (b) put the child into the custody of the other parent or into the custody of the person identified by the court; (c) pay at least a part of a remuneration for work in case of duration of labor relationship and the petitioner does not work for serious reasons; (d) deposit a sum of money or a thing with the custody of the court; (e) not dispose of certain things or rights; (f) do something, omit something or suffer from something. The preliminary measure may impose a duty upon somebody else than upon the participant only if such duty is fair to demand from him. In ordering the preliminary measure, the chairman of the panel shall impose upon the petitioner to file a petition for commencement of the proceedings with the court within a specified period; this rule shall not apply if the proceedings on the merits may be commenced even without a petition. The court may also decide that the preliminary measure shall last only for a specified period.

Under Chapter 15 of the Civil Procedure Code of Sweden, interim measures can be: prohibition, subject to a default fine, of carrying out a certain activity; performing a certain act or an order, subject to a default fine, to have regard to the applicant's claim or the appointment of a receiver or the issue of a direction suitable in other ways to safeguard the applicant's right; restoration of possession.

In China, under the Chinese Civil Procedure Law, interim measures are preservation of property: sealing up, distraining, freezing or other methods as provided by law (Article 94).

Under Indian Orders 38 and 39, interim measures include attachment and injunction.

Interim measures in Singapore under Order 29 include: injunction, interim payment, interim preservation of property, taking of samples.

Under Japanese law, interim measures include: provisional remedy; provisional seizure, and provisional disposition.[105]

Under Order 29 of Malaysia: injunction; order for the detention, custody or preservation of any property which is the subject matter of the cause or matter, or as to which any question may arise therein, or for the inspection of any such property.

Under Article 159 of the Civil Procedure Code of Kazakhstan, interim measures are: seizure of property; seizure of money; prohibition to the defendant to perform certain actions; prohibition to other persons to transfer property to the defendant or perform other obligations in relation to him/her; suspension of sale of property; suspension of force of the challenged legal act.

According to the Law of Procedure in Shariah Courts in Saudi Arabia, Article 234, classes of interim measures are: inspection to establish the condition; an injunction against interference with possession and of its recovery; an injunction against travel; enjoining charity works; custodianship; dealing with a worker's daily wage; other given the character of urgency by law.

Under Article 63 of the Civil Procedure Act of Kenya, interim measures can be: to issue a warrant to arrest the defendant and bring him before the court to show cause why he should not give security for his appearance, and if he fails to comply with any order for security commit him to prison; to direct the defendant to furnish security to produce any property belonging to him and to place the same at the disposal of the court or order the attachment of any property; to grant a temporary injunction and in case of disobedience commit the person guilty thereof to prison and order that his property be attached and sold; to appoint a receiver of any property and enforce the performance of his duties by attaching and selling his property; to make such other interlocutory orders as may appear to the court to be just and convenient.

Interim measures under Article 64 of the US Federal Rules of Civil Procedure, interim measures are: arrest; attachment; garnishment; replevin; sequestration; and other corresponding or equivalent remedies.

---

[105] Articles 11–25 of Civil Provisional Remedies Act (Act No 91 of 22 December 1989).

3.3.2 In International Arbitration

There is no particular and overarching instrument dealing with the classes of interim measures that an arbitral tribunal may provide. Most institutional rules only deal with the requirement for provision of "appropriate" measures, which leaves wide room for discretion of tribunals.[106]

The UNCITRAL Rules are the only rules that specify particular measures under Article 26, para. 2: an interim measure is any temporary measure by which, at any time prior to the issuance of the award by which the dispute is finally decided, the arbitral tribunal orders a party, for example and without limitation, to: (a) maintain or restore the status quo pending determination of the dispute; (b) take action that would prevent, or refrain from taking action that is likely to cause, (1) current or imminent harm or (2) prejudice to the arbitral process itself; (c) provide a means of preserving assets out of which a subsequent award may be satisfied; or (d) preserve evidence that may be relevant and material to the resolution of the dispute. In various institutional rules this enumeration is reproduced to a significant extent.[107]

This can be compared and contrasted with, for instance, the Swiss rules, which provide under Art. 29 that the content of the measures to be ordered is not restricted. The admissibility of certain types of interim measures and their possible content is governed by the law applicable to the dispute.[108] In general, interim measures may contain any order which is necessary or appropriate to secure the purpose of the arbitration. There are four main types of interim measures:[109]

1. measures aimed at preserving or restoring the status quo pending the determination of the dispute (e.g. an order to continue the performance of a contract, an order to secure the object of the dispute);
2. measures aimed at preventing current or imminent harm to a party (e.g. an order to take appropriate action or to refrain from taking certain actions that are likely to cause such harm);
3. measures to facilitate or to ensure the enforcement of a future award (e.g. an attachment of assets[110] or a provision of security[111] or other means of preserving assets out of which a subsequent award may be satisfied); and

---

[106] Yesilirmak (2005), p. 203.

[107] E.g. rules of Saudi Centre for Commercial Arbitration, the Qatar International Center for Conciliation and Arbitration, the Abu Dhabi Global Market Arbitration Centre, the DIAC Arbitration Rules.

[108] Swiss Private International Law Act, Art. 183 N 7; von Segesser and Kurth (2004), p. 72; Poudret et al. (2007), p. 624; Berger (1992), p. 236.

[109] Redfern and Hunter (2015), p. 220; Knoepfler (1997), pp. 309–310; von Segesser and Kurth (2004), pp. 72–74; Wirth (1996), pp. 33–34; Poudret et al. (2007), p. 628; UNCITRAL Report (2004), pp. 17–18; UNCITRAL Report (2004), pp. 6–10.

[110] With regard to the admissibility of attachments under Swiss law, cf. Swiss Private International Law Act, Art. 183 N 7; von Segesser and Kurth (2004), p. 72.

[111] E.g. security for costs, cf. Art. 41 N 23–28.

4. measures aimed at facilitating the conduct of arbitral proceedings (e.g. an order to preserve evidence).[112]

Given this background, to attempt an exercise of pigeonholing the types of interim measures is both useless and unrealistic. The arbitral tribunal may provide any measures that would not be (a) impossible to be performed; and (b) contrary to the mandatory rules and the public policy of the law of the seat. However, it is possible to consider a number of broad categories of interim measures that arbitral tribunals would grant. These can be subdivided into two big groups. First, there are interim measures that purport to safeguard the substantive rights claimed by an applicant requesting interim relief. Moreover, the other group of interim measures have procedural importance and purport to ensure the orderly and effective manner of conduct of the arbitral proceedings.

First, similar to what Article 26, para. 2 of the UNCITRAL Rules posits, the tribunal may grant a measure purporting to safeguard the status quo between the parties.[113] Such a measure may exist in a positive and negative requirement—the respondent should act to maintain or restore the status quo or the respondent should not act/refrain from actions that disturb the status quo between the parties. It is usually assumed that another type of interim measure is to order that certain actions posing risk or threat of harm should or should not be taken.[114] However, in the view of this author the two categories of interim measures are actually underpinned by one and the same rationale. Therefore, it is submitted that a broad standard for ordering interim measures is ordering that a party (or the parties) maintain particular conduct that would not aggravate their relationship and would not aggravate their dispute or prevent the effectiveness of the award to be rendered by the tribunal. This type of measure can also be termed as "injunction".[115]

The second broad category is to order that one of the parties undertakes a particular action.[116] This may be carrying out of a particular contractual performance (specific performance). It may be interim payment[117] or some similar measure that requires from one of the parties to act in compliance with particular contractual obligation while the case is pending.

Third, another broad category is targeting particular objects related to the contract between the parties. Most often such measures aim at inspection or preservation of goods.

These do not purport to affect the relationship between the parties but only to support the arbitral process. First, such measure is a measure of securing and

---

[112] Zuberbühler and Muller (2005), p. 235.
[113] Born (2014), pp. 2483–2487.
[114] Born (2014), pp. 2487–2490.
[115] Yesilirmak (2005), pp. 207–212.
[116] Born (2014), pp. 2490–2491.
[117] Born (2014), pp. 2498–2499; Yesilirmak (2005), pp. 217–218.

collecting evidence.[118] Second, another type of such measure is security for payment,[119] security for costs or other manners of payment that guarantee the covering of financial consequences related to the arbitral proceedings.

3.3.3 Interim Measures in ICSID

On basis of the ICSID case law and the scholarly analysis and review thereof, it is possible to draw a list of typical categories of interim measures granted by ICSID tribunals:[120]

1. A measure requiring the parties to co-operate in the proceedings and to furnish all relevant evidence[121]
2. A measure to secure compliance with the award.[122]
3. A measure to stop the parties from resorting to self-help or seeking relief through other remedies, incl. domestic proceedings.[123]
4. A measure to prevent a general aggravation of the situation;[124]
5. A measure to safeguard the confidentiality of proceedings[125]

The review of available ICSID case law demonstrates that the most requested interim measures by parties have been termed as: non-aggravation of a dispute (36%), and stay of parallel proceedings in national courts (30%).[126] It should be noted, though, that the success rate differs. For instance, fully granted requests for non-aggravation of disputes are as low as 28% of investment arbitration case law while measures to stay parallel proceedings have been much more common, in 76% of all cases where it was requested, full or partial stay of proceedings was provided.

---

[118] Yesilirmak (2005), p. 206.

[119] Yesilirmak (2005), pp. 212–213.

[120] Schreuer et al. (2009), p. 780.

[121] E.g. Decision on Provisional Measures of 16 January 2006, reproduced in Sempra v. Argentina, Award, 28 September 2007, para. 37.

[122] E.g. Atlantic Triton v. Guinea; Pey Casado v. Chile, Decision on Provisional Measures, 25 September 2001, paras. 78–89.

[123] E.g. Award of 6 January 1988, MINE v. Guinea 4 ICSID Reports 69; CSOB v. Slovakia, Procedural Order No. 4, 11 January 1999, quoted in CSOB v. Slovakia, Decision on Jurisdiction, 24 May 1999, para. 9; SGS v. Pakistan, Procedural Order No. 2, 16 October 2002, 8 ICSID Reports 388/9.

[124] E.g. Azurix v. Argentina, Decision on Provisional Measures, 6 August 2003, para. 50.

[125] World Duty Free v. Kenya, Award, 4 October 2006, para. 16, quoting the Decision on a Request by Respondent for a Recommendation of Provisional Measures of 25 April 2001.

[126] Goldberg (2019), pp. 10–11.

It has been expressly reasoned that the former requires a high threshold.[127] Certain examples for the latter that could be found within the case law include stay of: bankruptcy proceedings in the respondent's courts; freezing of the investor's assets by the respondent's courts; enforcement of debt pending the resolution of the dispute; proceedings related to unenforceability of the court's judgment concerning resolution of the dispute; proceedings against the investor.[128]

Other granted but much less common measures that can be found in practice include production of documents, security for costs, preservation of evidence.

3.3.4 Exemplary Specific Types of Interim Measures

One of the key arguments/conjectures set out in the beginning of this study is that there is interplay, interrelation, and interdependence between the nature of the interim relief granted, and the substantive rights and obligations upon which the interim measures are to have effect. In other words, the essences and typology of a dispute predetermines what measures should be applied in that dispute.

The purpose of this part of the study is to outline several popular types of disputes (e.g. concerning sale and supply of goods; construction; intellectual property) in international commerce and transactions, and what measures could be specifically targeted in these cases.

Furthermore, this part also features one of the most challenging areas of international arbitration practice and scholarship, a perennial casus belli: anti-suit injunctions. Such a broad topic deserves an in-depth separate work and is not adequate to delve into it within the scope of the current study. Moreover, the issue of anti-suit injunctions and their offshoots such as anti-anti-suit injunctions, etc. has developed in a distinct field, which is only loosely related to the topic of interim relief. Nevertheless, in this author's view it would be unrealistic not to mention the key features of anti-suit injunction and their paraphernalia if only restricted to keeping the perspective of them through the lenses of interim relief.

3.3.4.1 Specifics of Interim Measures Concerning Sale of Goods

Interim measures in disputes concerning sale of goods are typically related to the subject matter of these disputes. Varying to some extent, disputes regarding sale of goods will be either related to (1) payment issues—non-payment; partial payment; damages liability due to partial, delayed, defective delivery; (2) quantity and quality of goods issues—defective goods, etc.

---

[127] Churchill Mining PLC and Planet Mining Pty Ltd v. Republic of Indonesia (ICSID Case No. ARB/12/14 and 12/40), Procedural Order No. 14 dated 22 December 2014, para. 72.
[128] Goldberg (2019), p. 12.

3.3 Types of Interim Measures

This is why the specifics of such disputes will mostly require the following groups of measures:

1. measures aimed at collection of evidence, or
2. measures regarding preservation of disputed goods. Most likely, these can be reduced to: inspection of goods, or deposition of goods to be safeguarded at a warehouse, or similar facility.[129]
3. measures ensuring proper payment. Traditionally, a seller would seek freezing of buyer's account to preserve money available for payment of an ultimate judgment or award.

However, a measure more specific to such cases is blocking a letter of credit or a performance guarantee, i.e. an instrument that secures payment of purchase price or secures liability, e.g. for defective goods. In this regard, there is an abundant case law especially on measures targeting payment instruments for sales contracts. The approaches of the different jurisdictions towards stop-payment orders vary.[130] It has been an established principle arising from, for instance, English courts case law[131] on injunctions, that sellers may seek an interim relief measure, i.e. injunction, to prevent a bank from making payment under a bank guarantee or letter of credit. The case law has confirmed that this measure is admissible but, though, on very slim grounds, due to the strict nature of the bank's payment obligations; an applicant would be successful only where fraud could be proven.

Other jurisdictions (e.g. Germany[132]) deem interim relief blocking payment of guarantees/letter of credit as inadmissible because the essence of the guarantee/letter of credit as an abstract and independent instrument different from the underlying agreement between the principal and the beneficiary dictates payment upon duly made demand. In other jurisdictions (e.g. France, USA[133]) stop-payment injunctions on a third party guarantor/issuer are allowed upon proof of a strong case for a fraud on behalf of the beneficiary. As in such situation the guarantor/issuer is under obligation to desist from making payment, the guarantor/issuer may be required to refuse payment.

Hence, if the dispute revolves around performance of contractual obligations secured by a guarantee/letter of credit, the payment of the guarantee/letter of credit would increase the potential liability of a party. This is why the beneficiary should not pursue payment of the bank guarantee issued in relation to the contract. The principal can request from the tribunal to make provisional order instructing the

---

[129] A certain example can be the Indian case in High Court of Delhi, Pawan Hans Helicopters Ltd. vs Aes Aerospace Ltd. on 22 April, 2008; 2008 (2) ARBLR 63 Delhi.

[130] Bertrams (2004), pp. 407–418; also Draguiev (2016), p. 91.

[131] R D Harbottle (Mercantile) Limited v National Westminster Bank Limited [1978] 1 QB 146; Edward Owen Engineering Ltd v Barclays Bank International Ltd [1978] 1 All ER 976.

[132] E.g. OLG Dusseldorf, 14 April 1999, ZIP 1999, p. 1518.

[133] Uniform Commercial Code, § 5-109.

beneficiary not to act regarding the guarantee. If the beneficiary fails to comply, this can have impact on the liability of the beneficiary under the arbitration proceedings.

What is to be noted is that the specific typology of sale of goods relations entails use of such payment instruments and, therefore, disputes with regard to such disputes would often involve disputes, incl. measure, concerning such payment instruments. This determines the nature of this often sought interim relief as well—freezing a payment to avoid aggravating the dispute.

3.3.4.2 Specifics of Interim Measures in Construction Disputes

Construction disputes have a number of features that set them apart from other types of disputes. They may involve complex issues of fact and technical expertise; they may involve a number of layers of engaged parties; disputes may hinder large scale works which is why rapid decision-making would be required by the parties.[134] From a procedural point of view, proof is essential as construction works, especially completion of a site, may be difficult to be evidenced at the time a tribunal examines the case. This is why preservation of evidence measures may be very much needed by the parties. This type of interim measures—concerning the taking of evidence, and preservation of evidence, and generally these supporting the status quo between the parties, can qualify as characteristic for construction disputes.

According to ICC, the most common interim relief granted under the auspices of ICC in construction arbitrations includes: preservation of the status quo, preservation of evidence and assets, provision of security for costs, measures to secure the enforcement of any final award and orders for interim payments.[135]

Hence, a typical construction dispute situation would entail a number of particular points of dispute:

1. a dispute regarding the stage/phase and level of completion of construction works, which could also include issues of delay;
2. a dispute regarding quality/defects of completed works;
3. payments and costs disputes

Therefore, interim relief would have to ensure that there is a sufficient body of evidence for the dispute to be resolved, and to ensure payment disputes are not aggravated.

Similar to what was analysed under the sales disputes heading above, construction payment bonds and guarantees can also be subject of injunctive relief. Typically a construction works assignor, e.g. an employer under FIDIC-type of works, would provide a guarantee for its contractual payments to the assignee, the construction contractor; the contractor would provide a guarantee for any liability under the contract, e.g. liability for defects or delay. This is very pertinent where the

---

[134] Jenkins (2013), pp. 1–2.
[135] ICC Secretariat's Guide to ICC Arbitration (2012), para. 3-1036.

3.3 Types of Interim Measures   93

construction employer would like to call a bond/guarantee in cases of liability of a contractor for delayed or defective works. The contractor, however, would be interested to preserve assets of the employer from dissipation by way of injunctive relief as to ensure (interim) payments from the employer. The contractor would also be interested to block any attempt a guarantee/bond to be called by an employer who claims payment for defects or damages for delay; vice versa, an employer under duty to render payments may be interested to block an attempt by the contractor to call a payment instrument if the employer is not willing to pay. In these situations, the considerations under the previous heading of disputes (sale of goods disputes) would apply. Both parties are interested in evidence preservation.

Two more peculiar types of measures reflecting the nature of construction disputes are (1) measures requesting contractual performance to be continued, and (2) interim payments orders.

First, typically a performance order would be an order upon the contractor to continue construction works where the activity is on the critical path to completion.[136] Such order is a very intense tool and if permitted, it must not prejudge the end result of the dispute and the measure's effect should be reversible; moreover, if the interim relief would require significant time and effort amounting to deciding on the substance of the dispute, the measure should not be granted. Nevertheless, the case law has confirmed the possibility of such measures.[137]

Second, interim payment order would request disputed payments under a case to be rendered irrespective of the pending dispute. The attitude towards such a measure is generally understood as very cautious and restrictive. However, it is not an unthinkable measure[138] and might be recommended where not receiving payments would drive a contractor to lose liquidity, cease operations and exit the market, and become insolvent so that it would not be able to continue works on the particular project. The situation should be averted as it is an aggravation of the status quo between the parties.

3.3.4.3 Specifics of Interim Measures Concerning Intellectual Property

The core issue related to intellectual property is its non-material/intangible nature. This is why the traditional mechanisms for enjoinment of property are difficult to be applied. Further, it is difficult to ensure compliance with a measure concerning intellectual property. Also, the need for interim measures in IP disputes is very acute as the infringement of the IP rights of a party may be effected easily while the case is pending until it is resolved. Finally, as IP rights provide a sort of monopoly, balancing the interests of the parties and the adequacy of the measures is very

---

[136] Beisteiner (2019), pp. 63–114.

[137] Higher Regional Court Frankfurt 5.4.2001, 24 Sch 1/01 = NJW-RR 2001, 1078; Swiss Federal Court has rendered decision BGE 136 III 200.

[138] ICC Secretariat's Guide to ICC Arbitration, re Art. 28, para. 3-1036.

important as deciding preliminarily for one of the parties or another may affect gravely the other while the case is pending.[139]

Most frequently, the interim measures granted by arbitral tribunals involve restriction on the conduct of a party, or both parties, to prevent breach of various IP rights (trademarks, patents, etc.). Same applies to rights under license agreements or confidentiality undertakings, or know how. A party should be enjoined from the use of particular intellectual property, or to be prohibited to take actions that may infringe upon the alleged IP rights of the other party. In other words, these interim measures are aimed to ensure preservation of the status quo.[140] Examples that emerge from the case law could be an order requiring a party not to use certain trade mark and know how under license[141] and an order on IP rights holder not to prevent a party from continuing to use certain licensed IP.[142] Although these seem to be radically opposite situation, both entail one and the same: IP rights are granted upon contractual arrangements with continuous performance, therefore interim relief targets allowing or disallowing such continuous use of the IP as to safeguard status quo to avert further aggravation and damages.

Further, unlike other types of disputes, what is not uncommon in the area of IP rights is that the interim relief that a party needs might also entail enjoining a third party to the dispute, which is also a third party to the relations between the disputants. Such a situation may entail a measure targeting a third party such as a hosting services provider, a platform or website, an element from supply chain or transaction, etc. where certain content infringing the disputed IP rights is located. This why a claimant would need to initiate a separate interim relief procedure to obtain measures against such a third party.

For instance, this has been explicitly envisioned under Article 9 (1) (a) of the Directive 2004/48/EC of the European Parliament and of the Council of 29 April 2004 on the enforcement of intellectual property rights ("an interlocutory injunction may also be issued, under the same conditions, against an intermediary whose services are being used").[143] A noteworthy example can also be the injunction on Google to delist the website of an alleged infringer of IP, which was granted by the Supreme Court of Canada[144]—i.e. a third party services provider, which had control over the IP-related content and had contact with the potential infringement, was subjected to a protective measure as a matter of interim relief in order to secure the rights of the IP-holder.

It is important to note that this nature of the IP rights and the interim measures concerning such rights affect the options to enforce these measures and implement

---

[139] See details in Cook and Garcia (2010), pp. 4–11.

[140] See details in Cook and Garcia (2010), pp. 221–223.

[141] Resort Condomiums v. Bolwell and Resort Condominiums (Australasia) Pty Ltd in van den Berg (1995), pp. 628–650 (Supreme Court of Queensland, 29 Oct. 1993).

[142] Chartered Institute of Arbitrators (2016), p. 15.

[143] Hartmann-Vareilles (2017), pp. 1–6.

[144] Google Inc. v. Equustek Solutions Inc. 2017 SCC 34.

them in practice. As the measures target certain conduct of the parties, the extent of enforcement of the measures depends very much on the available measures that the lex executionis provides regarding IP rights. If there is none, or alternatively, if it comprises procedures that have to be undertaken by an authority or other third party, it is possible that such measures be in reality not capable of being implemented in one or more countries concerned. Therefore, the sole compliance with the arbitral interim measures may well be the voluntary compliance by the parties. After all, the interim measures are targeted at their conduct. Failure to comply may result into aggravation of liability, being additional damages due to infringement of IP rights while the case has been pending.

Hence, it is an issue to be considered what may be more effective as to IP-related interim measures: to request interim measures from the arbitral tribunal, or to seek assistance from respective state courts in the relevant countries which may ensure that the court-granted measures are enforceable against third parties as well. However, the ubiquity of interim measures and internationality of IP rights may cause that interim measures granted by courts would not meet the interests of the aggrieved party as it will have to seek measures in a number of jurisdictions, or enforce measures granted in one jurisdiction in a number of other jurisdictions. On the other hand, arbitral measures will be binding the respective party regardless of the jurisdictions where a breach may occur. Finally, it is to be noted that the aggravation of liability would not always suit the interests of a party as a single IP rights violation while the dispute is pending may turn out to be difficult to compensate by damages by the final award on the merits of the dispute.

3.3.4.4 Specifics of Interim Measure Concerning Some Categories of Moveable Property (Vessels, Aircrafts, Etc.)

3.3.4.4.1 Arrest of Ships

Perhaps the most natural and popular measure imposed in maritime disputes is arrest of vessels (ships). By definition contained in the widely ratified International Convention Relating to the Arrest of Sea-Going Ships (1952),[145] arrest means detention of a ship by judicial process to secure a maritime claim, but does not include the seizure of a ship in execution or satisfaction of a judgment. The not so commonly ratified International Convention on Arrest of Ships from 1999[146] contains a very similar definition of arrest. Ship seizure is related to criminal actions while execution is a post-judgment act of asset liquidation. In contrast, arrest is the tool employed in civil and mostly commercial disputes with maritime character.

---

[145] International Convention Relating to the Arrest of Sea-Going Ships, Signed at Brussels, on 10 May 1952, UNTS 6330.
[146] International Convention on Arrest of Ships, 1999, Geneva, 12 March 1999.

Both conventions provide detailed list of maritime-related claims which serve as basis for granting arrest of a ship. Typically, the ship should have entered into the territorial waters of the respective contracting state, and also should have entered any of its ports. Arrest in open seas is much more seldom effected.[147] Evidently, the purpose of the arrest is to render the ship, a property which is, naturally, capable of being easily removed, restrained as a security for the claim on the merits of the dispute.

Under both the 1952 and the 1999 Conventions, the ship is subject to release against a provision of security, which demonstrates the functioning of the arrest as a safeguard to enforcement of a possible judgment on the merits. The physical hindrance on the movement of the ship also shows that the measure is directly reflecting moveable nature of the object of the measure (the moveable nature of the vessel).

Furthermore, the policy behind both Conventions is that the ship is arrested in the contracting state that factually exercises jurisdiction over it due to presence within its ports and waters. This is, again, preconditioned on the moveable nature of the ship as property so that a creditor should be able to restrain it in the country where the ship is located as a matter of fact regardless of whether the courts of that country enjoy jurisdiction on the merits of the case. The 1999 Convention goes even further as it provides that the jurisdiction granting the measure to be able to review the merits of the maritime dispute, unless the local law does not allow this (Art. 7 thereof).

Exactly the operation of this strong territorial link exemplifies what is peculiar about the arrest of a vessel as a type of interim measure. Such a measure imposed on moveable property can be implemented effectively only if all courts of countries having physical and territorial touch points with the property (the vessel) can exercise jurisdiction and impose the measure while the vessel is physically within their hold. Otherwise, a measure on a moveable asset would hardly have meaningful operation.

3.3.4.4.2 Immobilization of Mobile Equipment

The Convention on International Interests in Mobile Equipment (Cape Town Convention)[148] contains some rules on interim relief concerning moveable property commonly used in active commercial operations. As per Article 2(3) of the Cape Town Convention, it regulates certain interests in airframes, aircraft engines and helicopters, railway rolling stock, and space assets. These could be classified, in general, as moveable, also mobile, property, which, similar to vessels, are usually in constant usage, turnover and movement across countries and territories.

Under Article 13(1)(c) of the Cape Town Convention, relief pending the outcome of a dispute may be granted in relation to the listed objects within the scope of the

---

[147] Baatz (2014), p. 485.
[148] Cape Town Convention on International Interests in Mobile Equipment, 2307 U.N.T.S. 285.

3.3 Types of Interim Measures

Convention. By its nature and operation, Article 13 of the Cape Town Convention contains an interim measures rule. An "immobilisation" of such moveable property essentially means imposition of a block on the physical movement of such property. The country where the moveable property is located is designated under Article 43 (1) of the Cape Town Convention to have jurisdiction over applications for interim relief.

Similar to ship arrest, the nature of the object of interim measures, i.e. the nature of moveable property, dictates the nature, characteristic features and operation of interim measures under the Cape Town Convention. Since the property in question (for instance, aircrafts) is expected to be constantly moving in space across various territories, it is unrealistic to assume that it is possible to ensure subsequent enforcement over the moveable asset without imposition of measures that prevent the moveable asset from moving in space. In other words, the moveable property should be "grounded" due to the effect of the interim relief under the Cape Town Convention. Hence, there is a strong link of territoriality between the physical location of the asset and the jurisdiction of the country where the interim measures should be imposed. Exactly because of this link the Cape Town Convention provides as basis of the interim relief jurisdiction the localization of the asset. But the starting point for considering the interim measure should not be the jurisdiction on its own, but the object (target) of exercising jurisdiction, i.e. the very asset within the scope of the Cape Town Convention.

Therefore, the regimes of arrest of vessels in maritime law, and immobilization of aircrafts, spacecrafts, and other movables, demonstrate that the features of these properties indicate what anatomy, grounds and effect the interim measures targeting such property need to entail.

3.3.4.5 Anti-Suit Injunctions as Interim Measures

Anti-suit injunctions have originally been a creature of common law.[149] Common law jurisprudence has devised this type of injunctions (bearing in mind that an injunction, in general, is an equitable remedy being a court order instructing parties to act or refrain to act in a certain way[150]) to ensure that a party does not submit its claims before another court. Hence, this has been predominantly a mechanism for supporting jurisdiction of courts. To be noted, compliance with court orders, including anti-suit injunctions, is ensured under English court by the threat of contempt of court offence. Anti-suit injunctions have been spawned in several other common law jurisdictions[151] and in some form can be claimed to exist in some civil law

---

[149] Hartley (2009), pp. 222–228; Bureau and Muir Watt (2017), pp. 190–195.

[150] Hudson (2009), pp. 1079–1081.

[151] E.g. Australia—s CSR Ltd v Cigna Insurance Australia Ltd (1997) 189 CLR 345; USA—Laker Airways v. Sabena, 731 F 2d 909 (DC Cir. 1984).

jurisdictions.[152] Acting contrary to an anti-suit injunction could be a criminal offence as could be seen as contempt of court.

The variety and the widespread use of anti-suit injunctions, especially in relation to arbitration,[153] requires that an attempt of framing of anti-suit injunctions to be made, and at the same time the variety of possible anti-suit injunction scenarios makes this generalization difficult, and possibly useless. Hence, it is more important to outline, first, the concepts underpinning the use of anti-suit injunctions; second, the potential targets and addressees of anti-suit injunctions, as well as anti-suit injunctions through the prism of case law.

It is deemed that the anti-suit injunction safeguards jurisdiction. The body seized with a claim has, under the Kompetenz-Kompetenz principle,[154] the autonomous power to decide and rule over its own jurisdiction.[155] Hence, until this ruling is made, the dispute should not be handled by another body, and the jurisdiction should not be encroached upon by any third dispute resolution body. Indeed, these are the actual roots of anti-suit injunctions as English courts started giving anti-suit injunctions to ensure that no foreign court decides on a dispute prior to the seized English court.[156]

Another explanation for anti-suit injunctions is lis pendens. The fear of parallel proceedings underpins the rules of some international instruments such as Regulations Brussels Ibis, and the Lugano Convention.[157] The coordination of international proceedings is based on the concept that identical disputes should not be allowed to be heard in different courts/tribunals, so as to avoid possibly conflicting decisions. The understanding of parallel disputes may be strict, i.e. that parallel proceedings are to be avoided only where the parties, and the cause of action, are identical. This is the approach of EU Regulations. It has been suggested by the International Law Association[158] that a broader approach may be undertaken, so that if there is a substantial overlap, the proceedings should not run in parallel. Hence, anti-suit

---

[152] Gaillard (2006) and cited there case law—Quebec, see Superior Court of Quebec, Civil Chamber, July 9, 1999 and Court of Appeal of Quebec, November 29, 1999 in the matter of Lac d'Amiante du Canada Ltée et 2858-0702 Quebec Inc. v Lac d'amiante du Québec Ltée, discussed by Stewart Shackleton in Shackleton (2000). For Germany, see Lenenbach (1998). For France, see Cass. 1e civ., November 19, 2002, Banque Worms v Epoux Brachot et autres, which upheld, in the context of an international bankruptcy, the decision of a French judge to order a creditor to stop a real property seizure proceeding brought in Spain against the debtor's building, 2003 Dalloz 797, note by G. Kairallah; Gaz. Pal., June 25–26, 2003, at 29, note by M.-L. Niboyet. For Brazil, see Curitiba Court of First Instance, June 3, 2003, Companhia Paranaense de Energia (COPEL) v UEG Arancaria Ltda, 21 Revista de Direito Bancário e de Mercado de Arbitragem 421 (2003). More generally, for Latin American countries see Grigera Naón (2005).

[153] Bermann (2017), pp. 284–288.

[154] Bermann (2017), pp. 91–101.

[155] Briggs (2013), pp. 103–104.

[156] Hartley (2009), pp. 222–223.

[157] Hartley (2009), pp. 237–241.

[158] ILA Final Report on Lis Pendens and Arbitration (2009), para. 5.12(1).

injunctions are used in order to prevent another court or tribunal from rendering a conflicting decision on the same dispute.

Use of anti-suit injunctions can be explained through the prism of safeguarding the arbitration or choice-of-court agreement.[159] A negative effect of these agreements is that the parties should not act in breach of the choice of court or arbitration, hence should not bring their disputes to other bodies but for the envisioned one in the agreements. When a party violates the clause, it may be compelled by anti-suit injunction, so that party will fulfil its contractual obligations.

The latter, along with a treatment of the Kompetenz-Kompetenz principle, is enshrined in the view that there should be a kind of prima facie presumption for courts to defer their jurisdiction in matters relating to arbitration, until the arbitral tribunal decides on its own jurisdiction and possibly the validity of the underlying arbitration agreement.[160] If this approach is adopted, parallel proceedings shall be avoided, and anti-suit injunctions target to effectively safeguard this.

Finally, anti-suit injunctions are related to the principle of non-aggravation of disputes.[161] If there is a dispute between parties, which has entered a formal procedural stage, it would be an aggravation of this status quo if one of the parties initiates another procedure under the same dispute. This will generate costs and possible damages to the interests of the parties, and can be consuming time-wise as well. Hence, the dispute would be aggravated, i.e. turned more difficult, complex, expensive, austere, etc.—if the two parallel cases continue. The purpose of the anti-suit injunction is to restrain the conduct of the party causing the aggravation.

The target (object) of the anti-suit injunction can be either another body (authority) or the parties to another procedure. The case law has seen both approaches. For instance, a court enjoins a particular court or arbitral tribunal not to hear a particular claim submitted by the respondent in the proceedings before that court. Alternatively, a court or tribunal issues an order that directs a party to the procedure not to submit any related claims to another (particular) court or tribunal or directs that the claims submitted there should be withdrawn. On this basis, it is possible to infer two models.

The first one (A) targets the jurisdictional power of another dispute resolution body. Under this model, one body instructs another body (without subordination or hierarchy between them) to exercise its jurisdictional powers in a certain manner, most often not to exercise its jurisdictional power under a given dispute.

The other model (B) is that one body directs a party to actual or potential proceedings before it to act or refrain to act in a certain manner, most often not to seize another body, or to withdraw its seizure, when there is one.

---

[159] Born (2014), pp. 2500–2501; Bermann (2017), pp. 289 and 291.
[160] McLachlan (2009), p. 511.
[161] See e.g. SGS Société Générale de Surveillance S.A. v. Islamic Republic of Pakistan (ICSID Case No. ARB/01/13), Procedural Order No. 2 of Oct. 16, 2002, 18 ICSID REV.—FOREIGN INV. L.J. 293 (2003).

An overview of the anti-suit injunctions as the one above indicates well why these are not met with enthusiasm outside common law jurisdictions. First argument against the use of anti-suit injunctions is that it may encroach upon the jurisdictional powers of another body, which is in clear breach of the Kompetenz-Kompetenz principle.[162] The counter-argument is that an anti-suit injunction that targets a party and not another body should not be contrary to Kompetenz-Kompetenz.[163] This is a formally valid argument, but unrealistic, as in reality to target the conduct of a party is to target, indirectly, the jurisdictional powers of another body.

Second, it has been argued that anti-suit injunctions are of little practical value[164] as the case law demonstrates that a war of anti-suit injunctions may ensue. For instance, in KBC v Pertamina case—Karaha Bodas Co. LLC (KBC) v Perusahaan Pertambangan Minyak Dan Gas Bumi Negara (Pertamina) and PT, PLN (Persero);[165] Karaha Bodas Co LLC (KBC) v Perusahaan Pertambangan Minyak Dan Gas Bumi Negara (Pertamina),[166] a dispute between an Indonesian company and Indonesian government led to parallel proceedings in Switzerland, Indonesia, and USA purporting one party to enjoin the other from taking actions in a particular forum without any significant result for any of the parties.

Third, many jurisdictions do not provide for anti-suit injunctions and do not support them, therefore, using anti-suit injunctions may not bring effect.

Fourth, anti-suit injunctions meddle with procedural rights.[167] Some jurisdictions, for instance those in Continental Europe, do not favour measures that affect exercise of procedural rights, which should be autonomous and independent and within the sphere of decision of the respective party. It may be unsuccessful or without merits or inadmissible but nevertheless the party should be capable of exercising its rights. As to arbitration particularly, a tribunal would hardly defer the matter of which is seized on basis of the instruction of another body to which the tribunal is not subordinated, and in breach of its duties to the party to consider the dispute, its jurisdiction, and render an enforceable award. The same reasons apply to a court under jurisdiction based on a forum selection clause.

Finally, the track record of courts or tribunals complying with anti-suit injunctions is considerably unfavourable to this practice.

Some of these problems have been considered in the case law of the ECJ in two seminal cases, Allianz SpA, formerly Riunione Adriatica di Sicurtà SpA, Generali Assicurazioni Generali SpA, v West Tankers Inc., Case C-185/07 (West Tankers), and Gazprom OAO v Lietuvos Respublika Gazprom v Estonia, Case C-536/13.

---

[162] Briggs (2013), pp. 103–104; Lévy (2005), pp. 115–129; Scherer and Giovannini (2005).

[163] Lew (2005), p. 25.

[164] Gaillard (2006), pp. 209–210.

[165] Decision of 18 December 2000, 16(3) Mealey's IAR C-2 (2001).

[166] 190 F. Supp. 2d 936 (S.D. Tex. 2001).

[167] Feb. 4, 1983 Interim Award in Case No. 338, E-Systems, Inc. v. Iran, 2 Iran-U.S. Cl. Trib. Rep. 51, 57 (1983); Lévy (2005), pp. 115–129.

West Tankers was rendered under EU Regulation Brussels I-44/2001. The ECJ considered whether an anti-suit injunction from a court to another body would breach the Regulation Brussels I. The ECJ adopted the view against anti-suit injunctions considering the Kompetenz-Kompetenz principle, the mutual trust between judicial authorities in the EU, and the effectiveness that EU regulations should have. All these principles are undermined by the anti-suit injunction as in West Tankers a court directed a party not to litigate but to arbitrate its dispute because of an arbitration clause. The ECJ argued that the seized court in another EU Member State should be able to decide on its own jurisdiction and decide on the matter, it could not be directed, instructed, subordinated or in any other way affected by the court issuing the anti-suit injunction (paras. 29–31).

The Gazprom decision is, however, quite different. There the ECJ considered the Regulation Brussels Ibis—Regulation 1215/2012, to find that Recital 12 has put arbitration entirely outside the application of Regulation Brussels Ibis (paras. 36–39). The case was about an injunction by arbitral tribunal, not by a court. First, according the Opinion of the AG in the Gazprom case,[168] the recast Regulation Brussels Ibis should not be interpreted as governing matters of arbitration law, which could be gleaned from juxtaposing Regulations 44/2001 and 1215/2012, and the inclusion of the explicit language of Recital 12 which directly excluded arbitration from the Brussels regime. In a more restrained tone, the ECJ concluded that the Regulation does not apply to issues related to arbitration, including the recognition and enforcement of arbitral awards being in fact anti-suit injunctions. In a more neutral way, the position of the ECJ was that EU law neither supported, nor precluded recognition and enforcement of anti-suit injunctions. Hence, a court in a EU Member State is free to base its attitude towards anti-suit injunctions concerning arbitration on its national law, on international treaties, but not on the Regulation Brussels Ibis.

What is, then, the conclusion left after the string of West Tankers-Gazprom ECJ case law? It seems that a court anti-suit injunction is contrary to the EU Regulation. An arbitral tribunal anti-suit injunction would not be per se. If it is refused recognition within the EU law, the grounds for this should not be Regulation Brussels Ibis. Hence, is the nature of the body granting the anti-suit injunction the differentiating factor which determines whether anti-suit injunctions are acceptable or not?

It seems simplistic to answer in the positive. The situation with anti-suit injunctions is much more complex. There is no coherent concept of anti-suit injunctions. These exist in various form, depending on the rendering dispute resolution body, the nature of the rules applying to the recognition and enforcement of the injunctions, the target of the injunction, etc. It should be considered, though, that anti-suit injunctions seem to be fit for a single national system of jurisdiction, or simply operate in a vacuum. Why—because the origin of anti-suit injunctions is in a jurisdiction—England—where the English courts did not need to consider what effect the injunction will have abroad. The injunction-giving court would not have

---

[168] Opinion of Advocate-General Wathelet delivered on 4 December 2014, Case C-536/13.

been bound by a system of coordination of jurisdiction such as Regulation Brussels Ibis. The only consideration for that court could be that no other proceedings are undertaken abroad so that the decision of that English court could be enforced abroad. The sanction is clear—contempt of court, to be applied within the English jurisdiction. If things are seen in a single-jurisdiction perspective, anti-suit injunctions seem to be a very pragmatic tool. If, however, such an injunction should be enforced abroad, this will raise a significant number of issues, most of them undermining the effectiveness of an anti-suit injunction. The same reasoning applies to arbitral anti-suit injunctions. The arbitral tribunal is concerned with protecting its own jurisdiction and the enforceability of its award. Further, it may impose sanction for non-performance of its injunctions, by extending the damages awarded. Hence, in great similar to English courts at the time of starting the practice to issue anti-suit injunctions, arbitral tribunals operate into a single composite jurisdiction system (although their awards can be set aside or refused enforcement). Therefore, in a world where anti-suit injunctions would have to go from one jurisdiction to another, their practical value is very much undermined. This is so also because they are posed to solve a problem which can be dealt with by using other instruments with greater viability.

The problem is not exactly safeguarding jurisdiction or enforceability of a decision/award. These are consequences, not the root of the problem. The heart of the matter is that parties should act in compliance with the respective applicable jurisdiction rules (on conflict of jurisdictions) or with the respective arbitration or choice of court agreement. The negative effect is that parties should not contravene the jurisdiction rules, based on statute or agreement, so that should be compelled into following these. In instruments of coordination of jurisdiction, a lis pendens rule (like in Regulation Brussels Ibis) or refusal of recognition and enforcement rule (like in Regulation Brussels Ibis) deal with this problem so that if a party brings a claim where it should not, the procedure would be stayed or terminated at all. The New York Convention safeguards this policy by way of its Article II (3) which bars a court to deal with a matter within the scope of arbitration (a kind of a "statutory" anti-suit injunction). It is safeguarded also by awarding damages for aggravation of the dispute and causing further complexity to it.

Therefore, the practice of anti-suit injunctions exists but its very practicality is of very dubious and questionable nature. A more viable alternative can be found under the principle of lis pendens and/or the refusal of enforcement of arbitral awards. If the rationale of lis pendens is applied, this will require all bodies to refuse jurisdiction as long as there is a body already seized with arbitration. Alternatively, an award that contradicts a prior court ruling in the respective country should be refused recognition and enforcement. The issue shifts from jurisdictional issues to issues of enforcement. This may, at least, alleviate the problem of Kompetenz-Kompetenz intrusion.

After Brexit has been implemented since the beginning of 2021, this should breathe new life in anti-suit injunctions. The latter are most often issued by courts of arbitral tribunals seated in the United Kingdom. Once UK need not have regard of EU law anymore since the beginning of 2021, there seems to be no theoretical (or practical) barrier to anti-suit injunctions. In parallel to this, courts outside UK have devised an "antidote" to anti-suit injunctions.[169]

A German court in 2019 did issue an order[170] that prohibited a party to an IP dispute to apply for anti-suit injunction in US courts in parallel to proceedings pending in Germany. The reasoning of the appellate instance was that if anti-suit injunction would be granted in US, this could significantly impair the right of defence, which dictated imposition of restraint as a countermeasure.

In 2020, the Paris Court of Appeal did restrain parties to an IP dispute from filing a motion for anti-suit injunction in UK courts. The argument of the French courts was that an anti-suit injunction would affect the procedural rights of parties and the fairness of the process, which are guaranteed by French law. Hence, there were sufficient grounds to enjoin the parties from pursuing other proceedings.

The importance of anti-suit injunctions for this study, however, lies elsewhere. Put briefly, while other specific types of interim measures reviewed target tangible objects (i.e. goods, vessels, aircrafts, etc.), or target substantive conduct of the parties (i.e. not to transfer assets, to be restrained to undertake certain action, etc.), anti-suit injunctions are devised to impose their effect on legal procedures. Irrespective of whether termed as requiring another adjudicating body not to handle a dispute, or enjoining a party from applying to such adjudicating body, anti-(anti-)suit injunctions ultimately meddle with procedural rights and conduct of legal procedures. This peculiar and inherent feature of injunctions as interim measures is the factor which lies at the heart of, and determines the string of issues that stem from usage of anti-suit injunctions. This is what brings Kompetenz-Kompetenz as a matter for discussion in this topic; this is what calls for consideration of fairness and equality between the parties; this is what challenges whether lis pendens is not a more adequate tool to deal with the problem of spawning various concurrent procedures, and this is what poses a question on the capacity of such measures to be enforced in other jurisdictions.

Anti-suit injunctions are another example of the interplay between the target of measures, and their type, nature and content.

References

Baatz Y (ed) (2014) Maritime law. Routledge, London
Baker S, David M (1992) The UNCITRAL Arbitration Rules in practice: the experience of the Iran-United States Claims Tribunal. Kluwer Law International, The Hague
Bantekas I, Ortolani P, Ali S, Gomez MA, Michael Polkinghorne M (2020) UNCITRAL model law on International Commercial Arbitration. Oxford University Press, Oxford

---

[169] Niehaus (2021).
[170] OLG München, decision of 12 December 2019, case no. 6 U 5042/19 confirming LG München I, decision of 2 October 2019, case no. 21 O 9333/19.

Beisteiner L (2019) Provisional measures specific to construction arbitration: focus on the Austrian Legal Framework and Jurisprudence. In: Baltag C, Vasile C (eds) Construction arbitration in Central and Eastern Europe: contemporary issues. Kluwer Law International, The Hague

Berger KP (1992) Internationale Wirtschaftsschiedsgerichtsbarkeit. De Gruyter, Berlin

Bermann GA (2017) International arbitration and private international law. Brill Nijhoff, Leiden

Bertrams R (2004) Bank guarantees in international trade. Kluwer Law International, The Hague

Blackaby N, Partasides C, Redfern A, Hunter JM (2015) Redfern and Hunter on international arbitration. Oxford University Press, Oxford

Boog C (2011) Die Durchsetzung einstweiliger Massnahmen in internationalen Schiedsverfahren, aus schweizerischer Sicht, mit rechtsvergleichenden Aspekten. University of Zurich, Zurich

Born G (2014) International Commercial Arbitration. Kluwer Law international, The Hague

Briggs A (2013) The conflict of laws. Oxford University Press, Oxford

Bureau D, Muir Watt H (2017) Droit international prive, Tome I, Partie generale. Themis, Paris

Chartered Institute of Arbitrators (2016) Applications for interim measures. International Arbitration Practice Guideline, London

Cook T, Garcia AI (2010) International Intellectual Property Arbitration. Kluwer Law International, The Hague

Draguiev D (2016) Arbitrating bank guarantees and letters of credit. Dispute Resolution J 71(3): 91–106

Dumbauld E (1932) Interim measures of protection in international controversies. Springer, Dordrecht

ELI – Unidroit Model European Rules of Civil Procedure, From Transnational Principles to European Rules of Civil Procedure (2021) Oxford University Press, Oxford

Gaillard E (2006) Reflections on the use of anti-suit injunctions in international arbitration. In: Mistelis L, Lew J (eds) Pervasive problems of international arbitration. Kluwer Law International, The Hague

Gaitis JM (2005) The Federal Arbitration Act: risks and incongruities relating to the issuance of interim and partial awards in domestic and international arbitrations. Am Rev Int Arbitr 16(1): 54–55

Goldberg D, Kryvoi Y, Philippov I (2019) Empirical study: provisional measures in Investor-State Arbitration. BIICL/White & Case, London

Grierson J, Van Hooft A (2012) Arbitrating under the 2012 ICC Rules. Kluwer Law International, The Hague

Grigera Naón H (2005) Competing orders between courts of law and arbitral tribunals: Latin American experiences. In: Briner R, Aksen G (eds) Global reflections on international law, commerce and dispute resolution. Liber Amicorum in honour of Robert Briner. ICC Publication 335, Paris

Hartley T (2009) International Commercial Litigation. Cambridge University Press, Cambridge

Hartmann-Vareilles F (2017) Achievements in civil intellectual property enforcement and recent initiatives within the digital single market strategy on the regulatory environment for platforms and online intermediaries. ERA Forum 18:1–6

Herinckx Y (2014) Liability for inappropriate interim measures in commercial arbitration. Paris J Int Arbitr 2:243–279

Hudson A (2009) Equity and trusts. Routledge, London

ICSID (1968) ICSID Convention history, vol II. ICSID, Washington D.C.

ILA Final Report on Lis Pendens and Arbitration, Arb. Int'l 25 (2009) 83

Jenkins J (2013) International construction arbitration law. Kluwer Law International, The Hague

Joint ALI/UNIDROIT Working Group on Principles and Rules of Transnational Civil Procedure, ALI/UNIDROIT Principles of Transnational Civil Procedure, UNIDROIT 2005 Study LXXVI – Doc. 13

Knoepfler F (1997) Les Measures Provisoires et l'arbitrage international. In: Kellerhals (ed) Schiedsgerichtbarkeit. Schulthess Verlag, Zurich

Lachmann JP (2008) Handbuch für die Schiedsgerichtspraxis. Verlag Dr Otto Schmidt, Cologne

Lenenbach M (1998) Antitrust injunctions in England, Germany and the United States: their treatment under European Civil Procedure and the Hague Convention. Loyola Los Angeles Int Comp Law Rev 20:257–323

Lévy L (2005) Anti-suit injunctions issued by arbitrators. In: Gaillard E (ed) Anti-suit injunctions in international arbitration. IAI International Arbitration Series No. 2

Lew J (2005) Anti-suit injunctions issued by national courts to prevent arbitration proceedings. In: Gaillard E (ed) Anti-suit injunctions in international arbitration. IAI International Arbitration Series No. 2

Mayer P (2004) Litispendance, connexité et chose jugée dans l'arbitrage international. In: Reymond C, Bernardini P (eds) Liber Amicorum Claude Reymond. Litec, Paris

McLachlan C (2009) Lis Pendens in international litigation, collected courses of the Hague Academy of International Law, 336. Brill, Leiden

Miles C (2017) Provisional measures before international courts and tribunals. Cambridge University Press, Cambridge

Niehaus G (2021) First anti-anti-suit injunction in Germany: the costs for international arbitration. Kluwer Arbitration Blog. http://arbitrationblog.kluwerarbitration.com/2021/02/28/first-anti-anti-suit-injunction-in-germany-the-costs-for-international-arbitration/. Accessed 14 Sept 2022

Note of the Secretariat on the Possible Future Work in the Area of International Commercial Arbitration (1999) U.N. Doc. A/CN.9/460, ¶121, XXX UNCITRAL Y.B. 395, 410

Poudret JF, Besson S, Berti S, Ponti A (2007) Comparative law of international arbitration. Sweet & Maxwell Publishing, London

Scherer M, Giovannini T (2005) Anti-arbitration and anti-suit injunctions in international arbitration: some remarks following a recent judgment of a Geneva Court. Stockholm Int Arbitr Rev 3: 28

Scherer M, Richman L (eds) (2015) Arbitrating under the 2014 LCIA Rules: a user's guide. Kluwer Law International, The Hague

Schreuer C, Malintoppi L, Reinisch A, Sinclair A (2009) The ICSID Convention: a commentary. Cambridge University Press, Cambridge

Schwartz E, Derains Y (2005) Guide to the ICC Rules of Arbitration. Kluwer Law International, The Hague

Shackleton S (2000) Int Arbitr Law Rev 3

UNCITRAL (2004) Report of the Working Group on Arbitration on the work of its 40th session, New York, A/CN.9/547. UNCITRAL, New York

van den Berg AJ (ed) (1995) Yearbook commercial arbitration, vol XX. Kluwer Law International, The Hague, pp 628–650

Von Segesser G, Kurth C (2004) Interim measures. In: Kaufmann-Kohler G, Stucki B (eds) International arbitration in Switzerland - a handbook for practitioners. Kluwer Law International, The Hague

Wirth M (1996) Enforceability of a Foreign Security Award in Switzerland in: ASA Special Series No. 9, Zurich

Yesilirmak A (2005) Provisional measures in International Commercial Arbitration. Kluwer Law International, The Hague

Zuberbühler T, Muller K (eds) (2005) Swiss rules of international arbitration: commentary. Kluwer Law International, The Hague

Chapter 4
Enforcement of Interim Measures

Under Chap. 2 this study did elucidate the grounds of an adjudicating body to issue interim measures.

Under Chap. 3 the study further analysed the typology, procedure, form and content of such measures.

This chapter seeks to cover the next and subsequent stage of the life of interim measures—how these should be implemented in practice. Following the structure of previous parts of the study, this chapter delves into a number of areas.

First, the chapter provides review of the enforcement conditions and process under the regulations within the Brussels regime, with main focus on Regulation Brussels Ibis.

Second, the chapter also contains an overview of one of the most challenging aspects of interim relief in international arbitration—its enforcement. Due to its consensual nature, there is a disparity of views among scholars and practitioners as to the extent to which interim measures may be forced upon a party to arbitration procedure. It is even more challenging to consider what effect interim relief issued by arbitral tribunals may have on third parties which are non-signatories of arbitration agreements. This part of the study also reviews national legislation which aims to facilitate enforcement of interim relief decisions/orders/awards by arbitral bodies. The grounds and preconditions for such enforcement in major jurisdictions are included in this review.

Moreover, the chapter also contains analysis of another enforcement-related matter: whether a party to international arbitration procedure may suffer certain negative consequences/sanctions or other type of liability for evading compliance with interim measures imposed by arbitral tribunals.

4.1 Enforcement in Cross-Border Civil and Commercial Litigation

Under Regulation Brussels Ibis, interim measures capable of enforcement are:

1. those granted by the court having jurisdiction over the substance of the case, or
2. those under Article 35 which are not granted by the court having jurisdiction over the substance of the case but notified to the respondent prior to enforcement.

Within the Brussels II regime, interim measures could not be enforced in jurisdictions outside the one where the relief is granted. It should be borne in mind, however, that in 2022 Regulation 2019/1111 has entered into force, which renders interim measures under that regulation enforceable under conditions that mirror the Regulation Brussels Ibis regime. This is why the current part of the study does not provide a separate review of the issue of enforcement under the regulations within the Brussels II regime.

4.1.1 Formalities

Regulation Brussels Ibis provides a comprehensive framework of documentary requirements for enforcement purposes under Article 42 thereof.

The applicant provides competent enforcement authority with a copy of the judgment which satisfies the conditions necessary to establish its authenticity; and a certificate under Article 53, certifying that the judgment is enforceable and containing an extract of the judgment.

More specifically about the judgment ordering a provisional, including a protective, measure, the applicant shall provide the competent enforcement authority with a copy of the judgment which satisfies the conditions necessary to establish its authenticity; and a certificate under Article 53, containing a description of the measure and certifying that the court has jurisdiction as to the substance of the matter; and that the judgment is enforceable in the Member State of origin; and, where the measure was ordered without the defendant being summoned to appear, proof of service of the judgment. The competent enforcement authority may require the applicant to provide a translation of the judgment only if it is unable to proceed without such a translation.

Article 53 refers to Annex I as to the form and content of the certificate necessary for enforcement.

It should be noted that the procedure envisioned by Regulation Brussels Ibis sets a uniform and simplistic documentary manner for cross-border enforcement and circulation of judgments.

4.1.2 Requirements for Enforcement

Article 42 is an enforcement procedural rule. It regulates under what conditions the relevant authorities in a Member State are competent to undertake actions to put the foreign judgment into effect as per that particular Member State.

A contrario, Article 42 should be understood to operate only where the judgment shall be enforced in a country different from the one where granted. Given that according to Article 2 interim measures may take the form of a judgment, an interim measure would have effect in a country different from the one where granted insofar as the requirements of Article 42 are met.

The key elements of Article 42 are two. First, under Article 42(2)(b)(i) is regulated the origin of an interim measure that may be given effect extraterritorially. Second, under Article 42(2)(c) is regulated the condition for extraterritorial effect of an ex parte interim measure.

4.1.3 Scope of Application of Article 42(2)(b)(i), i.e. First Requirement

According to that requirement, the interim measure shall be enforced where a certificate is furnished that the measure is issued by a court having jurisdiction on the substance of the matter. Hence, only a measure granted by a court with jurisdiction on the merits can be enforced abroad. This is an apparent clash with Article 35 which regulates that even a court without jurisdiction on the merits can issue interim measures on the matter. Hence, a number of important distinctions can be drawn:

- A party to a dispute may apply for interim measures by a court that has jurisdiction on the merits of the dispute as per Regulation Brussels Ibis. Regardless of whether the party will proceed to a case on the merits before that court, the interim measures granted by that court will be enforceable in another Member State as the requirement of Article 42(2)(b)(i) is met.
- A party to a dispute may apply for interim measures by a court that does not have jurisdiction on the merits of the dispute. However, in order that such a court may have jurisdiction to grant interim measures, it should meet the real connecting link requirement. The court will have jurisdiction to grant interim measures but these would not be enforceable in another Member State.

Hence, as a tactical move, the applicant should apply to this court only if this is the court where the object of the interim measure is located. Otherwise, the interim measure obtained will remain without implementation as it would not have extraterritorial effect. This is why the current Article 42 in fact curtails extraterritoriality of interim measures. The only courts that can issue interim measures with extraterritorial effect are the ones that have international jurisdiction on the matter as per the jurisdictional bases in Regulation Brussels Ibis.

Does the real connecting link doctrine operate under Article 42(2)(b)(i)? It is not a requirement for enforcement, apparently, as it is possible that a court has jurisdiction on the merits without the existence of a territorial link between that court and the object of the interim measure. Hence, the lack of real connecting link would not prevent or prejudice extraterritorial enforcement if the interim measures are granted by a court with jurisdiction on the merits. This analysis confirms that the real connecting link is a jurisdictional requirement, not an enforcement requirement. Vice versa, where the real connecting link actually is present in practice, extraterritorial enforcement would not be necessary as the object of the interim measures would be situated in the same country as the court that granted the measures.

4.1.4 Extraterritoriality and Ex Parte Measures

There is an additional requisite element for ex parte measures. According to the ECJ case law—Denilauler, prior to the current version of the Regulation, an ex parte measure could not be enforced abroad as the legal certainty enshrined in the Regulation does not permit enforcement actions on basis of ex parte measures. I.e. the respondent should be notified of the measures before enforcement commences. The rule has been incorporated in the current Article 42(2)(c) as it regulates the situation where the measure is granted in the course of a procedure where the respondent is not summoned and is not participating.

Regulation Brussels Ibis is, therefore, a complete overhaul of the Brussels regime in this respect as Denilauler managed to restrict the scope of measures that can be enforced extraterritorially to measures from an adversarial procedure. Currently the Regulation expands its application by introducing a positive requirement. While under Denilauler, a measure would be a contrario enforceable if the respondent was officially notified by it, under Article 42(2)(c) this would be so if the enforcement authority is furnished with a proof that the judgment incorporating the interim measure was served on the respondent. Hence, currently the Regulation does not require that the measure is product of an adversarial process but that the respondent is aware that the judgment is granted before its enforcement commences.[1] Instead, it suffices that there is documentary proof that the respondent is notified of the measure, not that the procedure has been conducted inter partes. The procedure may be ex parte or not, this does not have impact on the proper commencement of enforcement under the Regulation.

---

[1] Garcimartin (2014/2015), pp. 66–67.

4.1.5 Putting the Interim Measures into Effect

The extraterritorial effect of the interim measure is not automatic. Measures are governed by procedural rules and hence each Member State has its own autonomy in regulating its law on interim measures. Therefore, it cannot be possible that a single interim measure would have one and the same operation in each and every Member State where enforced. This is why under Article 54, the competent enforcement authority is allowed to modify and adapt the interim measure subject to enforcement to the closest local equivalent. The assessment should be made by the enforcement authority at the place of enforcement and be governed by the lex executionis. The criterion that Regulation Brussels Ibis sets is that the effect of the measure that the authority selects should pursue similar aims and interests as the one granted by the foreign court. The assessment should be made with view to two elements: first, the aim of a measure, and second, the interests, i.e. the mischief that a measure is supposed to attain.

4.1.6 Enforcement of Interim Measures Under Regulation Brussels Ibis: Circulation of Interim Measures Granted Under Article 35 of Regulation Brussels Ibis

Neither in Van Uden case, nor subsequently did the ECJ rule on the issue of potential enforcement of interim measures granted under Article 35 (i.e. circulation of interim measures).[2] Therefore, the question was left open. Under Regulation Brussels Ibis, it could be argued that enforcement under Chapter III is available only for interim measures incorporated in judgments that are issued by the court having jurisdiction over the main proceedings. A contrario, interim measures cannot be enforced, if granted under Article 35. This conclusion could be supported by the rationale that real connecting link inevitably ties interim measures to the place where they would be enforced, although there exists a theoretical detraction[3] to this understanding of Article 35 of Regulation Brussels Ibis.

Recently in a judgment under Regulation (EC) No 2201/2003 (Brussels II), the ECJ adopted in Case C-256/09, Purrucker I, the view that interim measures under Article 20 of Brussels II could not be enforced (later recast as Article 15 under Regulation 2019/1111—Brussels IIbis, but following the same logic and policy). It has been argued that Article 20 of Brussels II has a very different drafting from Article 35, and that it is underpinned by different values (especially as to issues of expediency in matrimonial relations). However, in this author's view the difference between two Regulations, albeit it exists and cannot be challenged, does not render

---

[2] Mankowski and Magnus (2007), pp. 609–620.
[3] E.g. Honorati (2012), pp. 525–544.

interim measures jurisdiction entirely different. The policy of the specific grounds for interim measures jurisdiction is to answer the problem of urgency and necessity. If only the court with jurisdiction over the substance of the matter can have jurisdiction to issue interim measures, and these will have to be enforced subsequently in another jurisdiction, the interests that interim measures are bound to preserve and protect are very much likely to be destroyed by the time they are implemented in practice. Hence, the very nature of interim measures calls for creating a specific jurisdiction that also avoids/bypasses enforcement problems. This is why circulation of interim measures under Article 35 is an issue which is in actuality pointless and if adopted, may well lead to exorbitance and/or abuse. Instead, the policy of the Regulation should be understood to be: if an applicant seeks urgent relief, should go to the jurisdiction where the relief will be implemented. Otherwise, if time is not of the essence, the applicant should pursue interim measures to be provided from the court with jurisdiction on the merits. The current drafting of Regulation Brussels Ibis confirms this understanding.

4.2 Enforcement in International Arbitration

4.2.1 Law Governing Enforcement of Interim Measures in International Arbitration

4.2.1.1 Supranational Source of Rules

States have entered into bilateral treaties that cover, inter alia, enforcement of foreign awards, including, potentially, interim measures awards/orders. Bar this, there are just a few multilateral instruments regulating this area. Most importantly, this is the New York Convention.

There has been much debate and discussion what regulation the New York Convention provides to the enforcement of interim measures at all.[4] There are two key provisions concerning the application of New York Convention to interim measures.

First, this is Article I (1), according to which "This Convention shall apply to the recognition and enforcement of arbitral awards made in the territory of a State other than the State where the recognition and enforcement of such awards are sought, and arising out of differences between persons, whether physical or legal."

Second, under Article V (e), "The award has not yet become binding on the parties, or has been set aside or suspended by a competent authority of the country in which, or under the law of which, that award was made."

---

[4]See discussion at Born (2014), pp. 2931–2935; Veeder (1999), p. 21; Bermann (2017), pp. 437–438.

One school of thought,[5] which has roots in both theory[6] and case law has relied upon these provisions to reason that the New York Convention does not apply to interim measures at all. First, Article I (1) is interpreted to indicate that New York Convention regulates only enforcement of awards that settle the merits of a legal dispute. Second, this is supported by Article V(e) as it speaks of non-enforcement in the case of non-binding awards, i.e. awards that have not become final and binding on the parties. Hence, it is argued, interim measures cannot be enforced on basis of the New York Convention because there are subject to modification and are not final, as they do not settle the merits of a dispute but decide only an ancillary issue, which is often decided not by an award but by a procedural order. Furthermore, the travaux preparatoire conclusively show that the drafters of the New York Convention did not envision application to interim measures at all.

Another school of thought,[7] however, has embraced a pragmatist view that there should be no rational reason that regardless of the drafting history of the New York Convention, nowadays interim measures should be enforced under the New York Convention, as (1) a ruling on interim awards finally disposes with an issue with procedural implications—an application for interim measures, and (2) these can be granted by way of an award (interim or partial), not exclusively procedural order.

The same division of opinions surfaces in the case law. An exponent of the first theory is a renown Australian judgment Resort Condominiums International Inc. v. (1) Ray Bolwell and (2) Resort Condominiums (Australasia) Pty. Ltd[8] which reasoned that that an arbitral decision needs to be a final and binding award for its enforcement under the New York Convention. The Court held that the determination of the arbitrator of its decision as an "award" does not make such decision an award within the meaning of the Convention. The Court based its finding on the determination that the arbitrator's injunction is of "an interlocutory and procedural nature and in no way purport to finally resolve the disputes ... referred by RCI for decision or finally resolve the legal rights of the parties". The Court added that such injunction is "provisional only and liable to be rescinded, suspended, varied or reopened by the tribunal which pronounced them". Consequently, according to the Australian Court, the arbitrator's description of the decision as "award" does not make it an award within the scope of the Convention provided that the decision finally resolves the parties' legal rights.

However, US courts thought different. In Sperry International Trade, Inc. v. Government of Israel[9] the parties entered into a contract requiring Sperry to design and construct a communication system for the Israeli Air Force. Under the

---

[5] Born (2014), pp. 2510–2512; Yesilirmak (2005), pp. 258–259.
[6] UNCITRAL (1999), p. 410; Boog (2011), p. 379 (interim measures do not fall within scope of Article I of New York Convention); Gaitis (2005), pp. 31–33; Lachmann (2008), para. ¶2060; Poudret et al. (2007), para. ¶633.
[7] Born (2014), pp. 2512–2515; Yesilirmak (2005), pp. 263–264.
[8] XX YCA 628–650 (1995) (Supreme Court of Queensland, 29 October 1993).
[9] 532 F. Supp. 901 (S.D.N.Y.), aff'd, 689 F.2d 301 (2 Cir. 1982).

contract, Sperry caused Citibank N.A. to open an irrevocable letter of credit in favour of Israel, which could be called upon Israel's certification that Sperry is in breach of the contract. Sperry initiated arbitration proceedings claiming breach of the contract and eventually requested from the arbitrators to enjoin Israel from calling the letter of credit. The arbitrators ordered, in an "award", that the proceeds of the letter of credit were to be held jointly by Israel and Sperry in an escrow account pending a decision on the merits. Israel argued that the award is not final and, therefore, could not be enforced. The court rejected this argument holding that the award was severable from the merits and because, by its nature, it required "affirmative action", the award would be rendered a meaningless exercise of the arbitrators' powers if it were not enforced. Accordingly, the court confirmed the award. A Swiss Supreme Court decision[10] has reasoned that awards should be considered also decision "which rule on one or more preliminary substantive or procedural issues" and "an interlocutory award disposing of one or several preliminary issues, whether procedural or on the merits."[11]

In this author's view, the views of the second school of thought should be adopted for several reasons. First, the literal interpretation of the New York Convention does not actually indicate that only rulings on merits should be enforced under the New Convention. Article I speaks of enforcement of awards arising out of differences between persons, with the gloss that the difference should be of legal nature. This delineates the scope of arbitral proceedings—deciding differences in legal relationships, but does not indicate that an award should deal only with substantive rights at stake in such a difference. As noted, interim measures is an ancillary issue but it is sufficiently related to the legal rights and obligations in dispute in the arbitral proceedings. Therefore, it cannot be honestly said that the New York Convention does not include, in its ratione materiae scope, such issues as interim measures that are tightly connected to, and actually arising out of, the legal difference between the parties to the arbitral proceedings.

Second, the argument on finality is unconvincing, too. It is a settled law that arbitration is a one-instance procedure and there is no option to appeal. An arbitral ruling may be (1) revoked by the arbitral tribunal itself; or (2) set aside by a court; or (3) refused to be enforced by court, but this does not undermine the finality of an arbitral ruling. The arbitral tribunal disposes with an issue finally and in a binding the parties way. Hence, an order or award on interim measures is final and binding as it cannot be appealed by the parties. Therefore, the finality and binding force is not a feature salient to arbitral awards on the merits; to the contrary, this is a feature of any arbitral ruling and it stems from the dispute resolution powers of the tribunal.

Lastly, from a teleological point of view, there is no point in having an arbitral tribunal that does not issue rulings that are capable of enforcement under the New York Convention. In the same vein, there is no point in having a New York Convention that covers only rulings on merits but not rulings on interim measures.

---

[10] Judgment of 13 April 2010, DFT 4A_582/2009, ¶2.3.1 (Swiss Federal Tribunal).
[11] Judgment of 6 April 2011, DFT 4A_614/2010, ¶2.1 (Swiss Federal Tribunal).

4.2 Enforcement in International Arbitration   115

Indeed, the New York Convention drafting did not envision interim measures. But this is an argument of dubious value. In the 1950s of twentieth century, the practice of granting interim measures by arbitral tribunal had not developed yet. Such interim measures would be rather exotic and actors on the arbitration field would not think of these as binding at all. The evolution of the treaty is, however, evident. As the New York Convention is an international treaty and an instrument of international law, the so called evolutionary interpretation[12] can be applied to it which means that the treaty may be interpreted in light of the evolution of law and society without taking it as cast in stone at the time the treaty was drafted. The concepts embedded in the text of the treaty have gone further and lived their own lives beyond what the drafters (having background from the beginning of the twentieth century in fact) intended. Operating in the twenty-first century, the New York Convention would not be a comprehensive instrument if it cannot encapsulate the pragmatics of the current reality of international disputes decided by arbitration.

4.2.1.2 National Law

The national laws, usually the domestic arbitration statute, may include some rules on enforcement of interim measures.

Broadly speaking, there are two types of national law rules concerning enforcement of interim measures. First one is the "real" regulation on enforcement of interim measures—it provides for the procedure to enforce interim measures granted by an arbitral tribunal. Second one is regulation stipulating rules for assistance by national courts to give effect of interim measures granted by arbitral tribunals. These are not actual enforcement rules but rather rules on coordination between arbitral tribunal and national courts. These may also be called rules for sui generis enforcement[13] as these do not concern direct enforcement of the ruling of a tribunal but "filter" the ruling of the tribunal and the ruling that is practically implemented would be the court decision, not the arbitral ruling, although the order will be the one provided by the arbitral tribunal.[14]

Below are examples of such:

English Arbitration Act
Under Section 42[15] if the seat of arbitration is in England the court may, under Section 42, make an order requiring a party to comply with a 'peremptory order' made by an arbitral tribunal. This option is available if a party does not comply voluntarily with prior order made by the tribunal. Both the tribunal, upon notice to

---

[12] Bjorge (2014); Legal Consequences for States of the Continued Presence of South Africa in Namibia (South West Africa) Notwithstanding Security Council Resolution 276 (1970), Advisory Opinion of 21 June 1971, ILR, Vol. 49, 21–22.
[13] von Segesser and Boog (2013), p. 121.
[14] Yesilirmak (2005), pp. 254–256.
[15] See commentary in O'Callaghan and Finnis (2013), pp. 436–437.

the parties, and one of the parties have right to request judicial support on basis of Section 42 of Arbitration Act 1996. In the latter case, the party should have exhausted other options within the arbitral proceedings before turning to the state court. Moreover, this option is available only for "peremptory orders" of a tribunal, which are not defined by the Arbitration Act 1996 but may include interim relief measures as well (e.g. in Emmott v. Michael Wilson & Partners Limited (No. 2)). Non-compliance with the court order may attract liability for contempt of court, which is criminal liability.[16]

Swiss Private International Law Act

Under Article 183, para. 2 of Swiss Private International Law Act, if a party does not voluntarily comply with interim measured by the arbitral tribunal, the arbitral tribunal may request the assistance of the state judge; the judge shall apply his own law. The provision is interpreted broadly as to include not only the tribunal but also the parties[17] to have right to recourse to state court. The provision is applicable to both measures provided by a tribunal seated in Switzerland or abroad. The procedure is bilateral. State courts have jurisdiction only in case of non-compliance with a tribunal-granted measure and with the consent/approval of the tribunal, if the measure is party requested. The procedure is understood as specific sui generis enforcement.[18]

German ZPO

Under Section 1041, para 2 of German ZPO, the court may, at the request of a party, permit enforcement of an (interim) measure, unless application for a corresponding interim measure has already been made to a court. It may recast such an order if necessary for the purpose of enforcing the measure.[19] The option is not limited to measures rendered by tribunals seated in Germany—a party may request the enforcement of a measure issued by a foreign tribunal (cf. Arbitration Act 1996). Moreover, failure to comply is not a prerequisite for applying to the court for enforcement of the arbitral interim measure. Section 1041 contains a lis pendens restriction so that a court does not render enforcement of an interim measure where another interim measure application is made to the court (which does not preclude making application to the court and the arbitral tribunal on one and the same matter). The court should not make review of the interim measure granted by the arbitral tribunal but would yet seek to avoid any contravention of public policy or manifestly defective arbitral measures.[20] If the interim measure is not compliant with the German law, the court may enforce it by recasting (modifying) it. Pursuant to § 1041 (3) ZPO, the state court may, upon request, repeal or amend its prior decision to grant leave to enforce the arbitral tribunal's order of an interim measure. Such

---

[16] Yesilirmak (2005), p. 249—a separate approach.

[17] Boog (2011), pp. 123–124; von Segesser and Boog (2013), p. 122.

[18] von Segesser and Boog (2013), p. 121.

[19] See commentary in Schäfer (2015), pp. 215–237.

[20] OLG Saarbrucken 27.02.2007, OLGR 2007, 426 (427).

application requires an appropriate reason, e.g. change of circumstances since granting leave of enforcement. Under § 1063 ZPO, measures may be granted as a provisional relief until the enforcement is decided. The criteria for issuing these is as under § 916–917 ZPO.[21]

4.2.1.3 Non-statutory Sources of Law/Soft Law

The amendment of the UNCITRAL Model Law from 2006 has brought a number of changes to the Model Law, including with regard to interim measures. Under Chapter IVA Interim Measures and Preliminary Orders, the UNCITRAL Model Law now provides for recognition and enforcement of interim measures in Articles 17H and Article 17I (Section 4 of Chapter IVA). However, the level of adoption of the 2006 amendments to the UNCITRAL Model Law in national legislations is still relatively low. Nevertheless, this albeit being soft law as a source of law, can become effective once implemented into national laws, and as such has the potential to become statutory source of law under the previous Sect. 4.2.1.2.

4.2.2 Addressees of the Rules: Ratione Personae Scope of the Rules of Enforcement

As analysed herein under Sect. 2.2.1.2, the jurisdiction of arbitral tribunals comprises only the parties to the arbitral proceedings, based on the parties to the arbitration agreement (clause). This jurisdictional scope is important for determining the scope of interim measures granted as well as the ratione personae scope of the enforcement of the interim measures. The implications of this restriction on enforcement is that the only parties that can be affected by the measures when effectuated would be the parties to the tribunal's jurisdiction. The enforcement would be only in such a way that can be imposed on the parties to the case, and not upon, or by, other parties. This is important because the lex executionis at each State varies and it is the actual law that would determine whether and how the interim measures will be effected into practice after all. If the lex executionis requires that a third party should do or refrain from doing certain actions for the purpose of implementation of the interim measures. So it may happen that a tribunal provides certain measures but under the lex executionis of the place of enforcement does not provide for mechanism of enforcement that involves only the actions of the parties, or, alternatively the mechanism requires a third party to take action. The ratione personae restriction would lead that such interim measures may be within the jurisdictional scope of the tribunal, may be granted, but may fail to be enforced.

---

[21] BGH, decision of 7 July 2016—I ZB 90/15.

4.2.3 Procedure of Enforcement. Competent Bodies

The foregoing sections exemplify the main issues at stake at the stage of enforcement of the interim measures.

First, national laws may have specific rules and provisions that target particularly handling interim relief enforcement. These usually entail support/assistance or at least some level of involvement of national judiciary. Hence, parties and/or the tribunal may request that national courts issue their own decisions/orders to bring about enforcement of the interim measures. This is how the arbitral measures become "incorporated", "planted" in domestic judicial decisions/orders and hence are to be enforced along the respective national procedures which apply to enforcement of court decisions/orders. E.g. non-compliance with court orders under English law may be considered as contempt of court and be treated as a criminal offence, as noted above.

Second, where the interim measures are treated as a certain category of foreign/international arbitral awards/orders, then the domestic rules on civil procedure would lay down the steps and stages for enforcement. These would have to go in the same vein as any other foreign decision of that type. E.g. if the domestic law of a particular country assumes that interim awards are to be considered as tribunal awards subject to enforcement, the award creditor would have to submit the interim relief award to be enforced under the same procedure as other awards undergo.

4.2.4 Consequences of Non-compliance

Voluntary compliance with arbitral tribunal ordered interim measures seems to be an alternative to enforcement. Indeed, if a party complies with the interim measures, there would be no actual need to seek enforcement. However, it would be unrealistic to believe that parties would comply voluntarily if there is no mechanism to sanction non-compliance. One avenue to sanction non-compliance would be, generally speaking, the option for a party to seek enforcement of the measures granted. Enforcement lies outside the bounds of the arbitral procedure. Successful or unsuccessful enforcement would not have effect on the conduct of the proceedings. Therefore, there should be another avenue open for redress and it is within the arbitral procedure.

Non-compliance with interim measures is a part of the more general issue of non-compliance with the rulings of the arbitral tribunal.[22] The power of the tribunal would not be real if could be undermined by parties' non-compliance. This extends to interim measures as well. However, the issue is more complex. The nature of arbitration is consensual, contractual. The parties refer their dispute to arbitration in order that the substantive rights and obligations arising out of their arbitrable

---

[22]Born (2014), pp. 2446–2447; Yesilirmak (2005), pp. 240–243; Draguiev (2022), pp. 135–155.

relationship are adjudicated. Interim measures are granted in order that the perceived end of the arbitral procedure is safeguarded, i.e. the award would be able to be enforced and the rights at the heart of the dispute—given rise to, as the tribunal has finally ruled. If a party fails to comply with interim measures granted by the tribunal, this poses risk to the ends of the procedure and the subsequent enforcement of the rights of the parties. This is why the procedural problem of non-compliance is intertwined with the substantive question of rights and obligations at stake in the procedure. Infringement of substantive rights would, as a general principle of law, cause legal responsibility in terms of damages. Non-compliance with interim measures may (and in most situations—would certainly) lead to damages payable by the non-compliant party to the other party whose rights have not been preserved by the interim measures. This gives ground to the argument that non-compliance should bring aggravation of liability so that one of the parties' damages to the other are increased taking into account the failure to comply voluntarily with interim measures.

There is another perspective.[23] The arbitration agreement bears not only features of a contractual arrangement but goes beyond—it has a procedural nature[24] and its effect is procedural, i.e. it grants dispute resolution and procedural powers to the arbitral body. The arbitral agreement contains also some substantive obligations on itself, not referring to the substantive rights and obligations forming the subject matter of the case.

Usually this substantive side is overlooked by theory and practice. The effect of the arbitration agreement is that it designates substantive conduct that the parties should follow in case of a dispute. Even if not stated explicitly, this is implied by the very nature of the arbitration agreement. Substantive rights and obligations are, for instance: not to seize a forum which is not designated under the agreement; to comply with the powers of the selected forum; not to act in contravention to the agreement and the orders/judgment/award rendered, etc. This can also be assumed on basis of the two main effects of the arbitration clause, its prorogatory and derogatory effects. The prorogatory effect is assigning jurisdiction to a tribunal to resolve the dispute. The derogatory effect is to deprive any other court or tribunal from jurisdiction to resolve the dispute.[25] Hence, if a party fails to comply with what an arbitral interim measure orders, this can be seen as a violation of the obligations of that party under the arbitration agreement.

Therefore, two underpinnings can be established. First, that the damages of a party stemming from the dispute within the primary relationship between the parties would be exacerbated and would increase as a result of the failure to comply with the interim relief. Second, that irrespective of any actual or potential increase in the losses suffered by a party to the dispute, even the mere non-compliance would

---

[23] See generally Draguiev (2022), pp. 135–155, where the argument is elaborated at length.

[24] Takahashi (2008), pp. 57–91 and 67.

[25] Hartley (2009), p. 163; Briggs (2013), p. 162; Mankowski and Magnus (2007), pp. 382–383.

ground damages liability of the non-compliant party; however, calculation of precise damages depends on actual loss subject to being proved.

This poses a number of procedural issues. First, the consequences of non-compliance would be assessed at the deliberation for the award, and the increase of damages would be included in the award. Second, there is a question of proof. The substantive basis of the notion of aggravation of liability requires that aggravation reflects actual losses suffered by the party on account of the non-compliance of the other party such as costs and other damages.[26] Aggravation is not an automatic sanction and is not a fine imposed by the tribunal. The amount of the sanction should be proven and depends on the damages suffered by the party. Hence, even if a party fails to comply, but (1) no losses ensue; or (2) regardless of existence of losses, there is no sufficient evidence for these, the arbitral tribunal should not aggravate liability, i.e. increase amount of damages, for the sole reason of actual non-compliance. In principle, the tribunal may award punitive damages. However, the extent of the permissibility of these depends much on the lex arbitri, and the enforcement of such award may be problematic with regard to the lex executionis.

Besides, if the tribunal does not implement any liability for non-compliance, it is deemed possible that a party may bring claim against the non-compliant party for breach of the arbitration agreement (as the procedure is based on it) and/or breach of the accepted procedural rules.

Most cases in practice within this area of the law stem from situations where a party has commenced parallel or related proceedings in breach of an arbitration clause, very often contrary to an antisuit injunction. The situation is identical to cases where the action is commenced contrary to an exclusive jurisdiction/choice of court agreement. The established case law of English courts[27] settled that damages for foreign proceedings in contravention to arbitration agreement may be awarded.[28] In CMA CGM SA v. Hyundai Mipo Dockland Ltd[29] the parties were engaged in a number of contractual disputes pending in parallel in UK and France. The French courts did award damages plus costs. The UK arbitral tribunal did hold that the French proceedings were instituted in breach of the arbitration clause between the parties, and awarded the same amount of damages mirroring the award in France.

It was confirmed in Re Boodhoo case that *"If a costs order in favour of a successful applicant for a stay or for an anti-suit injunction directed to giving effect to an arbitration agreement or an English jurisdiction clause was made on the standard basis, there would necessarily be a part of the successful applicant's costs of the application which it could not recover because of the restrictive process of assessment. That unindemnified portion of costs would then be loss that could only be recovered as damages for breach of the jurisdiction or arbitration agreement, if such a damages claim were permissible. Where the cause of action for relief*

---

[26] Yesilirmak (2005), pp. 242–243.
[27] [1980] 1 LLR 375A.
[28] E.g. Collins (1997), p. 72.
[29] [2008] EWHC 2791 (Comm).

enforcing the agreement by stay or injunction in the English court and the cause of action for damages for breach of that agreement were, as they normally would be, the same, the effect of the authorities was to prevent separate proceedings for damages by reference to unrecovered costs, notwithstanding the breach of the arbitration or jurisdiction agreement"[30]

Following the same rationale, but in the setting of exclusive jurisdiction agreements, US courts have decided in the case of Indosuez International Finance BV v National Reserve Bank[31] to award costs incurred in course of proceedings commenced in Russia in contravention to the exclusive New York forum selection clause.

The matter has been considered in a judgement of the German Supreme Court (BGH).[32] The German courts reasoned that German substantive and procedural laws recognize the liability for breach of an exclusive jurisdiction agreement (i.e. also of an arbitration agreement). The BGH decided that a German counterparty was entitled to be awarded indemnification for the costs spent on the US proceedings, regardless of the fact that US proceedings would not allow such reimbursement.

In Decision of the Swiss Supreme Court 4A_444/2009 of 11 February 2010, and Decision of the Swiss Supreme Court 4A_232/2013 of 30 September 2013, the Court was faced with disputes concerning distribution agreements, where in the former case the claim was brought in Israeli, and in the latter in Greek courts but in contravention of Swiss-related arbitration clauses. Subsequently, the Swiss seated arbitral tribunals in the respective cases did favour awarding compensations to the non-breaching parties as part of the proceedings on the merits (the compensation being measured by the expenses incurred in the foreign court proceedings). This was put to scrutiny before the Supreme Court, which did not overrule the arbitral approach as contrary to Swiss public policy. Further, there is a reported Italian case[33] where damages were awarded for a vexatious claim brought in breach of an arbitration agreement. The losing party in the proceedings was condemned to a category of damages as per Article 96 of the Italian Civil Code, which provides for liability for fraudulent or negligent conduct of claims. The grounds for that stemmed from commencement of the proceedings in breach of an existing arbitration clause, i.e. breach of an arbitration agreement.

Albeit the bulk of the case law deals with breaches of exclusive jurisdiction agreements and parallel proceedings, not interim measures, in this author's view[34] the underpinning principle and policy is the same regarding arbitration agreements, and that the same rationale is easy to be transposed to the area of interim relief. It seems clear that costs incurred due to contravention of an interim measure should be considered as recoverable. This is a clear and measurable loss.

---

[30] [2007] EWCA Crim. 14.

[31] 304 AD 2d 429 (2003), 758 N Y S 2d 308 (NY App Div 2003).

[32] 17 October 2019 (III ZB 42/19).

[33] See case report in Caccialanza (2014).

[34] See further in Draguiev (2022), pp. 135–155.

The case law also indicates that theoretically claims for further damages are possible. Although the overview does not indicate particular examples to be analysed, in this author's view it is adequate to outline that international proceedings in various jurisdictions are costly and may lead to severe business disruption, bad publicity, waste of time and resources, etc. negative consequences. These all flow as sequences to the conduct of the breaching party. It should be answered in the positive that further damages may exist and be recovered.

Moreover, besides compensatory damages, it is possible to imagine also non-compensatory damages, i.e. damages punishing the non-compliant conduct itself, which in common law jurisdictions may be termed as punitive damages. It has been argued[35] such may be awarded in these cases and some case law, e.g. the cited case of the courts of Verona, suggests this may also be on the table for an aggrieved respondent to interim relief proceedings.

4.3 Interim Measures in ICSID. Enforcement

Neither the ICSID Convention, nor the Arbitration Rules thereto contain a rule on non-compliance with interim measures.

According to a practice direction—in Note B to Arbitration Rule 39 (of 1968 1 ICSID Reports 99)—the sanction is that this is reflected in the final award on the merits. This is argued by authorities as well.[36] The case law is scant but yet it supports the view that failure to comply is a breach of the Convention[37] and that the consequences of interim measures non-compliances should be taken into account in fixing damages in the final award.[38]

4.4 Compliance Under National Law. Consequences of Non-compliance with Interim Measures

Interim measures are granted by a ruling of a dispute resolution body. Usually jurisdictions adopt specific set or rules (procedure) for enforcing the provided interim measures, and usually these rules are akin to rules on enforcement (execution) of court rulings.

---

[35] E.g. Caccialanza (2014).

[36] Friedland (1986), p. 337; Parra (1993), p. 41.

[37] Quiborax S.A. and Non-Metallic Minerals S.A. v. Plurinational State of Bolivia (ICSID Case No. ARB/06/2), award dated 16 September 2015, para. 582.

[38] AGIP v. Congo, Award, 30 November 1979, paras. 9–12; MINE v. Guinea, Award, 6 January 1988, 4 ICSID Reports 69.

There are three typical consequences flowing from non-compliance with interim measures.

First, these are civil. Civil consequences are two broad categories. The first is monetary, i.e. that the perpetrator is liable for damages. Second, the effect of actions or transactions contrary to interim measures may be null and void. In some jurisdictions this is absolute invalidity but in others the invalidity can be claimed only by the applicant who is harmed by the actions or transactions at stake.

Second, criminal. In some jurisdictions it is a criminal offence to contradict interim measures ruling. The consequences of this criminality, however, differ. The penalty in some countries (e.g. in England—contempt of court; Portugal—Article 375 of Civil Procedure Code; Article 292 of the Swiss Criminal Code; Art 102–104 of Civil Procedure Law of China) may be financial (fine) (e.g. in England and USA[39]—contempt of court; Article 292 of the Swiss Criminal Code; Art 102–104 of Civil Procedure Law of China) while in others the punishment may be imprisonment (sentence) as well (Art 102–104 of Civil Procedure Law of China). The sanction can be administrative fine, too (e.g. Russia).

References

Bermann GA (2017) International arbitration and private international law. Brill Nijhoff, Leiden
Bjorge E (2014) The evolutionary interpretation of treaties. Oxford University Press, Oxford
Boog C (2011) Die Durchsetzung einstweiliger Massnahmen in internationalen Schiedsverfahren, aus schweizerischer Sicht, mit rechtsvergleichenden Aspekten. University of Zurich, Zurich
Born G (2014) International Commercial Arbitration. Kluwer Law international, The Hague
Briggs A (2013) The conflict of laws. Oxford University Press, Oxford
Caccialanza M (2014) Damages for breach of the obligation to arbitrate: a step forward of national courts in favour of arbitration? http://arbitrationblog.kluwerarbitration.com/2014/05/27/damages-for-breach-of-the-obligation-to-arbitrate-a-step-forward-of-national-courts-in-favour-of-arbitration/
Collins L (1997) Essays in international litigation and the conflict of laws. Clarendon Press, Oxford
Draguiev D (2022) Liability for non-compliance with a Dispute Resolution Agreement. Arbitration: Int J Arbitr Mediation Dispute Manag 88(1):135–155
Friedland P (1986) Provisional measures and ICSID arbitration. Int Arbitr 2:335–357
Gaitis JM (2005) The Federal Arbitration Act: risks and incongruities relating to the issuance of interim and partial awards in domestic and international arbitrations. Am Rev Int Arbitr 16(1): 54–55
Garcimartin F (2014/2015) Provisional and protective measures in the Brussels I Regulation Recast. Yearb Private Int Law 16:57–84
Hartley T (2009) International commercial litigation. Cambridge University Press, Cambridge
Honorati C (2012) Provisional measures and the recast of Brussels I Regulation: a missed opportunity for a better ruling. Rivista di diritto internazionale privato e processuale 48(3):525–544
Lachmann JP (2008) Handbuch für die Schiedsgerichtspraxis. Verlag Dr Otto Schmidt, Cologne

---

[39] See e.g. Stryker Corp. v. Davol Inc., 234 F.3d 1252, 1260 (Fed. Cir. 2000); see also KSM Fastening Systems Inc., 776 F.2d at 1532; Federal Rule of Civil Procedure 65(d) and Art. 18 U.S.C. § 401.

Mankowski P, Magnus U (eds) (2007) Brussels I Regulation – European Commentaries on private international law. Sellier, Munich

Note of the Secretariat on the Possible Future Work in the Area of International Commercial Arbitration (1999) U.N. Doc. A/CN.9/460, ¶121, XXX UNCITRAL Y.B. 395, 410

O'Callaghan K, Finnis J (2013) Support and supervision of the courts. In: Lew J, Bor H (eds) Arbitration in England, with chapters on Scotland and Ireland. Kluwer Law International, The Hague

Parra A (1993) The practices and experience of ICSID. In: Conservatory and provisional measures in international arbitration. ICC publication no. 519

Poudret JF, Besson S, Berti S, Ponti A (2007) Comparative law of international arbitration. Sweet & Maxwell Publishing, London

Schäfer E, Verbist H, Imhoos C (2015) ICC arbitration in practice. Kluwer Law International, The Hague

Takahashi K (2008) Damages for breach of a Choice-Of-Court Agreement. Yearb Private Int Law 10:57–91

Veeder VV (1999) Provisional and conservatory measures. In: Enforcing arbitration awards under the New York Convention – experience and prospects. United Nations, New York

von Segesser S, Boog C (2013) Interim measures. In: Geisinger E, Voser N (eds) International arbitration in Switzerland: a handbook for practitioners. Kluwer Law International, The Hague

Yesilirmak A (2005) Provisional measures in International Commercial Arbitration. Kluwer Law International, The Hague

Chapter 5
Interim Measures in Other International Judicial and Quasi-Judicial Bodies

This study seeks to argue two main points related to interim measures. First, interim measures are not merely preserving a status quo and are not merely a procedural issue; interim measures are an effective tool to influence the course of a pending dispute, to manage it until it is finally resolved and prevent its aggravation. Second, interim measures have inherent characteristics dictated by the nature and function that they have, which have been expounded earlier on in this study. Such inherent characteristics of interim measures are being manifested in the various shapes and forms that interim measures may take, depending on the particular type of dispute and applicable procedure. The specifics of interim relief outlined hereabove in relation to private cross-border disputes do by no means pertain only to this particular category of cases. On the contrary, private transnational disputes are one of the various examples of the common traits that interim relief measures share across various types of controversies and systems of procedural law.

To reinvigorate this point, this study makes a short excursus to briefly outline the other type of international disputes—those of public law nature, and the specific interim relief rules contained in the procedural mechanisms in the field of international law and its specific regimes (e.g. particular areas such as law of seas; human rights; regional international organizations and self-contained systems of law, etc.). The purpose of this excursus is to stress, once again, what grounds and procedural mechanisms for granting interim relief are available in international disputes; that the international scope of a dispute would make necessity for such measures all the more pertinent; and that as per their general characteristics, these would not significantly differ from those in private disputes.

© The Author(s), under exclusive license to Springer Nature Switzerland AG 2023
D. Draguiev, *Interim Measures in Cross-Border Civil and Commercial Disputes*,
EYIEL Monographs - Studies in European and International Economic Law 30,
https://doi.org/10.1007/978-3-031-28704-6_5

5.1 Interim Measures in the International Court of Justice[1]

5.1.1 Jurisdiction

The grounds for interim measures by the International Court of Justice are incorporated in Article 41 of the Statute of ICJ. The ICJ can indicate, if it considers that circumstances so require, any provisional measures which ought to be taken to preserve the respective rights of either party. The provision does not elucidate the requirements of Article 41 and these have been developed in the jurisprudence of the ICJ.

The grounds for ICJ jurisdiction to indicate interim measures (Article 41) are different from the general jurisdiction of the ICJ (Article 36). The existence of interim measures jurisdiction does not require Article 36 jurisdiction, and vice versa. Jurisdictional analysis is preliminary (as per Aegean Sea Shelf case) for the purpose of rendering ruling on the interim measures request.

A prima facie jurisdiction of the ICJ should be established in order that interim measures are indicated by the court.[2] In the absence of prima facie jurisdiction, the ICJ would reject an interim measures request.[3] This is important as usually the urgency of the situation does not allow that the question of interim measures await until the jurisdictional stage of the case is reached.[4] Hence, in practical terms, the ICJ will have to deal with the interim measures application before it deals with the jurisdictional and/or substantive matters of the case. This is why the court should be satisfied, at least prima facie, that the case may surpass the jurisdictional stage. Otherwise, it will be inadequate to exercise its powers to indicate measures under a procedure that appears totally outside the court's powers.

On basis of the dicta in the Interhandel case[5] presence of an instrument of acceptance of court jurisdiction would possibly suffice for ascertaining prima facie jurisdiction.

---

[1] See generally Miles (2017), pp. 131–342.
[2] Fisheries Jurisdiction Case, Federal Republic of Germany v Iceland, Order of 17 August 1972 I.C.J. Reports 1972 30, 34; Armed Activities in the Territory of the Congo, ICJ Rep. 2003, 4–36.
[3] Oellers-Frahm (2011) p. 935.
[4] Oda (1996), p. 550.
[5] Order of 24 October 1957, I.C.J. 105, 113 (by Judge Wellington Koo).

5.1.2 Standards

The purpose of interim measure proceedings is preservation of rights—the rights of the parties that are subject of the proceedings on the merits.[6] But in fact it is indeed the preservation of the subject matter of these rights.[7]

The Article 41 should be interpreted as prevention of irreparable harm and in order to cater for urgent situations.[8] In the case law of the PCIJ, it has been argued that the harm to be prevented by the interim measures should be "absolutely irreparable".[9] According to this dicta, reparation will not suffice to render the damages good. This requirement is hard to be found as relevant under the current status of ICJ jurisprudence. Irreparability should be viewed through the prism of execution of the judgment of the ICJ. If the execution shall be rendered impossible, there are grounds to consider the harm to be beyond repair. In some cases where essential rights such as human life[10] are at stake, it seems obvious what irreparable harm means. Otherwise, the court shall consider the variety of facts. Some commentaries suggest that continuous violation, if there is prima facie evidence for this, may pass the test and require indication of interim measures.

The purpose of the measures is to secure the status quo and to avoid the aggravation of the dispute.[11]

The measures should not prejudice the resolution of the dispute or anticipate the judgment.[12]

Along with prima facie jurisdiction, there should also be prima facie possibility that the merits of the claim will be granted as well.[13] E.g. in the Great Belt case[14] the court examined for the purpose of the interim measures request the existence of the claimed substantive rights and as long as these are established, regardless of possible doubt as to the exact extent of the right, the potential merits of the claim lead to the prima facie substantive foundation of the interim measures request. If the claimed

---

[6] Oda (1996), p. 551; Oellers-Frahm (2011), p. 931.

[7] Frontier Dispute Case, Burkina Faso/Mali, Order of 10 January 1986, I.C.J. 3, 13.

[8] Fisheries Jurisdiction Case, Federal Republic of Germany v Iceland, Order of 17 August 1972 I.C.J. Reports 1972 30, 34.

[9] Sino-Belgian Treaty case, PCIJ Series A, No. 8, 7.

[10] LaGrand (Germany v. United States of America), Provisional Measures, Order of 3 March 1999, I. C. J. Reports 1999, p. 9.

[11] Land and Maritime Boundary between Cameroon and Nigeria, Provisional Measures, Order of 15 March 1996, I. C. J. Reports 1996, p. 13, 22; Oda (1996), p. 552.

[12] LaGrand (Germany v. United States of America), Provisional Measures, Order of 3 March 1999, I. C. J. Reports 1999, p. 15; Avena and Other Mexican Nationals (Mexico v. United States of America), Provisional Measures, Order of 5 February 2003, 1. C. J. Reports 2003, p. 77, 91; Nuclear Tests (New Zealand v. France), Interim Protection, Order of 22 June 1973, I. C.J. Reports 1973, p. 135, 139; Oellers-Frahm (2011), p. 932.

[13] Oellers-Frahm (2011), p. 938.

[14] Passage through the Great Belt (Finland v. Denmark), Provisional Measures, Order of 29 July 1991, I.C.J. Reports 1991, p. 12, 13.

circumstances at the merits cannot be established at all, the interim measures request will fail as well.[15]

There should be urgency in order that the measures are indicated. Urgency would be present in case of imminent risk for the rights claimed at the merits of the procedure.[16] The imminent risk is mapped against the circumstances of the particular case.

5.1.3 Procedure

Interim measures procedure is governed by Rules 73–78 of the Rules of the ICJ. The judges dealing with an interim measures request should not participate in the procedure on the merits. Interim measures may be requested since the institution of the proceedings throughout the course of the case until the judgment on the merits. If the request is dismissed, the parties may make a new one but based on different facts (Article 75, paragraph 3).

The procedure is completed by rendering of an order ruling on the interim measures request—the ruling is only provisional, i.e. not on the substantive matter.[17]

Interim measures should be directed at the rights of the parties at stake in the procedure.[18] There should be a link between the right to be protected by the requested interim measures and the merits of the case.

ICJ is not bound by the requests of the parties. The measures may be indicated independently and proprio motu (Article 75 of the Rules of ICJ[19]).

The court can modify or revoke the measures upon request by the parties (Article 76). The span of the measures is until the judgment on the merits is rendered. Then the effect of the measures is substituted by the effect of the final judgment.

---

[15] Kosovo case (Accordance with international law of the unilateral declaration of independence in respect of Kosovo (Request for Advisory Opinion).

[16] LaGrand (Germany v. United States of America), Provisional Measures, Order of 3 March 1999, I. C. J. Reports 1999, p. 9, 15.

[17] Legal Status of South-Eastern Territory of Greenland (Nor. v. Den.), 1932 P.C.I.J. (ser. A/B) No. 48 (Order of Aug. 2).

[18] Land and Maritime Boundary between Cameroon and Nigeria, Provisional Measures, Order of 15 March 1996, I. C. J. Reports 1996, p. 13, 22.

[19] LaGrand (Germany v. United States of America), Provisional Measures, Order of 3 March 1999, I. C. J. Reports 1999, p. 9, 14.

5.1.4 Enforcement

It is a matter of long-standing discussion whether interim measures by the ICJ are binding.[20] The analysis of the preparatory works and the literal meaning of the Statute, and the Rules, speak that the ICJ cannot order to the parties to comply with the interim measures but only to indicate measures to them. Also, only the final judgment on the merits of the case has binding effect.

The position of the jurisprudence of the ICJ has been controversial as well. The Nicaragua case[21] stated that the parties should take into account the measures (not comply with them).

Scholarly opinion has ranged from supporting the legally obligatory nature of the measures[22] to arguing that these cannot bind states.[23]

In the LaGrand[24] case ICJ explicitly stated that any non-binding effect of interim measures would be contrary to the functions of Article 41 and the powers of ICJ of settlement of disputes. A breach of interim measures granted by the court would incur international responsibility for the State, then. As under Article 41, paragraph 2 the measures are submitted to the Security Council of UN, so it may take actions in case of non-compliance if this will breach international security and peace.

5.2 Interim Measures Under the United Nations Convention on the Law of the Sea

5.2.1 Jurisdiction

The jurisdiction of the ITLOS[25] or other bodies competent under the UNCLOS to grant interim measures is regulated in Article 290 of the United Nations Convention on the Law of the Sea. Under paragraph 1 of the Article, if a dispute has been duly submitted to a court or tribunal which considers that it has prima facie jurisdiction under Part XV (Settlement of Disputes) or Part XI, section 5 of the UNCLOS, the court or tribunal may prescribe any provisional measures which it considers appropriate under the circumstances to preserve the respective rights of the parties to the dispute or to prevent serious harm to the marine environment, pending the final decision.

---

[20] Oellers-Frahm (2011), pp. 953–954.

[21] Military and Paramilitary Activities in and against Nicaragua (Nicaragua v. United States of America). Merits, Judgment. I.C.J. Reports 1986, p. 14, 144).

[22] Lauterpacht (1958), p. 254.

[23] Mendelson (1986).

[24] Germany v. United States of America, Judgement, I. C. J. Reports 2001, p. 466, 502.

[25] It is to be noted that the basis of this study has been submitted as a doctoral dissertation at the University of Hamburg, while ITLOS has its seat in Hamburg.

The jurisdiction which the UNCLOS provides for to bodies such as ITLOS has two conditions. First, the jurisdiction to grant interim measures is derivative from the general jurisdiction of ITLOS, hence ITLOS would not be competent to prescribe interim measures where it has no jurisdiction at all, more specifically jurisdiction ratione materiae and personae. The UNCLOS provides for jurisdiction of the bodies prescribed under Article 287, paragraphs 1 of UNCLOS: (a) the International Tribunal for the Law of the Sea established in accordance with Annex VI; (b) the International Court of Justice; (c) an arbitral tribunal constituted in accordance with Annex VII; (d) a special arbitral tribunal constituted in accordance with Annex VIII for one or more of the categories of disputes specified therein. Under Article 288, the jurisdiction encompasses the interpretation and application of the UNCLOS. The parties bound are States parties to the UNCLOS. Hence, an interim measures application should be submitted to a body designated under UNCLOS, relate to UNCLOS matters and originate from a party to UNCLOS.

Second, the interim measures jurisdiction is based on the general jurisdiction under the UNCLOS but is further qualified. Interim measures would require that a prima facie case for presence of jurisdiction be established. The jurisprudence of the ITLOS developed the notion of prima facie examination of jurisdiction. According to The M/V "SAIGA" (No. 2) case,[26] the ITLOS does not have to finally decide on jurisdiction on the merits when considering interim measures, and that prima facie jurisdiction is sufficiently established where there is a prima facie basis for the jurisdiction. The prima facie jurisdiction is established if it is not obviously excluded[27]; there is a plausible likelihood for the jurisdiction on the merits to be established[28] or reasonable probability.[29] This sets a relatively low threshold which can be passed as long as it is not manifest that the respective body, ITLOS or other competent body under the UNCLOS does not have jurisdiction on the matter at all.

5.2.2 Standards of Assessment

First, there should be potential prejudice to the rights of the parties leading to irreparable harm, i.e. irreversible harm.[30] Harm should be probable and imminent.[31] There should be a link between the rights to be preserved by the measures and the rights subject of the merits of the dispute. A dicta to the M/V "SAIGA" case by Judge Laing suggests (paragraph 29) that this should not be a too heinous standard. However, additionally there is requirement for "serious harm" risk for the marine

---

[26] Saint Vincent and the Grenadines v. Guinea, Order of 11 March 1998, paragraph 29.
[27] Rosenne (2002), p. 515.
[28] Mensah (2002), pp. 43, 44, 50.
[29] Ndiaye (2001), pp. 95, 97.
[30] Mensah (2002), pp. 43, 47.
[31] Ndiaye (2001), pp. 95, 98.

environment. It is a different standard (otherwise it would fall within the "irreparable harm" category) and it may be argued it is of a lower threshold due to the essential nature of the interest (marine environment) protected in this manner.

Moreover, paragraph 5 of Article 290 provides a further condition—presence of urgency. It is to be considered against the factual background of the case. For instance, the prevention of judicial or administrative measures qualified to require urgent measures in the M/V "SAIGA" case, and the avoidance of depletion of tuna stocks called for urgent measures in the Southern Bluefin Tuna case.

Considering the wording of paragraphs 1 of Article 290 of UNCLOS, measures should also aim to preserve rights of both parties, so there should only be a degree of interference and adequacy of the interference[32]

5.2.3 Procedure

On basis of paragraph 3 of Article 290, the jurisdiction under the UNCLOS may be exercised only upon an application by a party and interim measures cannot be granted proprio motu. However, interpreting paragraph 1's qualification ("considers appropriate under the circumstances"), it can be inferred that once seized, the body under the UNCLOS can grant measures different from, or in addition to, the ones requested by the parties—this is also supported by Article 89, paragraph 5 of the Rules of ITLOS. The measures are subject to further modification and revocation by the competent body (paragraph 2) on basis of alteration in the circumstances. Hence, if a request based on a set of circumstances is dismissed, new one can be made on basis of different circumstances (partial res judicata applies), which is also enshrined in Article 92 of the Rules of ITLOS. The procedure is bilateral, i.e. includes submissions of both parties (Article 290, paragraph 3). However, Article 90, paragraph 4 of the Rules of ITLOS hints a kind of an ex parte stage of the procedure so that in the light of a pending procedure on interim measures and before both parties make submissions, the President of the yet not constituted Tribunal "may call upon the parties to act in such a way as will enable any order the Tribunal may make on the request for provisional measures to have its appropriate effects". This purports at the mischief that ex parte applications seek as well—the urgency of the situation calling for a very timely actions by the dispute resolution body. The decision of the body on interim measures is in the form of an order.

---

[32] Mensah (2002), pp. 43, 44.

5.2.4 Enforcement

In contrast to the term "indicate" in the Statute of the ICJ, the UNCLOS uses the term "prescribe" in paragraph 1 of Article 290. It is inferred that by no means this should mean something less than a binding direction on the parties of the dispute. As the case law of the ICJ is now settled that interim measures have compulsory nature, a fortiori the language of the UNCLOS should be interpreted to mean exactly this. Paragraph 6 also speaks explicitly about compliance with the measures granted. Further, Article 95 of the Rules of ITLOS also stipulates that parties should report to ITLOS the compliance with the measures. Hence, measures under Article 290 are binding and non-compliance would incur international responsibility, including aggravation of responsibility under the merits of the dispute.

5.3 Interim Measures in the European Court of Human Rights

5.3.1 Jurisdiction

Article 39 of the Rules of Court of the European Court of Human Rights provides that upon the request of a party or of any other person concerned, or of their own motion, the Court can indicate to the parties any interim measure which they consider should be adopted in the interests of the parties or of the proper conduct of the proceedings. The jurisdiction of the Court to grant interim measures derives from the general dispute resolution jurisdiction of the Court. Under Article 19 of the European Convention of Human Rights, the Court is established to ensure the compliance with the ECHR, which determines its ratione materiae jurisdiction. According to Article 32, paragraph 1 of the ECHR, the jurisdiction of the Court shall extend to all matters concerning the interpretation and application of the Convention and the protocols thereto, which encompasses inter-State cases and individual applications regarding breaches of the human rights enshrined in the ECHR. This is the ratione materiae scope of the jurisdiction of the Court as well. Hence, interim measures may be granted either under a case initiated by a State against a State for violations of the ECHR, or under a case initiated by an individual (natural or legal person) against a State for violations of the ECHR. For this reason within the ratione personae jurisdiction of the Court are both States parties to ECHR and individuals.

5.3.2 Standards for Assessment

The criteria for assessment of applications for interim measures are developed within the jurisprudence of the Court. In practice the Court applies Rule 39 only if there is an imminent risk of irreparable damage (e g. case of Mamatkulov and Askarov v. Turkey[33]). It is to be demonstrated against the background of the particular circumstances of the case what should qualify as "imminent risk" and as "irreparable damage". However, in most cases interim measures are granted concerning right to life (Article 2), the right not to be subjected to torture or inhuman treatment (Article 3) and, more rarely, the right to respect for private and family life (Article 8). Most cases are related to deportation and extradition proceedings. This gives a good flair of what is considered as danger to rights protected under the ECHR rights. These are essential rights, most often related to life and physical integrity, which may be put in real peril if interim measures are not granted. On basis of the case law of the Court, interim measures have been granted in aid of various rights, including: fear of persecution in case of deportation (F.H. v. Sweden[34]; Y.P. and L.P. v. France[35]); exploitation (M. v. the United Kingdom[36]); health degradation in case of deportation (D. v. the United Kingdom[37]); risk of death sentence upon extradition (Öcalan v. Turkey); risk of breach on fair trial (Soering v. the United Kingdom); severance of family life due to deportation (Amrollahi v. Denmark); prevention of ill treatment upon detention (Kotsaftis v. Greece); ensuring fair trial (X. v. Croatia (no. 11223/04)); stay of eviction (Yordanova and Others v. Bulgaria).

The status quo must be maintained on basis of the interim measure pending the judgment on the merits. Most usually, in practice the issue is not to purport avoidance of aggravation but of irreversible damage which should be prevented by operation of the granted interim measures.

Due to the strenuous standards for assessment, the great number of applications for interim measures is dismissed—161 cases granted, and 630 dismissed.

5.3.3 Procedure

The interim measures are indicated by the Chamber dealing with the case, or, where appropriate, the President of the Section or a duty judge appointed pursuant to paragraph 4 of the Rules of Court.

---

[33] Applications nos. 46827/99 and 46951/99.
[34] Application no. 32621/06.
[35] Application no. 32476/06.
[36] Application no. 16081/08.
[37] Application no. 30240/96.

5.3.4 Enforcement

Compliance with interim measures is a matter of debate. In one case, Cruz Varas and Others v. Sweden,[38] the Court reasoned that the interim measures are not binding upon the Contracting States. The main argument is that the ECHR on itself does not speak of any interim measures jurisdiction, and only the rules of the court—which are not adopted by the Contracting States and hence not binding upon them, feature a rule on interim measures. Measures are only indicated and this is why they are optional, and are not imposed on States and States are not obliged to follow them.

However, this dicta has been overcome.[39] The main indicator for the binding nature of a legal instrument is whether any responsibility is incurred due to non-compliance with it. In Mamatkulov and Askarov v. Turkey,[40] the Court took the view that Article 34 of the ECHR is intertwined with Article 39 of the Rules. Non-compliance with interim measures undermines the right of petition enshrined in the ECHR under Article 34. This would be a breach that incurs international responsibility under the ECHR. This reasoning has been expounded in later cases such as Ben Khemais v. Italy,[41] and Olaechea Cahuas v. Spain.[42] According to some commentary, failure to respect Rule 39 may be considered as aggravation of a breach of the rights under the ECHR.[43] Therefore, the position of the current case law of the Court is that Article 39 envisions obligatory interim measures. Prevention of irreparable harm as long as the dispute is pending is set to be a compulsory rule of the procedure in the EChHR.

5.4 Interim Measures in the Court of Justice of the European Union

5.4.1 Jurisdiction

Under Article 279 of the Treaty on the Functioning of the European Union, the Court of Justice of the European Union (ECJ) may in any cases before it prescribe any necessary interim measures. Under Article 38 of the Statute of ECJ, interim measures may be granted by the President of ECJ.

The jurisdiction to grant interim measures ratione materiae encapsulates disputes of the various types that fall within the scope of the substantive jurisdiction of the

---

[38] judgment of 20 March 1991.
[39] see Jacobs et al. (2002), pp. 401–402; Mole and Meredith (2011), pp. 221–226.
[40] Application nos. 46827/99 and 46951/99, judgment of 4 February 2005.
[41] Application no. 246/07, judgment of 24 February 2009.
[42] Application no. 24668/03, judgment of 10 August 2006.
[43] Jacobs et al. (2002), p. 402.

ECJ, mainly: procedures against a Member State for failure to fulfil obligations (Article 258–259 TFEU); actions against EU institutions for failure to act or for unlawful act (Articles 263–265 TFEU); procedures for ruling on preliminary references by Member States on questions of interpretation of EU law (Article 267 TFEU).

The general jurisdiction of the ECJ is basis to derive the specific jurisdiction of the ECJ on interim measures.

5.4.2 Standards for Assessment

According to Article 160, paragraph 3 of the Rules of Procedure of the ECJ, an application for interim measures should state the subject-matter of the proceedings, the circumstances giving rise to urgency and the pleas of fact and law establishing a prima facie case for the interim measure applied for. On this basis two main conditions for granting interim measures can be evinced.

First, the existence of a prima facie case for interim measures. The concept of prima facie case has been developed within the case law of the ECJ. The application should demonstrate reasonable opportunity for success on the merits of the case.[44] The assessment however should not indicate at least a 50% chance of success. To the contrary, the prima facie merits would mean absence of total deprivation of merits of the application. The application should not be entirely unfounded, entirely without any merits (Order of the President of the Court of 19 July 1995, Commission v. Atlantic Container Line AB and other[45]; Order of the President of the CFI of 3 June 1996, Bayer AG v. Commission[46]). The matter put forward by the application should be of such nature that is not obvious at the interim measures stage and necessitates further examination on the merits of the case (Order of the Vice-President of the Court in Commission v Pilkington Group[47]). This dicta, to be noted, sets a relatively low threshold. Prima facie should be anything that is not manifestly lacking merits, which can indicate that any legal issue that may be subject to opposing arguments, or factual issue that may require further collection of evidence, would qualify to pass the test.

The second condition is urgency. Urgency shall be present where serious and irreparable harm may be suffered before the case is decided on the merits and this is established in the application with a sufficient degree of probability (Order of the President of the CFI of 3 June 1996, Bayer AG v. Commission[48]). The risk should be actual, determinable by the time of the application, and not hypothetical. The harm

---

[44] Lenaerts and Arts (1999), p. 299.
[45] Case C-149/95R, [1995] ECR I-2165.
[46] Case T-41/96 R, [1996] ECR II-381.
[47] C-278/13 P(R), EU:C:2013:558, paragraph 67.
[48] Case T-41/96 R, [1996] ECR II-381.

caused should not be capable of being repaired or reversed by the decision on the merits of the dispute (Order of the President of the CFI of 16 February 1995, Amicale des Residents du Square D'Auvergne v. Commission[49]; Order of the President of the CFI of 12 May 1995, Chemins de fer, British Railways. v. Commission[50]; Compagnie Maritime Belge Transport NV v. Commission[51]). This is an indication what a qualitative concept as irreparable should be understood as. Hence, if the damages can be made good by compensation, the harm will be less likely to be considered as irreparable.

The Rules of Procedure of the ECJ do not state this, but the case law has established that the subject matter of the procedure on the merits should not be prejudiced by the interim measures (Order of the President of the CIF of 26 February 1997, C.A.S. Succhi di Frutta SpA v. Commission[52]; Commission v. Atlantic Container Line AB and other). The order on the measures should not prejudge the case. The interim measures granted should be of nature that allows subsequent modification and cancellation (Könecke v. Commission[53]), the measures should not be irrevocable. This requirements is at par with the requirement the measures not to prejudice the dispute on the merits.

5.4.3 Procedure

Article 160, paragraph 2 of the Rules of Procedure require that the interim measures application should be made to parties to a case before the ECJ. On this basis, it can be inferred that there should be a case instituted before the ECJ before the application is made. A contrario, application cannot be submitted prior the commencement of a case. The procedure is summary and both parties are allowed to make submissions, i.e. procedure is bilateral (Article 160, paragraph 5). However, the President has powers to grant the application ex part as well (Article 160, paragraph 6). According to case law, this is proper where the urgency of the situation requires so (IMS Health v. Commission).

The application is heard and decided by the President of the court or the Vice-President (Article 161). The decision on interim measures is made in the form of an order (Article 162, paragraph 2). It is final and not subject to appeal. The time span of the order is until the dispute on the merits is finally decided with the judgment (Article 162, paragraph 4). The interim measures are subject to variation and cancellation (Article 163). The decision in the order which dismisses the application is not binding—the parties may submit a new application (Article 164) but only if the

---

[49] Case T-5/95 R, [1995] ECR II-255.
[50] Cases T-79-80/95, [1995] ECR II-1433.
[51] Case T-24/93 R, [1993] ECR II-543.
[52] Case T -191/96 R, [1997] ECR 211.
[53] Case 44/75 R, [1975] ECR 637.

new application should be based on new set of facts. Therefore, there is partial res judicata, i.e. having once ruled on the lack of grounds to grant measures on a certain set of facts, the court is bound to dismiss an application based on the same facts.

5.4.4 *Enforcement*

Under Article 260 of TFEU, if the Court of Justice of the European Union finds that a Member State has failed to fulfil an obligation under the Treaties, the State shall be required to take the necessary measures to comply with the judgment of the Court. If the Commission considers that the Member State concerned has not taken the necessary measures to comply with the judgment of the Court, it may bring the case before the Court after giving that State the opportunity to submit its observations. It shall specify the amount of the lump sum or penalty payment to be paid by the Member State concerned which it considers appropriate in the circumstances. If the Court finds that the Member State concerned has not complied with its judgment it may impose a lump sum or penalty payment on it.

5.5 Interim Measures by the European Commission

5.5.1 *Jurisdiction*

The jurisdiction of the EU Commission to grant interim measures is placed within the procedure for imposing sanctions for breaches of competition law, where the Commission has rather quasi-judicial functions. It is based on the current Council Regulation (EC) No 1/2003 of 16 December 2002 on the implementation of the rules on competition laid down in Articles 81 and 82 of the Treaty and is applied in the area of competition law. The case law of the ECJ has inferred (e.g. in Camera Care Ltd. v. Commission[54]) that the powers under the current Article 7 of the Regulation 1/2003 should encapsulate also jurisdiction to direct the parties within the scope of the Regulation 1/2003 to a certain behaviour ("require the undertakings and associations of undertakings concerned to bring such infringement to an end. For this purpose, it may impose on them any behavioural or structural remedies"). Currently Article 8 explicitly enshrines interim measures jurisdiction of the EU Commission: "In cases of urgency due to the risk of serious and irreparable damage to competition, the Commission, acting on its own initiative may by decision, on the basis of a prima facie finding of infringement, order interim measures".

---

[54] Case 792/79 R, [1980] ECR 119.

5.5.2 Standards for Assessment

Both the current wording of Article 8, and the case law of ECJ (e.g. La Cinq SA v. Commission[55]), indicate two major conditions for granting interim measures. First, there should be prima facie case of infringement. The notion of prima facie is interpreted by the ECJ as of likelihood, probability. It is not required that the infringement is clearly established. Second, there should be risk of a serious and irreparable damage to the interests of the parties or the public interest. The two requisites should be considered together. It is a matter of assessment within the scenario of particular facts. Damage would be irreparable if it cannot be remedied by the subsequent ruling on the merits La Cinq SA v. Commission[56]). Further, there should be urgency for the request to be granted—the interests shall be prejudiced (seriously, irreparably) without immediate action (Irish Continental Group v. CCI Morlaix[57]; Mars / Langnese-Iglo and Schoeller Lebensmittel[58]). For instance, seasonal habits have been a factor for assessment of urgency.

5.5.3 Procedure

Interim measures may be granted by request or proprio motu (Distribution system of Ford Werke[59]). The procedure is bilateral and may involve participation of third parties (Article 27 of Regulation 1/2003; Opinion of Advocate General Sir Gordon Slynn in Ford of Europe Incorporated and Ford-Werke Aktiengesellschaft v. Commission[60]). The Commission may request payment of a guarantee. Measures are subject to revocation and modification. Measures are temporary depending on circumstances (Article 8, paragraph 2 of Regulation 1/2003).

5.5.4 Enforcement

Under Article 23, paragraph 2, item (b), the EU Commission has powers to impose fines on parties in case of non-compliance with interim measures.

---

[55] Case T-44/90, [1992] ECR II-1, para. 28.
[56] Case T-44/90, [1992] ECR II-1.
[57] IP 1995/05/16.
[58] Case IV/34.072, OJ 1993 L 183/19.
[59] Case IV/30.696, OJ 1982 L 256/20.
[60] Joint Cases C-228 and 229/82, [1984] ECR 1164.

References

Jacobs F, White R, Ovey C (2002) European convention on human rights. Oxford University Press, Oxford

Lauterpacht H (1958) Development of international law by the international court. Stevens and Sons, London

Lenaerts K, Arts D (1999) Procedural law of the European Union. Sweet & Maxwell, London

Mendelson M (1986) Interim measures of protection and the use of force. In: Cassese A (ed) Current legal problems of regulation of use of force. Oxford University Press, Oxford

Mensah T (2002) Provisional measures in the international tribunal for the law of the sea. Zaoerv 62:43–54

Miles C (2017) Provisional measures before international courts and tribunals. Cambridge University Press, Cambridge

Mole N, Meredith C (2011) Asylum and the European Convention on Human Rights. Council of Europe Publishing, Human Rights Files No. 9, Strasbourg

Ndiaye TM (2001) Provisional measures before the international tribunal for the law of the sea. In: Nordquist MH, Norton Moore J (eds) Current marine environmental issues and the international tribunal for the law of the sea. Martinus Nijhoff, Leiden

Oda S (1996) Provisional measures: the practice of the international court of justice. In Lowe V, Fitzmaurice M (eds) Fifty years of the international court of justice: essays in Honour of Sir Robert Jennings Cambridge University Press, Cambridge

Oellers-Frahm K (2011) Interim measures. In: Zimmermann A, Oellers-Frahm K, Tomuschat C, Tams C, Kashgar M, Diehl D (eds) The statute of the international court of justice: a commentary. Oxford University Press, Oxford

Rosenne S (2002) Provisional measures and Prima Facie revisited. In: Ando N, McWhinney E, Wolfrum R, Baker Röben B (eds) Festschrift in Honour of Judge Oda. Brill, London

Chapter 6
Assessment

6.1 Essence of Interim Measures

The analysis expounded in this study demonstrates that interim measures may be very varied and adaptive to the different disputes and settings thereof, where necessity for interim measures arises. Therefore, interim measures can be a flexible tool to attain a particular purpose. The purpose is, however, not contained in the interim measures themselves, but is outside interim relief proceedings. The purpose is entailed in the nature of the underlying dispute.

Interim measures are in fact conflict management tools. They are applied in order to influence a dispute. First, to influence the underlying relationship between the disputants so that it is not ruined—in terms of a particular subject matter that should be preserved from greater peril, or in terms of safeguarding further deterioration in financial or another position of the parties. Second, interim measures may be applied in order to enhance the way the dispute is being resolved, to facilitate the dispute resolution procedure itself—for the purpose of collection of evidence, for safeguarding jurisdiction for challenges, etc.

In another context, the concept of management is defined as a set of activities directed at the efficient and effective utilization of resources in the pursuit of one or more goals.[1] A dispute or conflict settlement, if assumed as the end of the dispute settlement procedure, should be achieved by applying a variety of tools. Such tools should be distinguished from the various characteristics and stages of a legal procedure (rules of procedure, evidence taking, deliberation, party submissions, final decision/award, etc.). There should be tools to ensure the meaningfulness of the end of the procedure—this is the category where interim measures are to be placed.

---

[1] Van Fleet and Peterson (2013), p. 24.

Therefore, interim measures should be perceived in a wider context. Usually they are conceived as a mere procedural issue, or better, a tool, which is within the power ("arsenal") of the adjudicating body, being court or arbitral tribunal. The function of interim measures has broader and far reaching impact as interim measures have direct effect not only on the way the procedure for resolution of the dispute is handled, but also on the dispute itself—on the course of the dispute. This is why the very essence of interim measures is that these are required as means for ensuring that both the underlying relationship, as well as the procedure for resolution of the dispute, are preserved and saved from deterioration. For this reason the proposition that the essence of interim measures is prevention of aggravation of a dispute should be corroborated. Aggravation may be seen at various levels. Aggravation should be seen through the ultimate goal of a dispute, i.e. that the dispute ceases to exist and that the parties to it conform to the initial underlying relationship between them. Hence, aggravation is effected by making compliance with the primary relationship more difficult (i.e. worsening of financial position of a party; deterioration or destruction of the subject-matter of the dispute, etc.), and by making resolution of the dispute more difficult (in terms of time, cost, etc.).

Moreover, as noted in the very beginning of this study, the conceptual characteristics of interim measures qualify them as tools necessary for the management of the underlying dispute—and not only management of the procedure itself. Preservation of goods or evidence or freezing of money and other assets serve to ensure the very end of the dispute resolution process will be achieved—orderly, lawful settlement of the dispute.

6.2 Comparing Effectiveness and Procedure: Interim Measures in Litigation vs Interim Measures in Arbitration

6.2.1 Common Features

The rationale of interim measures—as a procedural tool; as a conflict management tool; as a tool to prevent dispute aggravation—underpins interim measures in both cross-border litigation and arbitration.

The scope of available interim measures remains largely the same in both litigation and arbitration as the review of national laws on interim relief, as well as the review of major arbitral institutional rules, demonstrate that a dispute resolution body is empowered to provide interim measures it deems necessary and adequate with regard to the particular dispute at hand. It is difficult to infer that there is a certain category of measures that is available only by a court, while it cannot be granted by an arbitral tribunal, and vice versa. At the same time, certain measures, especially those granted in arbitration, may be practically quite more difficult to be enforced (realized) due to arbitration's specific features. However, in abstract terms, the types of measures at hand is largely the same within the purview of both litigation and arbitration.

6.2.2 Differences

What underpins measures in arbitration is what underpins arbitration itself – its consensual nature. Formally, this is not a correct proposition as parties are bound to comply with interim measures and cannot "opt out of" compliance with interim measures as with any other measures granted by the tribunal. However, enforcement of interim measures granted by tribunals is problematic and may not be realized in each and every situation. Hence, measures by arbitration are difficult to be imposed to a recalcitrant party. Instead, this may lead to certain adverse inferences, or damages claim/award.

Therefore, the main difference is existence of mechanism, i.e. the mechanics of operation of interim measures provided by arbitration. State court measures are corroborated by the imperii of state authorities and can be forced upon a party. In arbitration, a party may refuse to comply with measures. Some jurisdictions would allow that state authorities assist for the purpose of enforcement of measures, but this is largely a matter of national law provisions, and is an exception and not a general rule.

Does this render arbitral interim measures less effective? In this author's view, this is difficult to be argued, and furthermore proven. If state court measures are favoured due to the enforcement mechanism, this would be premised on the long-standing argument that the essence of law is its forcible effect, its operation as a system of rules guaranteed by state authority to sanction non-compliance.[2] This perspective is correct but not catching all aspects of the problem as voluntary compliance with interim measures is usually the typical, and not the exceptional, case (similar to the fact that compliance with the law, and not criminal conduct, is the typical case of human behaviour). Authority cannot be always equated to power to sanction. Law should be distinguished from its enforcement mechanism, which is not always use of direct force upon parties.

Interim measures by an arbitral tribunal are indeed more difficult to be policed, as the mechanism includes a more complex mechanism to ensure compliance, but does not mean that compliance cannot be ensured at all. However, a line of distinction should be drawn: interim measures in litigation may have easier (in terms of time/ cost) manner of enforcement compared to interim measures in arbitration. So, the main point is that both types of measures will be effective, but court measures could be at a lesser cost (in terms of money, time, efforts).

---

[2] See scholars such as Austin, Kelsen, M. Weber.

6.3 Law and Economics Perspective to Interim Measures

This study argues that interim measures have managerial function, i.e. should interfere with the situation between the parties to a legal dispute and preserve/freeze or control it until final resolution. In other words, the managerial function stems from the concept of case management—to identify, assess and evaluate a case (dispute) and its implications and projected development, its potential outcome and spillover effects, and lay down the infrastructure for its evolution for the onset of the case (the dispute) throughout its continuation to its end/completion—indeed, final settlement. Therefore, interim measures are teleological, i.e. have a purpose, and so they strive to ensure certain efficiency. Interim measures are tools to ensure efficiency—efficiency of law, as interim measures freeze the particular situation of dispute balancing the costs of parties. Therefore, if an economics perspective of law is assumed, there can be a certain analysis based on risk, costs, allocation, policy and efficiency.

Efficiency should have a cost-compared-to-benefit perspective. The longer a dispute protracts, the higher amount of costs is being accumulated. A dispute entering into a formal stage (procedure) necessarily attracts a further amount of costs, involving fees, costs of administration of dispute, representation costs and further potential damages to the interests of the parties.

Therefore, a stage of the formal dispute, which comprises a review of interim measures application, certainly adds up to the mass of costs. At the same time, there is a certain trade off: interim measure application and procedure may lead to augmenting additional costs; however, interim measures ought to protect the parties so that (1) the procedure is being managed and is prevented from excessive loss of time and resources; (2) further distraction to the interests of parties is prevented, incl. on a post-award stage. Interim measures ought to ensure that a party would not be able to diminish its financial status to avert compliance with the award; inflict damage to the subject matter of the dispute; etc.

Therefore, there should be a balance between additional costs for interim measure application and procedure, on one hand, and prevention of costs for implementing the award, on the other. This trade off indicates the basic dynamics of the cost-benefit analysis of interim measures. If efficiency is guaranteed at an earlier procedural stage, i.e. by way of interim measures, this may hinder potential lack of efficiency at the later enforcement stage after the dispute resolution procedure is completed.

There is one more trade off which should be considered. Both parties to a dispute are bound to suffer harm and loss. As put by R. Coase, "To avoid the harm to B would inflict harm on A. The real question that has to be decided is: should A be allowed to harm B or should B be allowed to harm A? The problem is to avoid the more serious harm".[3] If an interim measure is granted, a party would be restrained and may suffer loss. If that measure is not granted, the other party may suffer loss, too. In result, to grant the interim measure or not, is to decide which party may suffer

---
[3] Coase (1960), p. 2.

6.3 Law and Economics Perspective to Interim Measures

more significant and deserving to be prevented loss. In this regard, interim measures are tools to cater for more efficient distribution of costs.

Richard Posner's seminal "Economic Analysis of Law" provides an additional perspective of interim measures and the strive for effectiveness. With regard to granting preliminary injunction, i.e. an interim measure, Posner applies a formula which encapsulates a cost allocation analysis:

$$P(Hp) > (1-P)Ha$$

P is the probability that the plaintiff will prevail in the full trial on the merits (and therefore 1 — P is the probability that the defendant will prevail); Hp is the harm that the plaintiff will suffer if a preliminary injunction is not granted to maintain the status quo pending the trial, and Ha is the harm the defendant will suffer if the preliminary injunction is granted.[4]

This formula is, in other words, based on striking a balance of costs between the parties, so that the costs of granting the measure would not be overcome by counter-balancing costs to be borne by the party suffering losses due to the measure. This formula may serve as basis for a wider conclusion on the operation of interim measures: the cost of not having the measure vs the cost of having the measure. In other words, if the measure is not granted, the applicant may incur certain costs, incl. damages; if the measure is granted, the respondent may incur certain costs, incl. damages. If the applicant costs (could potentially) outweigh the respondent's costs, the dispute resolution body ought to grant the application; if the respondent costs outweigh the applicant costs, the body ought not to grant the application. However, this balance is not stricken by simply juxtaposing costs; the costs, which a party risks suffering, should be at the level of irreparable harm or at least harm very difficult to compensate.

In result, the economic analysis of interim measures' functionality in law might elucidate that:

(1) Interim measures might have a role regarding cost efficiency, as interim measures might decrease enforcement costs, at the stake of increase of legal costs in the course of a dispute resolution procedure since a portion of legal costs shall be allocated to the segment of the procedure concerning interim measures;
(2) Interim measures might have wider cost allocation and efficiency role since interim measures may be used as a tool to balance the losses parties to a dispute suffer with and/or without adequate interim measures at place.

Hence, it could be assumed that interim relief may be used as a tool for 'wealth maximization',[5] i.e. increase of totality of utility, as the interim relief should strike a balance of the costs/losses/harm, actual and potential, between the parties to the

---

[4] Posner (1985), p. 522.
[5] Posner (1985), pp. 85–106.

dispute. None of the parties' total wealth would be irreparably damaged as being safeguarded by the interim measures.

6.4 Strategies for Use of Interim Measures

The question of strategizing use of interim measures in cross-border disputes can be considered in several scenarios.

6.4.1 Strategy for Interim Measures in Courts

A creditor under the Brussels regime faces the following dilemma. If the creditor turns to the court having jurisdiction prior to, or while the claim is pending, the decision on interim measures will be capable of being enforced within the framework of enforcement of judgments (article 42 of Regulation Brussels Ibis). The granted measures may face the various problems and hurdles that a foreign judgment may have to deal with when attempted to be enforced.

For the said reason, it may seem wiser, in terms of time and cost, that the creditor avails of the option under Article 35 of Brussels Ibis and applies for interim measures before the courts of the country where the measures would be imposed. This may pose some difficulties, too. Most of all, these will not be the courts having jurisdiction on the merits and it may be more difficult to present creditor's case to them instead of the courts dealing with the merits. This may involve issues of foreign law, if the law applicable to the merits is not the law of the courts seized in the interim measure proceedings. The upside, however, is that once granted, the interim measure will be more effectively implemented. And, after all, interim measures are all about effect and effectiveness.

Hence, the creditor is well advised to seek assistance for the purpose of obtaining interim relief from the courts where the interim measures will be targeted.

6.4.2 Strategy for Combination of Interim Measures by Courts and/or Tribunals

In the scenario of interim measures for disputes within the purview of arbitration, usually both arbitral tribunals and courts are competent to provide interim relief (save for the limited number of countries that do not allow court granted measures in support of arbitration). However, the main question is whether these are alternatives;

6.4 Strategies for Use of Interim Measures

coexisting options or mutually exclusive options, or simply different tools catering for different needs.

The main body for interim relief should be the arbitral tribunal. It is the body that should decide the merits of the dispute, and hence it is the body which is in best position to assess the necessity and adequacy of an interim measures application. As in the case of arbitration enforcement is always an issue to be dealt with, the situation is different compared with the Brussels Ibis regime where enforcement problems may be evaded on the cost of applying to the court that is not competent to handle the merits of the case.

This is why courts should provide interim measures only in exceptional, and limited number of, situations. Otherwise, it is possible that due to the overlap in the jurisdiction of courts and arbitral tribunal, conflicting interim measures be provided that will clash upon enforcement so as to a kind of a "race" to enforce will ensue—the party that first obtains interim relief and imposes it, will have primacy and leading role for the conservation of the dispute. This will lead to further complications that will aggravate the dispute as well. Therefore, use of courts after the tribunal starts to function should be avoided and where one and the same measure can be provided by court and arbitral tribunal with equal effect, resorting to court jurisdiction should be treated as acting in bad faith which may ground a damages claim as well.

Hence, a party should turn to courts where an arbitral clause is applicable in the following situations.

First, prior to commencement of arbitration. Although various arbitral tribunals provide for pre-commencement procedures, including emergency arbitrator procedures, in reality these are complicated procedures while in interim measure procedure time is always of essence. Hence, it is more effective to turn to a state court for prompt and timely assistance where interim relief is needed instead of undergoing complicated arbitral procedures.

However, when the arbitral tribunal is constituted, there should not be a reason to request assistance from a court save for one reason. It is unrealistic to contend that the enforcement of interim measures by arbitral tribunals should be the reason to avoid such measures. New York Convention should be interpreted as instrument allowing for enforcement of measures provided in the form of interim or partial awards. Therefore, it would make perfect sense to request interim relief from the arbitral tribunal, which is in best position to assess how the interim relations between the parties while the case pends should be regulated, and this is expected, first, to be complied with by the parties, and second, to be duly enforced. Furthermore, unlike court judgments, a single interim relief award should be subject to enforcement anywhere under the New York Convention. The caveat is that if the necessary measures involve actions (or omissions) of third parties not bound by the arbitration agreement, the practical value of the interim relief award of the tribunal is low. Instead, the applicant should seek assistance from courts at the place where the measure is targeted to be realized. This applies also to situations where damages for lack of voluntary compliance would not be adequate remedy, e.g. in situations where time is of essence; irreparable harm would be caused, etc.

Therefore, it is a matter of combination of measures and jurisdictions. The arbitral jurisdiction is the primary one, but a supplementary court jurisdiction can and should be used but for a limited number of situations.

6.5 Standards for Interim Relief

The review of interim measures provided under national law by courts; by arbitral tribunals, and in public international law disputes, differentiates a number of common characteristics that define the nature of interim relief granted by courts and tribunals.

The main features of interim measures that should be present are:

(i) A likelihood of success on the merits of the dispute exceeding 50%. In other words, the dispute resolution body makes assessment of the substantive rights and obligations and should conclude that it is of higher probability that the alleged rights exist in favour of the claimant;
(ii) A palpable level of risk that the claimed rights may be adversely affected, and that interim relief would avert such potential harm. This risk should be significant, not merely theoretical or existing in general.
(iii) There should be a pressing need for the interim relief to be granted. Usually if it cannot be demonstrated that there is such an urgent need, the relief will not be taken as necessary. This component is tightly related to the risk of harm, but is more of a temporal aspect to it.
(iv) There should be a balance between the parties. The relief should come as accounting for the risk, and should not create excessive harm itself. This may call for a subsequent and supplemental measure such as requirement for a guarantee for costs, etc.

6.6 See Table 6.1 for the Classification (Typology) of Interim Measures

Table 6.1 Classification (typology) of interim measures

By addressee: (the party bound by the measure)
Measures aimed at parties to the case;   *E.g. a party to present security or to provide goods for inspection or storage, or undertake/cease actions*
Measures aimed at third parties;   *E.g. bank accounts of a party to be blocked; court or another tribunal*
By purpose: (what end result is perceived by the measure)
To ensure a party has sufficient assets to be enforced against after the outcome of the proceedings;   *E.g. a party should not make transfers/dispositions with its assets*
To ensure that the subject matter of the case, or the situation between the parties, is not altered during the proceedings;   *E.g. goods to be provided for storage/inspection*
To ensure greater/graver damages are avoided;   *E.g. a party to refrain from conduct, e.g. to cease infringement*
To ensure the proper administration of the proceedings   *E.g. security for costs to be provided; evidence to be collected; disclosures to be made; parallel proceedings not to be undertaken in before court or another tribunal*
By subject matter: (the target/object purported to be affected by the measure)
Actions regarding the subject matter of the proceedings;   *E.g. preservation of goods; performance of contract*
Actions regarding the assets of a party;   *E.g. restriction on transfer of assets; blocking of bank accounts*
Actions in support of the proceedings, including regarding evidence to be used in the proceedings   *E.g. security for costs to be provided; evidence to be collected; disclosures to be made; parallel proceedings not to be undertaken in before court or another tribunal*
By rights to be safeguarded by the measure:
Right to receive money/damages/pecuniary receivables;   *E.g. claims for damages under contract – safeguarded by freeze of assets to ensure sufficient funds at enforcement*
Rights regarding (disposition/use of) property (moveables, real estate, IP rights, etc);   *E.g. claims for ownership of goods – safeguarded by depositing a specified place until the dispute is resolved*
Right to compel counterparty contractual obligations to be performed   *E.g. seller to transfer goods due under a contract – safeguarded by depositing a specified place until the dispute is resolved*
Right to compel non-infringement of contract/cessation of harmful conduct   *E.g. claims certain conduct to be prohibited, and respondent to refrain from further continuation of it, e.g. not to exploit certain signs due to potential trademark infringement – safeguarded by prohibition of that conduct while procedure is pending, e.g. not to use sign until issue is resolved*

References

Coase R (1960) The problem of social cost. J Law Econ 3:1–44
Posner R (1985/1987) Wealth maximization revisited. Notre Dame J L Ethics Public Policy 2:85–105
Van Fleet D, Peterson TO (2013) Contemporary management. Houghton Mifflin Harcourt, Boston

Chapter 7
Summary of Results. Conclusion

Interim measures are part of the lifeblood of dispute resolution. The necessity to obtain interim relief is usually considered as a secondary matter. However, if all the various arguments put forth in this study are taken into account, interim relief should be perceived as a tool to be employed in each and every dispute. This is so as interim measures come to the foreground to remedy a situation that surfaces and may surface in any dispute: to "hold" the pulse of the dispute in the interim period before it is finally settled; to manage and coordinate the situation between the parties until the resolution of the dispute; and to prevent its aggravation and safeguard the parties from suffering further harm. These are problems which are deeply embedded in the tissue of a dispute resolution process, and these problems hence call for the existence of interim relief instruments.

The present study focused on building up a holistic overview of interim measures and procedures associated with them in cross-border private law (civil and commercial) disputes that are the subject of international litigation and arbitration proceedings. The study sought both to reexamine key features of the said problem and to outline novel findings and analysis of interim relief in the area of international dispute resolution.

The analysis is built upon the assumption that human interaction in social life should be perceived as based on communication flows/relationships with regard to certain objects/states of affairs of life and as having a normative content (of a system of rules such as religion, morality, law, etc.). Where parties are in discord concerning a particular relationship as between them, these parties become part of a "secondary" relationship which is focused on dealing with the "primary" one, i.e. a relationship established to resolve the conflict and bring the parties back to a state of accord. The view of the author is that interim measures are an instrument of that "secondary" relationship to safeguard that the elements of the "primary" relationship are preserved because otherwise the dispute resolution process, i.e. the "secondary" relationship, would be left without purpose since the disagreement between the parties may destroy the "primary" relationship or the possibility that the parties be returned to their previous status.

The study has provided an overview of the key applicable bodies of law that regulate international civil and commercial disputes and interim relief proceedings part of these—the system of EU regulations, e.g. Regulation 1215/2012 along with other EU regulations, as well as the rules of a variety of arbitral institutions (ICC, LCIA, SCC, AAA, VIAC, SIAC, DIS, etc.). With reference to the Brussels Ibis Regulation, the study has special focus on the real connecting link doctrine developed in the case law of the Court of Justice of the European Union. Analysing the jurisdictional grounds establishing arbitral powers to grant interim measures, the study puts forth its position on coordination between concurrent arbitral and state court jurisdiction on interim relief concerning one and the same dispute: that parties' intention to arbitrate their disputes should be given primacy and state courts should be entitled to provide measures only where and when a tribunal cannot do so (at all or efficiently). Otherwise, if conflicting or concurrent measures are granted by tribunals and courts, the first to be enforced should preclude subsequent ones from being recognised.

The study looks into national law criteria to deal with interim relief requests as well as into conditions for interim relief under rules of international arbitral institutions. The work contains a large survey of national laws from a variety of legal systems. The survey indicates that there should be a demonstrable prima facie case regarding the substantive rights and obligations at dispute between the parties. Second, most jurisdictions require necessity, i.e. that without the measures the substantive rights at stake would be compromised/significantly harmed and the subsequent judgment or award might not be successfully enforced. Some national laws require an element of urgency as an absolute precondition while others treat urgency, if proven, not as an absolute prerequisite but as having a procedural effect rendering the interim measures procedure unilateral/ex parte. Striking balance between the parties' interests and gauging measures to be adequate to the risk and necessity is another relatively ubiquitous element of interim measures proceedings. These factors are understood to be looked for in international arbitration cases as well.

The analysis delves into the details of the interim measures regulation in a variety of jurisdictions as to outline the categories of measures that national courts may impose upon an interim relief request. Similarly, major international arbitral institutions rules have also been reviewed. The conclusion that this study draws is that there is no fixed or strict list of measures to be granted neither in national legislations, nor in the sources of international arbitration rules. Instead, adjudicators enjoy a level of discretion when granting measures that should be perceived as appropriate to provide the relief sought. These may be broadly classified as measures requiring a positive behaviour of a party (to undertake actions), or a negative behaviour of a party (to restrain from undertaking action), or a behaviour directed towards certain material objects (such as preservation of goods) or measures that should be in aid of, and ensure proper conduct of the legal procedure (collection of evidence, restraint on other proceedings, etc.). The review contained in the study also puts focus on a

7 Summary of Results. Conclusion 153

number of specific common types of international private law disputes such as international sale of goods, construction, intellectual property, arrest of vessels and block on movability of aircrafts as security to claims, as well as restraining anti-suit injunctions. This review infers that the specific nature of the underlying relations between the parties and the associated objects, i.e. the elements of the so called "primary relationship", have direct effect and influence the types of interim measures which are normally imposed in such disputes. This corroborates the argument that interim relief proceedings not simply safeguard the enforcement of the final resolution of the dispute but have immediate impact on the status of the underlying substantive rights and obligations between the disputing parties.

With regard to enforcement of interim relief, the study argues that an applicant may avail of the grounds for interim measures (e.g. Article 35 of Regulation Brussels Ibis) only where the object of the measure is within the jurisdiction of the court; otherwise, the general grounds of the Regulation should be followed. The study adopts the view that interim relief rulings in arbitration should be termed as awards; however, irrespective of the precise label, these should be subject to enforcement under the enforcement procedure rules of the New York Convention. The study reviews the national legislations of a number of countries to draw the conclusion that some provide for judicial assistance for compliance with arbitral awards and other provide for separate judicial measures to enforce arbitral relief. It is argued that failure to comply with arbitral measures may at one hand attract aggravated liability in the final award and claims for damages, and also liability under respective national law as in some countries this may lead to contempt of court punishment.

The study briefly makes an overview of interim relief proceedings under the auspices of bodies established under public international law (such as ICJ, ITLOS, ECtHR, etc.) to outline that the requirements for granting interim measures in such proceedings greatly resemble the conditions found in private disputes. This further corroborates the argument that the nature of the necessity to obtain such interim relief defines interim measures and procedures associated with them.

It is submitted it would be true but overly simplistic to assume that interim measures are a mere tool for safeguarding enforcement of final court judgment or arbitral award. Instead, the study, considering the analysis and review made therein, goes further and infers that interim measures have two overarching functions. First, to operate as a conflict management tool, as the study demonstrates that their aims and functions are directly influenced by the nature of the dispute and the underlying substantive rights between the parties, and consequently have a direct effect on these rights and the status quo between the parties—not merely on the legal proceedings pending under the dispute. Second, interim measures are called to prevent further aggravation of the dispute (influencing again the substantive relationship between the parties).

The study suggests that as to litigation proceedings, specific interim relief procedures cater better for the urgency and effectiveness that interim relief situations require. In relation to arbitration, the study infers that parties should turn primarily to the selected arbitral body and should resort to state courts only where no body is yet constituted or where third parties are involved or the practical implementation of the measure sought for is or could be compromised, very difficult or questionable, so urgency and effectiveness would dictate that a court imposed relief would be in better position to aid the situation of the applicant.

Assuming an economic perspective, the study concludes that interim measures might be perceived also as a wealth maximization instrument that balances allocation of the costs between disputants and prevents greater levels of loss. The study also features a suggested simplified typology of the classes of measures and what classes of measures would adequately respond to the various general types of disputes.

This study has purported from its outset to place the issue of interim relief in a broader, cross-jurisdictional and cross-sectoral background. It reflects the current global trends in business, private relations and disputes, which demonstrate several key tendencies.

First, commercial matters, especially due to the facilitating nature of digital and online communication, have gone global and there is barely a significant business activity, which does not transcend borders.

Second, the same trends have made personal relations almost global as well, given the ease of connectivity and mobility in our times.

Third, there is a proliferation of the types of disputes. While a few decades ago most cross-border commercial disputes related to sale of goods or, more rarely, construction works, for instance, nowadays more and more very complex and intricate types of disputes emerge. There are entirely new litigation models coming up, for instance consolidation of claims by specialized companies—a fine example is the area of cartel damages claims where agents search for and acquire this type of claims across Europe. Another example is the rise of consumer claims, e.g. class actions of large groups of consumers—the mass claim against Mastercard in UK is an example in this regard as well as claims arising from breaches of privacy or claims for violation of passenger rights (under EU Regulation 261/2004). Furthermore, there are innovative claims being employed—e.g. in areas such as privacy rights, IP, competition law, etc. In result, more and more novel situations arise where parties go into a conflict, private by its nature, over contractual and extra-contractual matters.

Interim measures should live in this world, they have to live in this world. Interim measures are called to answer all these diverse situations of disputes. For all those factors—easier communication, easier mobility, easier recourse to cross-border proceedings, multitude of jurisdictions having contact points with a dispute, etc.—a dispute can be aggravated easier than before. This aggravation may be effected by hiding of assets, relocation of parties, attempts to "torpedo" and subvert proceedings and cause overlapping cases to run in parallel, etc. Exactly because of this, interim measures come to play as an important instrument to avert such situations. Exactly because of this, interim measures are so important and become even more important.

For these reasons, once more, interim measures in cross-border disputes should be reconsidered. The perception of interim relief should evolve from safeguarding rights and/or enforcement of the ultimate award or court judgment towards an understanding of interim measures as an effective tool for management of the underlying relations between the parties and the pending dispute until the situation is resolved and the parties are instructed in a binding manner how to proceed with their relationship. In the end of the day, the purpose and functions of interim relief and associated with it procedures reflect the anatomy of any dispute resolution process, and so both are ultimately oriented towards one and the same aim—a dispute to be turned into an accord.